LECTURES

ON

TEMPERANCE,

BY

ELIPHALET NOTT, D. D., LL. D.,

PRESIDENT OF UNION COLLEGE.

WITH AN INTRODUCTION

BY

TAYLER LEWIS, M. D.,

PROFESSOR OF GREEK IN UNION COLLEGE.

EDITED BY

AMASA McCOY,

LATE EDITOR OF "THE PROHIBITIONIST."

HAMILTON, C. W.

JOHN MOFFAT.

1857.

WEED, PARSONS & Co., Printers and Stereotypers, Albany.

PREFACE.

THE Temperance Reform long since engaged sufficient learning and talent in its advocacy to rescue it from contempt. This vast agitation, which for more than a third of a century has stirred the mind and the heart of society, has evolved a literature of its own, which is more than respectable. Yet of the tens of thousands of speeches, sermons, addresses and lectures; the editorial reports and prize essays; the papers, tracts, pamphlets and volumes which this prolonged and arduous discussion has elicited, there are no productions on this subject which are marked with so much learning, eloquence and wisdom, as these eleven Lectures by President NOTT.

The mature fruits of the orator, who, at the age of thirty, pronounced a discourse on the death of Hamilton, which has made him famous for eloquence ever since—the wise and efficient President, ever since that year (1804), of Union College—the beloved and honored preceptor of fifty-three successive classes of collegians, and now a patriarch hardly less of Temperance than of education; the mature fruits of so gifted, so experienced, so profound, so sagacious an intellect; the vivacity and fervor of the author's style; the beautiful truth-seeking spirit which marks his investigations, his tireless patience of research, his unfailing charity and candor to all opponents, his devout deference to the teachings of the Holy Scriptures, and last, but not least, his own great personal renown; these circumstances unite to concentrate upon these Lectures a degree of interest and attention which is commanded by no other volume on this vast social reform; a social reform, let it be added, which, more than all others combined, engrosses the thoughts and the feelings, the hopes and the fears, of this generation of men.

Often as we had read these Lectures before, and always with admiration, instruction and delight, we rise from the more careful and critical perusal which is necessary to those who examine the proof sheets for the press, impressed with a deeper sense of their extraordinary merit, and a larger appreciation of their power for good over the minds of others. Our own experience would lead us to urge even veteran friends of Temperance—with whom it is a common mistake, that to them no more reading on the subject is necessary—to study anew a volume which, beyond any other ever published, either in America or Great Britain, goes further towards exhausting and placing on an impregnable basis, the arguments in favor of Total Abstinence from all intoxicating liquors.

Intemperance is not an evil of modern origin; nor is it the wise and good of this age alone who have addressed themselves to its cure. The physical and moral degradation with which it has cursed the world is painfully foreshadowed in the cases of Noah and Lot, as recorded in the Scriptures; and the same solemn problem is speculated upon in the Republic of Plato. In the fourteenth chapter of the third book of that immortal work, and which the scholars of every age have ranked among the master-pieces of human wisdom, will be found the following sentence: "We say, then, that *they must abstain from drunkenness.*"

Such is one of the maxims which have been familiar in all ages. But it was reserved for our own age to discover and promulgate the momentous truth which had escaped all previous sages and philosophers, that "to abstain from drunkenness," and yet to continue to drink, is for society at large a simple impossibility. That to abstain from drunkenness, men *must abstain from drink*, that is, intoxicating drink. These doctrines of Total Abstinence (the legislative prohibitions of the traffic, which follow as a logical sequence, the author has not pretended to discuss) are the great themes of these Lectures by President Nott. Availing himself of the labors of all who had written and spoken before him, he has reduced all existing learning on the subject to a system, and with such clearness, beauty and power, that there is no other one volume in the whole range of Temperance literature of such permanent and standard authority. And if Temperance, as here taught, will not raise man from earth to heaven, as Socrates claimed for his philosophy, it is no small matter—nay, in a nation with half a million of drunkards, it is a very great matter—if it will raise him from the gutter of the streets, and bring him within the influences of the house of prayer; and if, without being religion, it may thus be used to subserve the sublime and awful interests of religion, it should assuredly be urged upon the profound and attentive consideration of the pious and the good the country over.

We say, "the pious and the good." For it is not to be disguised, that notwithstanding all the mighty things which have been done in the way of public enlightenment on this important subject, there are not only whole classes of society, otherwise well read and intelligent, who have either forgotten or else never known the fundamental principles of Temperance, but there are very many profound Christians, many ministers of the gospel, who continue so far strangers to the ethics and the philosophy of the Temperance reform, that their own personal habits are still quoted against the suppression of the liquor traffic, and even the practice of Total Abstinence.

Besides, a new generation has grown up even in Temperance families, to whom these important and vital truths have never been seriously and systematically addressed.

The Prussians have a maxim, that whatever you would have appear in the life of a nation, you must put in its schools. The trustees of district schools, the teachers of Sabbath schools, and other guardians of the young, should be appealed to to put one or more copies of this volume in every school library in the land.

The value of this volume is much enhanced by an able and elaborate introduction by TAYLER LEWIS, LL. D., Professor of the Greek Language and Literature in Union College—a man who is equally eminent as an acute, original thinker, and for his profound acquisition in classical and biblical learning.

Professor Lewis has expressed especial admiration for the chart of Bible texts, in connection with wines, to be found in the appendix to the volume, and for which chart alone an eminent divine has said he would pay ten times the price of the whole work, rather than not have it in his possession.

E. C. DELAVAN, Esq., the distinguished President of the New-York State Temperance Society, has written a letter, in which he speaks in such terms as these of the Lectures of Dr. Nott:

"It is my belief that, in the proportion that this work is circulated and read, the cause of Temperance will advance and be perpetuated.

"I would urge all ministers of the gospel, all professing Christians, all heads of families, all organized Temperance societies, all instructors in institutions of learning, from the common school up to the university, to take immediate steps to give universal circulation to this work, called, by one of our most learned and benevolent citizens, 'THE BOOK OF BOOKS ON TEMPERANCE.'

"Let me urge all, in every state, county, town, village and hamlet, whether on the shores of the Atlantic or of the Pacific, or the intervening space between the two (who desire the cause of Temperance to advance), to flood the publishers with orders. A million of copies of these Lectures should be sold in this nation. If the work is successful in the English language, it will be published in the German and other languages, so that our fellow citizens from all nations and of all languages can have the benefit of the great and important truths contained in this volume.

"The publishers have engaged to pay to the New-York State Temperance Society ten per cent on their sales, to enable that Society to extend still further their labors of enlightening the public mind on the great and absorbing questions now at issue before the public, connected with the sale and use of intoxicating drinks."

Such is the estimation in which this work is justly held by the most eminent philanthropists of our country. The publishers have undertaken to present it to the public in a form that must be attractive, and at a price to bring it within the reach of all, and to make it convenient for associations of the friends of the cause to give it a wide circulation. It ought to find a ready entrance into every house in this and other lands.

INTRODUCTION.

The following Lectures produced a very marked effect at the time they were delivered, and few works, it may fairly be believed, have done more to place the cause of temperance on elevated, rational and Scriptural grounds. The entire absence of what some are pleased to call fanaticism, or of anything that could by any possibility be brought under that odious and much abused name, the transparent candor, the cogency as well as clearness of argument, the patience of examination, the deference to the Scriptures, and at the same time that spirit of fairness which would oppose their being wrested even to serve what might be deemed the best interests of humanity, — add to these the learning, without pedantry, the science, without pretence, the calm, sound reasoning, without the imposing show of argumentation, and we have the leading characteristics that must be conceded to the work by every intelligent and fair minded reader, whatever may be his opinion on the final merits of the questions that have called it forth. If we allude to the noble style of the writer, — that easy and vigorous command of language which marked his earliest widely spread productions, rendered still more attractive here by the mild and mellowed dignity of age,—it is simply done with the truthful purpose of commending the book as a most agreeable and instructtive classic to all who have a taste for elevated composition, who can appreciate true eloquence as well as distinguish good wine, or who have a relish for the beauties of thought and diction, whether they relish temperance or not.

A similar remark may be addressed to those who might doubt the entire correctness or cogency of the Scriptural argument as here presented. Be that, however, as it may, the work has certainly other merits demanding their attentive and careful perusal. Here is certainly much valuable Scriptural information, presented in a lucid and striking form, and which it may be worth any man's while to make himself familiar with. Here are hidden things drawn forth from classic research, which the mind is all the richer for possessing: more expanded, more liberal, endowed with a higher and more humanizing culture. They have an antiquarian value. They bring us into connection with other social conditions widely different from our own, yet exhibiting the same unmistakable traits of our common nature, the same intimate connection between ever varying outside physical facts and the principles of an eternal and immutable morality.

The temperance argument from Scripture, especially in the aspect in which it now presents itself of total abstinence *from all that can intoxicate*, may be regarded as twofold. It is *positive* and *defensive*. By the first we mean, the direct bringing to bear upon the conscience the law of love or charity, as given in the precepts and exemplified in the actual or declared conduct of Christ and his apostles. This argument raises no question of science. It has almost as little to do with any question of philology. It lies upon the very face of Scripture in its fairest and most obvious application to a patent and notorious evil. It takes its outside stand upon the admitted prevalence of a most destructive vice, and the admitted difficulties of prevention, made especially great by the introduction of new substances, new stimulants, new indulgences, new sensual habits, all concurring to produce a greatly changed condition of modern society. It is an application, to this changed and ever changing exterior, of an eternal, never changing, inward principle. This argument seeks no specific rule, it looks for no unmistakable denunciations of particular substances or particular enjoyments, as evil, *per se;* it requires no universal literal precepts of outward abstinence, whose observance, on no other grounds than the literalness and specialty of the terms, might degenerate into a dry asceticism, or an irrational superstition, instead of being favorable to an elevated and spiritual morality. It simply presents, we say, a certain condition of our modern society, on the one hand, and then brings to bear upon it the lucid teachings of Christ in the Parable of the good Samaritan, or the golden Law of Love, or the noble declaration of the Apostle, "*Wherefore, if meat make my brother to offend, I will eat no flesh while the world standeth, lest I make my brother to offend.*" "My brother!" Here is the soul of the argument, worth ten thousand rules, *per se.* My brother! my weak brother! my poor, vicious, lost, ruined brothers! brothers to me in Adam, and who may yet be brothers to me in Christ! I will abstain, for their sakes, from anything, from everything whose use in me might peril their souls, or even tempt to ways destructive of the poor measure of earthly good they might otherwise enjoy in this stage of discipline and probation. Logically, it may be summed in a sentence: May there be circumstances in which the higher Christian morality, the true transcendental ethics, would require a man to abstain from "meat" for the sake of others, how much stronger the argument now to abstain from intoxicating drinks on this principle alone, without any perplexing, ever irresolvable logomachies about "rights" or wrongs *per se?* Translate the Apostles' language, not the words simply, into a modern vocabulary, put the soul of the language into the corresponding thoughts that come out of the modern social condition, and we have the argument, *a fortiori* and *a fortissimo*, for entire abstinence from all those substances, whether old or new, whether simple or combined, that are now producing such appalling desolation in our modern world.

This argument is perfect. It needs no logical formulas; for the sane mind, the sound mind, the spiritual mind, bows down before it upon the first simple presentment of its two premises, Christian love and a ruined humanity. He who is truly temperate, truly *sober*, truly σωφρων, whether in the New Testament or classical usage of that beautiful word, acknowleges at once its conclusive power. Even on the lower scale of a purely secular ethics, and for minds that will ascend to no higher region, it is unanswerable. What need then, it may be said, of anything more? Why should not temperance men be satisfied with it, instead of trying to show more specific prohibitions, or looking for more literal condemnations of specific acts or substances, *per se?* Why not be content with the noble moral argument whose immutable spirit is the same for all ages, and capable of prompt and conclusive application to the prevalent vice or vices of any age? They *are* satisfied with it, we answer, at least all reasonable friends of temperance, all who wish to place the temperance cause upon its highest ground, all who would make it a matter of principle, as the New Testament does, instead of such a mere arbitrary asceticism or superstition as is taught in the Koran. They *are* satisfied with this positive, clear, unanswerable, Scriptural argument for total abstinence from certain things in certain well ascertained conditions of society and the world. They *are* content, we say; but it is their adversaries who are not satisfied. These are the men who are for pressing the Bible into specific rules, regulative of the outward thing instead of the inward principle. *They* are the men who strive hard to extract from the Scriptures, not so much specific con demnations as specific commendations of what is known to be evil. *They* are the *per se* logicians.

They would make out a *right*, *per se*, very much like the sin *per se* of others who would seem to be on the opposite extreme, and yet do actually harmonize with them in the spirit and principle of their reasoning.

Such is the condition into which perversity of feeling, rather than any logical demand of the intellect, brings the reasoning on this question, and hence the necessity, on the other side, of the second Scriptural argument, or the one we have styled the defensive. It is to wrest this weapon from their hands. It is to show that while the higher moral reasoning needs not the aid of specific denunciations of particular substances, as evil *in themselves*, or irrespective of their moral effects, so neither, on the other hand, must the adversary be allowed, without resistance, to maintain that any such substance is a good *in itself*, or declared in Scripture to be such, in any sense that would not allow or even demand a total abstinence from it in a given social state.

The temperance advocate takes issue on this ground. He denies that wine, the intoxicating wine of almost universal modern use, is pronounced a blessing in the Scriptures, and that, therefore, abstinence from it, total abstinence, is either a contempt or a denial of a good gift of God.

Such is substantially the position taken by Dr Nott in these Lectures. The *per se* ultraists on both sides are avoided. It is a calm, dignified, learned, and we think, in the main, successful argument, to show that the Bible condemns the use of certain substances, not *per se*, not from any qualities requiring the aid of science to ascertain them as such, not from any known or unknown chemical measure of alcohol, but because, according to the knowledge of the day, they were *intoxicating*, and therefore had an immoral influence. The physical or scientific causes may have been, in that age, very imperfectly known, as they are now very imperfectly known. But such a view does not detract at all from the reverence due to the real inspiration. It does not at all diminish—to a right thinking mind it even enhances—the moral power. There may have been, on the part of these inspired men, ignorance, even error, as to the nature of substances they approve, as well as of substances they condemn. The Infinite in knowledge might have made a supernatural advance in their science, but it would still, as science, have been *imperfect*, still the vehicle of error, still therefore the ground of cavil. It would have removed no real difficulty; it might, it probably would, have created others still greater. But they had a higher mission. They were inspired to denounce a specific psychological or moral state supposed to be produced by certain causes. The state was *known;* the causation was imperfectly understood, even as it is yet imperfectly understood; for when we say *imperfectly*, it is simply saying there is something more, and still something more, and that indefinitely, to be discovered about it. Liebig is farther on, but, in one sense, he is no nearer the perfect end of these things, even of these physical things, than Solomon the wisest of Jewish naturalists. The bare statement of the thought is sufficient to show that an exact scientific revelation of the chemical components productive of such a pyschological or moral state, would be at variance with the whole known manner in which the Infinite has chosen to communicate with the finite mind. It might be maintained morever—we say it with all reverent reserve of any *a priori* speculations as to the reasons or modes of the Divine teaching—that such a scientific method of revelation would have defeated the great end for which a revelation is made, and is alone worthy to be made. It would have had a tendency to increase that which is now the great evil of our fallen condition,—to make the physical predominant to the obscuration of the moral,—to give power and knowledge, especially *natural knowledge*, a higher place in our souls than grace and goodness. Even in the ethical region, it would have given prominence to the ascetic, and the æsthetic, instead of the higher spiritual. It would have had a tendency to make men content with the letter, and thus, perhaps, as has often been exemplified in our wayward human history, have led them to every kind of device to substitute a false and carnal for a true and spiritual obedience. It would, in short, have led the mind to rest in facts, the exact knowledge of which varies with the ever changing science of different ages, instead of that moral fact which was as perfect and as clear to Jeremiah as it is now to Faraday. The moral fact in this case was the *state of soul* we call intoxication. The ancients knew it as well as we, although our experimental evidence is so much more abundant. Holy men of old were inspired to denounce this evil. The Inspiring power used their thoughts, their language, their knowledge, as the medium through which to give the denunciation clearness, force and impressiveness. It was the outward knowledge of their day, perfect as to the effect, or thing denounced, imperfect as to the causation. The same Divine power filled them with a vehement feeling against this state denounced. Under the influence of this feeling thus inbreathed, this thought thus divinely given, and under the special guidance, too, of the eternal wisdom whence it came, they used the language of their day in the condemnation of substances best known as the producers of the psychological condition which was the real, the unchangeable evil *per se.* It was *intoxication;* not intoxication to excess, but intoxication in any degree; intoxication sought as intoxication simply, be it more or less. It was the act of a person in health using certain substances, not as medical remedies (more or less imperfectly known as the antidotes to an already deranged condition of the system), not for any nutritive, strengthening or restorative qualities, but solely for producing that evil state called intoxication, evil, not as excess, but in any, even the least or incipient degrees, — evil in effect, evil in motive, evil *per se.* It was the act of a person in health deranging his spiritual nature and putting it in a false state, disturbing the organs or faculties of thought, imparting an unnatural impulse to the passions, quickening the

Θυμος, or excitable part of our nature, not in the way its Maker designed it, as an auxiliary to the rational and moral action, but for its own pleasurable emotion; thus, in a word, running the risk of giving the sensual the predominance over the spiritual powers of our being. This was intoxication; a *spiritual fact.* A Hebrew prophet, we repeat, could know it as well as the most scientific of modern chemists or modern anatomists. It was evil—evil altogether; that which was sought, that which was desired for the purpose of producing it, that substance in which this, as a known or supposed effect, was the chief ingredient of value—that was evil also. It was evil, not so much from any chemical constitution, but because it was so sought and for such an end. Now to denounce the state without bringing in the supposed cause—the substance that quickened the evil motive, and was in turn called into demand by it—would have been beating the air. Intoxication was evil, and so were things that would intoxicate, especially as sought for that purpose. In speaking of it, therefore, as a thing wrong—always wrong as thus desired—he must use the language best understood by the men of his age, and which might be taken as the representative of the same unchanging truth amid all the changing science of after ages.

Here is the ground for the argument brought out in these Lectures. Wine is commended in some places as a blessing. This cannot be for any *intoxicating* effect, even in the slightest degree, but for the good it does, its known effects as healthful, pleasant, nutritive, restorative, non-intoxicating. It might be used to excess, as bread or honey might be eaten in excess, but such was not, such could not be, the common tendency of anything thus declared to be a blessing. Even a tendency to excess, simply as excess, must make a thing an evil (if such tendency belongs to the very essential working instead of being a mere incident, as in bread and honey and other substances commonly regarded as innocent); but in the thing denounced, there is clearly an evil distinct from that of excess, as will be seen in its proper place. So the good substance, the good wine, might become changed; it might be suffered to get into a perverted state, and in this changed state produce intoxication; but such was not, could not have been the state on which the benediction was pronounced. Neither could such have been any usual condition of the thing commended, for then it would not have been ranked with those other substances, "corn and oil," which, whilst they agree with it in its nutritive, healthful, in a word, blessed properties, would not have so wholly differed from it in this peculiarly and essentially evil effect.

And so, again, wine (sometimes under this generic name and sometimes under others) is condemned, not as something merely which might be used in excess; for there are other undisputed blessings that might also be thus used in excess, but which are not thus condemned in terms of evil attached to the very substances themselves. This is a distinction which is deemed to be one of much importance. A man might eat to excess, and gluttony is condemned, but bread is never called "a mocker;" no man is ever denounced for putting the loaf to his neighbor's mouth. One might cloy himself with honey; such excess, as excess, might be reproached as sensuality; but honey, though so sweet and tempting, is nowhere spoken of as something which it was dangerous for a man even to look upon, as an evil thing whose very nature it was to bite like a serpent and sting like an adder. These substances are nowhere spoken of in terms of severe condemnation, directed immediately against the things themselves, and without the accompaniment of any qualifying terms connected with such mere excess.

But there is a wine thus spoken of, condemned for an evil which is not merely that of excess. It must have been a substance known or supposed to produce intoxication; that unnatural thing which is evil in every degree. It was different from the healthful and nutritive substance; and the grand *moral* distinction was, that *it was sought for a different purpose*. It might not always be perfectly easy to draw the physical line between them, in consequence of the tendency of the healthful to degenerate into the injurious and the intoxicating. It may be a long time yet before science settles exactly where that line is, if she ever does exactly settle it. In modern as well as in ancient times, practical moral results furnish better rules than any chemical tests. It was not anciently, as it is not even now, a question of alcohol as determined by grains, but a higher question, a question of *intoxication*, as an admitted evil state. The wine that did not intoxicate, and was not used to intoxicate, or *sought to intoxicate*, was good; a blessing was in it. The wine that did intoxicate, and *was sought for that purpose*, was bad; it was pronounced a woe and a curse.

Such is the moral truth, the moral statement. Now in what language is this revealed to us in the Bible? It is answered: in a peculiar language, growing out of the peculiar nature of the subject matter. The good and the evil substances are both entitled logically to the generic name of wine, from the obvious fact of their common unadultered origin in the juice of the grape. Such, then, would occasionally be the name given to both, especially when precision of terms is unnecessary from the fact that the context clearly shows which effect, as characteristic of the respective kinds, was chiefly in view. Still, if there was a wide difference in such effects, marked by almost invariable characteristics,—if one produced only evil, whilst the other was in the main productive of good,—*if they were sought for directly differrent purposes*, the one for its intoxicating, the other for its nutritive and restoring qualities,—if the one was regarded by the virtuous as best, in its pure, unchanged state, whilst the other, as is the law of all things evil, kept ever calling for an increase of the characteristic evil quality, and so became continually more and more deleterious in its effects,—then there would arise, in time, an adaptation of language more specific in its terms, growing wider in its distinctive differences, and aiming to describe these two substances by their varying fruits, rather than by that generic union of origin which is the common ground of naming in the infancy or first stages of human speech. And such, on opening the Bible, we find to be actually the case. Such is the law of naming and derivation. The history of the thing, the rising and divergency of the evil appears in the words to which it gives rise; it is seen in the more sparing use of the old generalization and the more frequent employment of specific or descriptive epithets. The state of the Hebrew language corresponds well with what we would, *a priori*, expect it to be on such a theory. Both kinds of wine are occasionally described by the same generic appellation, *yayin;* but in other and numerous cases, each gets to itself its own peculiar name, more closely associated with its peculiar good or evil (that is, its nutritive or intoxicating effect), and the opposite purposes for which they are respectively sought; so that when the one is mentioned, there is no need of any qualifying language to show the reason either of the benediction or of the condemnation.

All need of dwelling farther on this, then, is saved by the admirable manner in which the whole subject is presented in the chart of texts to be found in the appendix. If the reader has any candor, the effect upon his mind must be most striking. The general term is *yayin;* the name almost always used with approbation, and sometimes with blessing, is *tirosh*, or the new unintoxicating wine or juice of the grape. There is, in fact, but one exception, Hosea, iv., 1, and there it will be seen, that in reference to the main, we may say, .the only point in this argument, or the matter of intoxication, it is only a seeming exception. Let the reader look carefully at the context, and he must see, from the connection of *tirosh* with the other indulgences there mentioned, that it is simply the excessive or surfeiting enjoyments there condemned, rather than any directly intoxicating or immediate soul changing quality, which is the evil element in the species elsewhere so unequivocally reprobated.

Other descriptive names are used for the good wine, but this is predominant—so predominnnt, we say, and so marked in the context for its innocent, non-intoxicating qualities, that any one who would cite these benedictions of *tirosh*, as real commendations of the intoxicating drink sought by the ancient drunkards, shows himself greatly wanting both in Bible knowledge, and a proper reverence for the Holy Scriptures. If any one is disposed to go still farther, and quote them in defence of the vile compounds of modern times, we will not attempt to characterize either his learning or morality.

The reader will notice in this synoptical chart some other terms of the later Hebrew, used for the same purpose as *tirosh*, but they are mostly descriptive, and expressive of a mild, innocent, non-intoxicating state of the vinous fluid. For the evil or intoxicating wine, the most common word is *yayin*.

Why should it take to itself so frequently this old name, thus driving the better and the unchanged substance to the use of a new and more descriptive epithet? The reason will be seen by a little careful attention to the usual course of things. In this world evil predominates. Language, like all things else, shares in the human degeneracy. Words follow the stream of the human depravity. It is thus that the evil thing usurps the generic or family title. On this account, in cases where *yayin* is employed of the innocent beverage, or the simple unintoxicating juice of the grape, it is usually accompanied by such a context as leaves no doubt of its meaning.

So, also, the use of the bad wine tends to multiplicity of epithet. The Anacreontic spirit seeks diversity in its song. The pure love of intoxication *per se*, as something different from restoring aliment or even the excess of cloying indulgence, demands new terms corresponding to its own ever growing strength. Hence such words as *sobhe*, the wine that is *sipped*, or *supped*—its etymology being visible almost all the way down our Saxon or Celtic stream—the *mesek*, the *drugged wine*, *mixed* with hot and spicy ingredients—the *shecar* or *strong drink*, synonymous with drunkenness itself. All these most graphically mark the descent from the commencing divergence of the barely intoxicating *yayin*, down to those lower and still lower degrees into which it is the nature of all evil, once born, to be ever plunging. That surely must be an evil, *per se*, to whose very essence it pertains to breed a deeper and still deeper evil. This evil is infused into the wine when it first begins to have its intoxicating quality. Chemists may settle that scientifically, if they can, from the degree of alcohol, but the practical test is the one for the moralist. That which intoxicates is evil, evil in the slightest degree of its effect; and the reason is, that such slightest degree of intoxication ever demands, not the same repeated simply (though that would be an evil), but a stronger and still stronger intoxication. This is the stone that Sisyphus is ever condemned to roll. The appetite calls for a stronger stimulant; the want invents a stronger substance, and this demands a new and stronger word. It is the hot mixed wine, the wine that giveth its color in the cup, that sparkles like the serpent's eye and stingeth like the adder's fang—it is the poisoned *mesek*, the potent *shecar*—these are the new ideas and the new terms, showing that they are the perversions, the adulterations, the poisonous changes of something which in its original state would not intoxicate and would not, therefore, be *sought by the drunkard.*

Now it may be said, perhaps, that there are a few cases, a very few, in which some of these names for the intoxicating wine are used with language seeming to imply approbation. But let the reader carefully examine that correct and valuable chart. He will see that such uses are unmistakably marked as medicinal. There were cases where an overpowering depression of body and soul might be relieved by stimulating wine; cases perhaps, of urgent necessity, before other and slower remedies could be applied.

So "strong drink might be given to him who was ready to perish." How strongly—if a man will but think—does the apparent exception prove the general moral prohibition of such substances. These cases but confirm the sober principle of interpretation that runs through these Lectures. The general position may again be stated under two aspects. The good wine might be used to excess, but it was the excess of surfeiting, not of intoxication; it was incidental, not entering into the very essence; it belonged to the misuse, not to *every use* of the substance employed. So, on the other hand, the intoxicating wine might be used for beneficent purposes, but it was in those same states of an already deranged spiritual or physical condition which demand other toxical or medicinal remedies—such being in their nature mainly poisons; that is, poisons for the healthy diathesis, and only to be taken as temporary antidotes to other still more malignant and deranging influences.

Such is the substantial outline of the argument in these Lectures. We have not made any close examination to see if there might not be some errors in the classical or Scriptural references. It is enough that the main positions are sober, cautious, well reasoned, impregnable. There are doubtless readers who will be dissatisfied. *Per se* ultraists on both sides may condemn the work as falling short. But their real quarrel is with the rational Bible method rather than the fair and candid manner in which it is brought out. Those who would make it a question of chemistry rather than of morals, may feel a secret disappointment. Even though they do not venture outwardly to complain, yet is there an inward vexation, perhaps, because the Bible has not been as explicit on some of these points as could have been wished, or as their favorite theory might demand. Why could not the Scriptures have always called the bad wine *yayin* and the good wine *tirosh*, so that there could be no possible mistake about the meaning and its application in every case? Why could not revelation have told us how much alcohol is in the one, and whether or no there is but little alcohol or no alcohol at all in the other? But to all such uneasy querists the fair answer is already given. This is not the way in which the Infinite communicates himself to the finite mind. It employs not the language of science; for it is ever changing, ever imperfect, that is, ever *unfinished*. It does not make use of its facts or statements as such; for they remain not the same from age to age. If it employs them at all, it is only as entering into the common mind, and as having thus become the representatives of universal thought. We would say it with reverence and diffidence: Scripture may even be regarded as avoiding marked precision of language or departure from the common speech, if by such niceties of terms, or such preference of the special and the technical, the mind would be led to dwell on the outward and the physical to the neglect of the great moral idea.

And yet even the language of the Bible, as distinct from its ideas, must have been an object of the Divine care. It is a book ever suggestive. Its holy texts are ever expanding to a higher and a wider meaning; but it is only for those who have eyes to see and ears to hear. They who seek for stumbling-blocks may find them in abundance; but still it remains true as ever, that "wisdom's ways are plain to him that understandeth, and right to them that find knowledge." That Scriptural simplicity of enunciation, which has the greatest charm for all who love the Bible most, furnishes the chief occasion for the caviller. It is perhaps impossible always to refute him logically. And so it may be that in this respect the present Lectures may fail to meet the views of extremists on either side; but we have little doubt of their securing everywhere a favorable and grateful hearing from the sincere friends of humanity and the candid and intelligent lovers of Divine truth.

CONTENTS.

Prefatory Letter by the Editor, ... 3

Introduction, by Prof. Tayler Lewis, ... 7

LECTURE No. I.

PRELIMINARY REMARKS.

Preliminary remarks — The question at issue stated — Testimony of Moses, Solomon and Pliny — Other testimony in Scotland — In America — The number of drunkards in this republic — The remedy intimated — No alternative — We must change our social usage, or meet the expense of their maintenance — What intoxicating liquors cost Great Britain annually — What those who purchase liquors pay their money for, ... 1

LECTURE No. II.

THE REMEDY.

Intoxicating liquors useful, but not as a beverage in health — Those who use intoxicating liquors, and live to be old, live not in consequence, but in spite of drinking — Intoxicating liquors analogous to exhilirating gas — The number of deaths by the use of intoxicating liquors very great — The waste of life by intoxicating liquors supplied from the ranks of temperate drinkers — Deleterious effects of distilled liquors, of beer and of bad wine, ... 29

LECTURE No. III.

THE BIBLE.

The kind of wine in question — The authority of Scripture — Wine of different kinds, good and bad — Spoken of by sacred writers — Grape juice called wine — Good wine — Better than after fermentation — If not wine, but grape juice out of which wine is made, and called wine figuratively, then is wine not commended, but grape juice merely — The wine of the press and vat in Palestine slightly fermented — What is meant by unfermented wine as here used,... 50

LECTURE No. IV.

INQUIRY EXTENDED TO PROFANE WRITERS.

The wine question continued — Grape juice spoken of as a beverage by profane writers — Called wine — Pronounced good wine — Better before than after fermentation — The formation of alcohol intentionally prevented by arresting fermentation — Dissipated when formed by the filter, or counteracted by dilution — The question at issue a question of degree, not of totality — The question of sin *per se* considered — Perfect purity not attainable — Wine placed on the same footing as other articles of food,............... 93

LECTURE No. V.

WINE — ITS SACRAMENTAL USE.

The wine made use of at the Paschal Supper, at the wedding at Cana of Galilee — And the wine recommended to Timothy,...... 131

LECTURE No. VI.

THINGS, NOT NAMES.

How wines called by the same name can be distinguished — Abstinence from wine urged on the ground of expediency,........ 148

LECTURE No. VII.

ADULTERATIONS.

The adulteration of the wines of commerce — Drunkenness and gluttony compared — Analogy between bad oil, bad milk and bad wine — An appeal to Patriots and Christians,.................. 170

LECTURE No. VIII.

MORAL AND NATURAL LAWS AS APPLIED TO STRONG DRINK.

Books of Revelation and Nature — Misery springs from violations of law — Nature interrogated — Her answer returned — In crime, disease and death — Spontaneous combustion — Distinction between stimulants and aliments — Example of moderate drinkers more injurious than of drunkards — Iniquities of fathers visited on children — Expostulation with moderate drinkers,.............. 192

LECTURE No. IX.

MORAL AND NATURAL LAWS AS APPLIED TO STRONG DRINK.

Nature still farther interrogated — Another page turned — The response in the structure of creation and the orderings of Providence — Man made for temperance and chastity — Excess fatal — The intrepid engineer — The voice of Nature, the voice of God — His disapprobation of intoxicating liquors stamped on the whole human organism — Especially the human stomach — Explanation of the drawings of Doct. Sewal — The maniac,............. 214

LECTURE No. X.

THE TRAFFIC — APPEAL TO DEALERS.

The injurious effect of abandoning the liquor trade considered — The expedient of total abstinence — The manner in which it should be enforced — An appeal to dealers,......................... 238

LECTURE No. XI.

RECAPITULATION — GENERAL APPEAL IN BEHALF OF TEMPERANCE.

Appeal to Parents — To Youth — To Women — Conclusion, ... 265

APPENDIX, ... 283

Letter from Mr. Delavan to Gov. King, ... 297

Adulteration of Liquors, ... 311

Bishop Potter's Address on the Drinking Usages of Society, 315

Use and Abuse of Alcoholic Drinks, in Health and Disease, by Wm. B. Carpenter, ... 336

LECTURE No. 1.

PRELIMINARY REMARKS.

Preliminary remarks — The question at issue stated — Testimony of Moses, Solomon and Pliny — Other testimony in Scotland — In America — The number of drunkards in this republic — The remedy intimated — No alternative — We must change our social usage, or meet the expense of their maintenance — What intoxicating liquors cost Great Britain annually — What those who purchase liquors pay their money for.

It is now some eighteen centuries since the temperance question was argued in Palestine, by a prisoner in bonds, before a Roman Governor. It has often since been argued; seldom, however, it is believed, with the same effect, and perhaps as seldom in the same spirit. Saul of Tarsus was scarcely less remarkable for his courtesy of manner than for his fixedness of purpose.

Mere dictation, as well as stern rebuke, comes with an ill grace, even among friends, from those, believed to be at least, as weak and erring as ourselves; whereas there is always a charm in meekness, and the persuasive accent of unaffected kindness seldom falls powerless, even on a stranger's ear. Whether the friends of temperance, I mean its most active friends, may not have lost something of their influence over the public mind by the advocacy of even their noble cause, in a manner too stern, and with a spirit too uncompromising, is a question which at the present time may well deserve consideration.

Even truth bears lightly on minds exasperated by a sense of injury; and conviction is slow to reach bosoms rankling with resentment, and before which prejudice has flung her broad and impenetrable shield.

Although we neither use, nor abet the use, even the moderate use, of intoxicating liquor, in any of its forms, as a beverage, still we do not know, and dare not therefore affirm, that they who do so use it, in some of them, are, on that account, greater sinners than other men. And even though they were, they are still our brethren: and we have no desire, during this season of divine forbearance, to sunder those bonds which have hitherto united us. On the contrary, we wish hereafter, as heretofore, to maintain a free and fraternal intercourse with them; to hear their arguments, and in our turn to address to them our own. We think that truth is on our side; and if it be so, our opponents may hereafter be convinced; and we trust in God they will hereafter be convinced —an additional reason why we are unwilling, by any indiscretion of ours, to alienate their feelings, and thus weaken the hold we might otherwise have on their reason and their conscience.

It is well to learn wisdom from the past. Years have now gone by, since I first became acquainted with the late Rev. Dr. Hoosack, of Johnstown, now gone to his rest. During a journey, taken with him soon after our acquaintance commenced, I observed that he used a little brandy and water with his dinner, to aid digestion; and took a small glass of bitters before breakfast to ensure an appetite; and though much younger than himself, I ventured to question the propriety of such a practice. He heard me patiently, and answered me playfully, as his manner was—"Your logic tells me one thing, my experience another, and in the absence of other evidence I shall continue my former practice;" and he did continue his former practice. We often afterwards met, and discussed the matter; but though the one drank spirits and the other water, we always met and parted in friendship. At length a public discussion of the whole question took place, at which both of us were present, when I was as delighted as surprised to find that my old friend Hoosack had come over to our side. "I continued," said he, giving a reason for his change of opinion "I continued to drink intoxicating liquor without apprehension, until I saw —— and —— and —— (naming three distinguished individuals) become intemperate, when thought I, if such men cannot, as life advances, withstand its growing influence, it is time for me to abjure its use."

And he did abjure its use; thereafter giving the whole weight of his influence to the cause of temperance, till full of years and honored by the churches, he left the world without a blot upon his character. His was a noble independence. I honored him for it, and I still honor him for it. My poor arguments did not convince him; the providence of God, however, did; and when light broke upon his mind he did homage to the truth.

But, in relation to the question now before us, what is truth? That some people lean to the one opinion, and some to the other, decides nothing. For though truth will ultimately prevail over error, the struggle may be violent and of long continuance. Saul of Tarsus is not the only individual, who, when erring grievously, has thought he was doing God service.

In some countries, when friends fall out, they are required by the laws of honor, to kill each other. In other countries each is required, by the same laws, to kill himself.

The time was, when our fathers owned slaves, and even, without compunction, engaged in the slave trade. Now the thought of this fills us with amazement: so the time was when rum and gin and brandy and whiskey, and that whole legion of alcoholic mixtures, were not only tolerated, but also held in estimation by the wise and good, as well as the ignorant and vile.

Then alcohol in some form was accounted needful to the doctor in compounding his medicine, to the lawyer in making out his brief, to the parson in composing his sermon—aye, *and in its delivery too.* While in every place of concourse,—at the house of feasting, at the house of mourning,—this spirit-stirring element seemed to be considered the one thing needful. To say nothing of gala days and weddings, not a christening could be performed, or even a funeral solemnized, among large and respectable classes of community, without this indispensable accompaniment. And the man of fortune who should have neglected to provide it, in anticipation, for his burial, would, in many a place, have been accounted, if not a denier of the faith, at least, less provident than an infidel.

Even in the exemplary and church-going city of Albany, the time was — I remember it well — when pastors and people vied with each other in the production of the best cherry, and raspberry, and strawberry brandy; as well as sundry other quite orthodox alcoholic mixtures, to be served occasionally, not only to company, but to be administered also to the smaller children as a vermifuge, and to the larger ones as a stomachic. While some there were — nay, many there were — and good men too, who, as a preparation for their nightly rest, as regularly took their whiskey punch, as they offered up their devotions. Indeed, if the moderate, and especially the occasional, use of intoxicating liquor, in some of its forms, is to exclude from our charity and fellowship, it will be difficult to find, even among our own members, executioners, without sin, to cast at their offending neighbor the first stone.

Now, notwithstanding this diversity of opinion and practice, all of us wish to live as long, and to enjoy, while we do live, as much as possible.

Will, then, the use of intoxicating liquor, extend the duration and increase the enjoyment of human life?

If this be the case, it is befitting that certain minds should be disabused of a groundless prejudice against its use; and on the contrary, if this be not the case, then is it befitting that certain other minds should be disabused of a no less groundless prejudice in favor of its use.

We who now oppose the prevailing practice, once thought and acted as those who now advocate it think and act. And who knows but those who now advocate it, may hereafter think and act as we do!

They cannot suppose that we who dislike self-denial as much, and love good cheer as well, as they do, have all at once, and without some good reason, real or imaginary, changed our habits, and abjured forever the use of an article, so long familiarized, and to which many of us at least were so much attached. As little can we suppose that they, who dread pain as much and love life as well as we do, will continue the use of the same article, (unless where inebriation has become habitual,) after they shall discover, what we profess to have already discovered, *that however prepared, and with whatever other ingredients combined, death is often, if not usually, one ingredient mingled in every cup in which it is contained.* For, however some might be disposed, for filthy lucre's sake, to furnish a deleterious preparation, to be drank by others, few it is believed would be disposed to drink of it themselves. And if such a preparation has been introduced, introduced extensively, they only who are privy to the fraud, and expect to profit by it, will withhold the meed of praise from the chemist who establishes and the herald who proclaims the alarming fact.

Had some drug, slow but certain in its work of death, been cast into those fountains whence your supply of water is derived, and had some wakeful guardians of the public welfare witnessed the transaction ; more than this, had they caused the water to be analyzed, detected the specific poison, tested its degree of virulence, and traced distinctly to its influence much of the disease and death with which your city is afflicted, ought they, because a portion of the citizens not having themselves as yet experienced any inconvenience, were incredulous; ought they, I repeat it, the less to sound the note of alarm on that account? This will not be pretended. As little will it be pretended, that for a similar reason the note of alarm may not, with equal freedom, be sounded where, in the use of any other beverage, a question of life and death is concerned. But is such a question here concerned? Many people think there is; think that in the manufacture and sale of the intoxicating liquors in use among us, fraud is practiced, and that under the guise of a healthful beverage, deleterious and destructive drinks are palmed on community; and that alike, though in different forms, in the hut of ignorance and the parlor of fashion.

Now be the truth of this what it may, they who believe this to be the truth are at liberty to proclaim that belief, even from the house-tops. "*The life of man is more than meat, and his body than raiment.*" But let it not be forgotten that they who do not believe this, are at equal liberty in the same manner to proclaim that they do not. Though error may, truth can have no reason to shun discussion. To think and speak and act on his own responsibility, and not to do the bidding of another, is alike the privilege of a freeman and a Christian.

Here then is common ground, where an issue may be fairly joined, between the water drinker and the spirit drinker of every class and character.

ARE THEN INTOXICATING LIQUORS OF THE KIND AND QUALITY GENERALLY IN USE AMONG US, DELETERIOUS, AS A BEVERAGE, OR ARE THEY NOT?

This is the real question; and not whether being deleterious, they ought to be avoided?

That pure alcohol is poison; that every beverage containing alcohol contains an element of poison, and that other elements of poison are often, if not usuallly, contained in intoxicating liquors, are known and admitted facts.

That these elements of poison, however, usually exist in such liquors, in sufficient intensity to disturb the healthy action of the system, by the production of crime, insanity, disease, or death, is not to be taken for granted, nor to be decided by reasoning *a priori*.

The same article may be healthful to plants and injurious to animals; healthful to animals and injurious to men; healthful to one man and injurious to another; healthful to some men at one time and in one degree, and injurious at another time and in another degree; or healthful in occasional, and injurious in habitual use. Now how is it with the several kinds of intoxicating liquors in use among us, are questions of fact not to be determined by clamor or dogmatism, but by observation and experiment.

To furnish data for such determination, however, no new experiments are required to be performed; a series of experiments reaching through more than forty centuries having been already furnished; experiments tried first in Asia on the top of Ararat, where the Ark rested; and since tried in Europe, in Africa, in America, and in the islands of the Sea. We have only to collect and collate these scattered and recorded results, to enable us to arrive at a knowledge of the truth.

Hear Moses speak: "And Noah began to be an husbandman, and he planted a vine-yard, and he drank of the wine." What next? "and he was drunken." I need not repeat the residue of the afflictive and humiliating details. Nor need I repeat the still more afflictive and humiliating details of drunkenness and incest, which the use of wine occasioned in the family of Lot after their departure from the vale of Sodom.

Hear Solomon speak: "Who hath wo? who hath sorrow? who hath contentions? who hath babblings? who hath wounds without cause? who hath redness of eyes?

"They that tarry long at the wine; they that go to seek mixed wine. Look not thou upon the wine when it is red, when it giveth its color in the cup, when it moveth itself aright. At the last it biteth like a serpent and stingeth like an adder." Neither here need I repeat the residue of the afflictive and humiliating details.

Hear Isaiah speak: "But they have erred through wine, and through strong drink are out of the way; the priest and the prophet have erred through strong drink; they err in vision, they stumble in judgment. For all tables are full of vomit and filthiness, so that there is no place clean."

But this, it is objected, is the testimony of sacred writers only. It is so. Would that of profane writers be deemed more conclusive?

Hear then Pliny the elder, speak. Pliny, than whom a purer patriot or a profounder sage lived not, out of Palestine, among the nations: "If we examine closely, we shall find there is nothing on which more pains are bestowed by mankind, than on wine. As though nature had not liberally furnished water, with which all other animals are content: we even force our horses to drink wine,* and we purchase at great pains and expense a liquor which deprives man of the use of his reason, renders him furious, and is the cause of an infinite variety of crimes.

---

* The custom of giving wine to horses was known to Homer. Vide, Iliad viii., li., 88. Philip de Comines says, that "At the close of a battle, having made his war horse, who was very much exhausted and very old, drink wine, it appeared to renew and rejuvenate him. The practice is common enough among all our cavaliers."

Columella, chap. 3, book 3d, recommends giving wine to cattle worried and overheated with labor.

"It is true it is so delicious that multitudes know no pleasure in life but that of drinking it. Yea that we may drink the more, we weaken this liquor by passing it through the straining bag,* and we invent other methods to stimulate our thirst; we go so far as to employ poisons. Some persons before drinking make use of hemlock,† that the fear of death may compel them to drink. Others swallow powder of pumice-stone and many other things which I should blush to name.

"The most prudent facilitate the digestion of vinous crudities by resorting to sweating rooms, whence they are sometimes carried forth half dead. Some cannot even wait to reach their couch, on the first quitting of the bath, nor even to put on their tunic. But naked and panting as they are, rush eagerly on great pitchers of wine, which they drain to the bottom, as if to exhibit the strengh of their stomachs. They next vomit ‡ and drink anew, renewing the like career twice and three times, as though born only to waste wine; as though men were under

---

* Columella, book ix., chap. 15. — The Greeks were acquainted with the custom of passing wines through the saccus.

[Vide Theophrastus de causis vi., chap. 9.] The Romans used to pass through the saccus old and too heavy wines. Vide Martial lib. 11, Epig. 40; also xii., 61.

† Wine is a remedy for the poison of hemlock, according to Pliny, lib. xxii., sec. 17.

‡ See on this custom, Cicero — Pro Dejotaro. Also Martial, book iii., Epig. 82. Seutonias, Life of Vitellius xiii., and of Claudius, chap. xiii.

obligation to be the channel by which wine should return to the earth.

"Others borrow from the barbarians most extraordinary exercises to show that they are constituted genuine wine-bibbers. They tumble in the mire, where they affect to lay the head flat upon the back, and to display a broad and muscular chest. All this they shamefully practice, because these violent acts lead them to drink with increased avidity.

"And now what shall we say to the infamous representations upon the drinking-cups and vessels for wine, which would seem as though drunkenness alone were insufficient to excite men to lewdness.

"Thus they drink, as if prostitution and drunkenness, ye gods! were invited and even bribed with a reward.

"Some receive a certain sum of money, on condition of eating as much as they drink; while others expend in wine what they obtain in games of chance. Thus the eyes of the husband become heavy, while those of the wife are wide open, and employed in full liberty.

"It is then the most secret thoughts are revealed. Some at such times disclose the contents of their last wills; others throw out expressions, which, in the common phrase, they will thereafter be forced to eat.

"How many perish in consequence of words uttered in a state of inebriety; so that it has passed into a proverb, that 'Wine brings truth to light.'

"Such men, at best* see not the rising sun, and thus abridge their lives. Thence proceeds their pendulous cheeks, their ulcerated eyes, their trembling hands, incapable of holding the full glass without spilling a portion of its contents. Thence those furious transports which disturb their slumbers, and that inquietude, just punishment of their intemperance, in which their nights are passed.

"The highest reward of their drunkenness is the creation of a monstrous passion, and a pleasure which nature and decency forbid. On the morrow their breath is still infected with the odor of wine. They experience, as it were, a death of memory, and almost total oblivion of the past. Those who live after this sort, call their conduct the art of making time and enjoying life; though the day of their debauch and the subsequent day are equally lost. In the reign of Tiberius Claudius, about forty years ago, it became the custom at Rome, to drink wine in the morning with empty stomachs, and to take no food till after drinking. This was of foreign derivation, and was introduced by certain physicians, who wish to commend themselves to the public favor by the introduction of some novelty.

"To drink is, by the Parthians, considered highly honorable. Among the Greeks, Alcibiades has thus distinguished himself; among the Latins, Marcellius Torquatus, of Milan, who had been prætor and pro-

* Vide Seneca, Epig. 122. Athenæus, lib. vi., p. 273; also some of the preface of Columella.

consul, has obtained the surname Tricongius, by drinking at once three congii of wine* in the presence and to the great astonishment of the Emperor Tiberius, who, in his old age, became severe, and even cruel, but in his youth was much addicted to drinking.

"It is believed, moreover, that Lucius Pisco obtained from him the prefectship of Rome, for having remained at table two days and two nights in succession with this prince, who had even then mounted the throne. It was said, also, that in nothing did Drusus Cæsar more closely resemble his father Tiberius, than in the quality of a deep drinker.

"Torquatus, of whom we have spoken above, had no equal in his exact observance of the Bacchanal laws; for the art of drinking has also its laws. Whatever quantity of wine he drank, he never stuttered or vomited. The morning found him still at his potations. He swallowed a great quantity of wine at one draught; and if a small cup was poured out to him, he never failed to demand the remainder. While he drank he never took breath nor spat, and he never left in his glass any heel-taps which could produce sound when thrown on the pavement; in which he diligently observed the rules for the prevention of trick in drinking.

"Tergilla reproached M. T. Cicero, that he drank too congii at a single draught, and that one day, being intoxicated, he had thrown a glass at the head of Marcus Agrippa. Truly these are the works of

---

* Three gallons, one quart and one pint.

drunkenness. But doubtless Cicero, the son, wished to take from Mark Antony, the murderer of his father, the palm of drunkenness; for it is well known that, before him, Antony had been very jealous of the title of a first-rate drinker, and even published a treatise on his drunkenness, in which he dares to apologize for that vice. But this treatise persuades me only, that the drunkenness of Antony was the cause of all the evils with which he has afflicted the earth. He vomited forth this work a short time before the battle of Actium; as if to show that he was already intoxicated with the blood of the citizens, and thirsted only the more for it.

"For this necessity accompanies the vice of drunkenness, that drinking augments thirst; and every one knows this 'bon mot' of the Scythian ambassador, that the more the Parthians drank, the more they thirsted.

"The western nations have also peculiar intoxicating drinks. The Gauls and Spaniards composed them of grain steeped in divers manners. The Spaniards give them various names. There is a method of rendering them susceptible of long preservation. Similar drinks are also made in Egypt from grain. There is no part of the world where inebriation is not practiced; for they drink such liquors pure — that is, without diluting them like wine. The earth seemed to produce grain for the nourishmen of man; but, by Hercules! how industrious is vice; we have found a method to make even water intoxicate us.

"Two liquors are furnished by the trees, both very pleasant, wine for inward, and oil for outward application. Oil, however, is the most useful, and men have been industrious in their efforts to procure it; but they have been infinitely more diligent in regard to wine, having invented ninety-five different kinds; perhaps double the number, on full examination, might be reckoned—and so few of oil! *

If, then, the use of intoxicating wine, deemed to be the least deleterious of intoxicating liquors, required, even in countries suited to the vine, so much caution, was attended with so much hazard, and led, even occasionally, to such lamentable results, what was to have been expected from those other and baser fabrications, which the brewer's and distiller's arts have subsequently palmed on the world? What? Precisely what has taken place,—*a mighty and gratuitous increase both of guilt and misery.*

But what evidence is there that such has been the case? You shall hear. To recent inquiries sent abroad by philanthropists, to different parts of the earth, the response returned from New Holland was, "that in that colony intoxicating liquors promote crime, induce disease, and hasten death." A similar response has been returned from Calcutta, from Burmah, from Malacca, from China, from the Cape of Good Hope, from Continental Europe, and from the British Isles.

---

* Plin., Lib. xiv., chap. 22.

In Scotland—exemplary Christian Scotland—the use of intoxicating liquors has tripled in the last fifteen years. In 1823, the whole consumption amounted to 2,300,000 gallons; in 1837, to 6,776,715 gallons. In Glasgow alone, there are two thousand two hundred spirit shops, that is one spirit shop for every ten dwelling-houses throughout the city. The consumption of spiritous liquors has increased in Glasgow during the last fifteen years five hundred per cent, whereas the population has increased only sixty-six per cent. But, mark ye, in the meantime crime has increased four hundred per cent, fever sixteen hundred per cent, death three hundred per cent, and the chances of human life diminished forty-four per cent. What an appalling result! *

But this is too general and remote. Be it so. Turn we then to evidence more specific, and to localities near home. If there be any truth in the declaration of physicians in our cities, or even in the verdict of juries returned over the bodies of the dead, and under the solemnity of an oath, then is drunkenness a most frightful source of death among ourselves. Nor is it, if the keepers of prisons and asylums are to be believed, a less frightful source of poverty, insanity and crime. It is apparent from the bills of mortality which have been kept, that in a single year twenty deaths have been occasioned in Portsmouth, N. H., by the use of intoxicating liquors: twenty-one in Salem, Mass.; thirty-one in New

---

* See Edinburgh Review for April, 1838; Trades Union.

Haven, Conn.; thirty in New Brunswick, N. J., and seven hundred in Philadelphia.

The average duration of life to those Irish emigrants who pave the streets and rear the edifices in the city, and who excavate the canals and grade the railroads in the country, the average duration of life to this hard laboring (and alas! that it should be so, till of late, hard drinking) population, is said, owing to this fatal propensity, to have been reduced to about five years from the time of their landing.

And it is also said, that those emigrants, who year after year enter the States hale and healthy from the Canadas, stripped of their summer's earnings by those harpies of the dram-shop, enter on the winter beggared and comfortless, and that a third of their number, before the next spring opens, are, not unfrequently, in their graves.

After examination had, it has been made apparent, that of eight hundred and eighty maniacs in our asylums, four hundred owe their loss of reason to the use of intoxicating liquors. That seventeen hundred out of nineteen hundred paupers in our poor-houses, and thirteen hundred out of seventeen hundred criminals in our prisons, owe their pauperism and their crime to the same cause. That forty-three out of forty-four murders were committed under the influence of alcoholic stimulus. That sixty-seven out of seventy-seven found dead, died of drunkenness, and that four hundred out of six hundred and ninety juvenile delinquents either drank themselves or belonged to families that did so.

"I have shown," says that indefatigable agent, Samuel Chipman, Esq., who visited all the poor-houses and prisons in the State of New-York, "I have shown beyond the power of contradiction, that more than three-fourths of all the pauperism is occasioned by intemperance, and that more than five-sixths of all those committed for crime, are themselves intemperate. In no poor-house have I failed to find the wife, the widow, or the children of the drunkard. In one, of one hundred and ninety persons relieved the preceding year, were nineteen wives of drunken husbands, and seventy-one children of drunken fathers. And in almost every jail were husbands confined for whipping their wives, or otherwise abusing their households."

This is certainly sufficiently near, and sufficiently specific. And yet intoxicating liquors, shame of human reason, disgrace of the nineteenth century, are manufactured and bought and sold and drank among us. More than this, their manufacture and sale are sanctioned by law, as well as usage. And a revenue derived from this polluted and polluting source, by some strange mistake in legislation, is received into the public treasury.

But have the witnesses relied on no prepossessions? Is there no exaggeration in their statements? I have sometimes thought there might be; and I have therefore done, myself, what I advise each of you to do: that is deliberately to look around you and take, within the circle of your own acquaintance, the di-dimensions of that misery which intemperance occasions, and sum up the number of dead which it has slain.

A friend of mine once gave me the number and the names of a social club of temperate drinkers which once existed in Schenectady, and of which, when young, he was himself a member; and I have remarked, how bereft of fortune, how bereft of reputation, bereft of health, and sometimes even bereft of reason, they have descended, one after another, prematurely to the grave; until at length, though not an old man, that friend alone remains, of all their number, to tell how he himself was rescued, from a fate so terrible, by the timely and prophetic counsel of a pious mother. And I have marked too how those pupils of my own, who, in despite warning and admonition, and entreaty, persisted in the use of intoxicating liquors while at college, have, on entering the world, sunk into obscurity, and finally disappeared from among those rival actors, once their companions, rising into life; and when, searching out the cause, I have, full of anxiety, inquired after one, and another, and another, the same answer has been returned, "He has become, or gone a sot into the grave."

Among these cases of moral desolation, I remember one of peculiar aggravation; it was that of a gifted and aspiring individual, and a professed Christian. Crossed and humbled by domestic affliction, he sought as many still seek, relief in alcohol. His friends foresaw the danger and warned him of it; that warning he derided; he even denied the existence of a propensity, which, by indulgence, was soon thereafter rendered uncontrollable; when suddenly, shrinking from the society of men, he shut himself up in his chamber and endeavored to drown his cares in perpetual inebriation.

His abused constitution soon gave way, and the death-scene followed. But oh! what a death-scene! As if quickened by the presence of the King of Terrors, and the proximity of the world of spirits, his reason suddenly lighted up, and all his suspended faculties returned in their strength. But they returned only to give to retribution a severer aspect, and render the final catastrophe more instructive and more terrible. For though at intervals he seemed to pour his soul out in confession, and to implore forgiveness in the most thrilling accents, shame, remorse, and despair were predominant: and there was, at times, an awfulness in the paroxysms of his agony, which no words can describe, and which can be realized by those only who witnessed it. "There," said he, pointing to his bottle and his glass, which he had caused to be placed beside his death-bed, "there is the cause of all my misery: that cup is the cup of wretchedness; and yet, fool that I have been! I have drank it; drank it voluntarily, even to its dregs. Oh, tell those miserable men, once my companions, who dream of finding in inebriation, oblivion to their miseries, as I have dreamed of this; tell them,—but it were vain to tell them—oh! that they were present, that they might see, in me, the dreadful sequel, and witness, in anticipation, the unutterable horrors of a drunkard's death." Here his voice faltered—his eye fell upon the abhorred cup—and, as his spirit fled, a curse, half articulated, died away upon his quivering lip!

Whatever exaggeration there may have been in those other statements, in these there is no exaggeration. This is not poetry, but history. Nor is this the whole. To say nothing of the untitled dead; the heads of families; the members of families, whose number has not been summed up; but—to say nothing of these—how many clergymen, how many physicians, how many jurists, in this and the neighboring cities, have, during the existing generation, fallen victims to this destroyer? Who of my equals in age, does not remember those venerable men, all moderate drinkers, who once held, in Albany, their meetings at noon-day? And who does not remember, too, the result of those meetings?—aye! and of those other meetings, held at a later hour by their sons—those young men of promise, that were, but are not!

Over all classes in that beloved city intemperance hath cast its withering influence. Nor over these only. There is no city, or town, or hamlet, known to the speaker, where it is otherwise. Of all the avenues to death, the world over, this is the broadest, steepest, most frequented. The sword hath indeed slain its thousands,—but alcohol its ten thousands!

Even in this republic, we are told by those familiar with such statistics, that there are more than five hundred thousand drunkards! What a deduction from our national virtue, honor, and happiness! What an addition to our national guilt, infamy, and misery!

Could you see those wretched beings separated from the residue of community, and congregated together in some great common Aceldama,—what a spectacle of horror! How much more so, could you see them individualized, dispersed among their friends and kindred, and linked each in his vileness, by ties tender and indissoluble, to other beings,—and often to beings of the purest virtue, of the liveliest sensibility, and the loftiest aspirings. Ah! could you see them thus, what guage could measure the extent, or arithmetic sum up the amount, of misery comprehended within your field of vision! Oh! could you number those concealed tears, which flow from so many sleepless eyes, as God numbers them; and hear those stifled sighs, that escape from so many sorrow-wounded hearts, as God hears them, you might then, but not till then, form an adequate idea of the superadded good which intoxicating liquors must hereafter produce, to cancel the dread amount of gratuitous evil they have already inflicted upon mankind!

FIVE HUNDRED THOUSAND *drunkards in this republic!!* But I will not vouch for the accuracy of their enumeration. I am aware that among the advocates of almost every cause there exists a propensity to exaggerate; and I will not, even in a good cause, insist on a hypothetical enumeration, or urge an inconclusive argument. Not having verified the details furnished of local drunkenness, I do not know with certainty the national amount.

But I do know, if drunkards exist elsewhere as they exist in the Empire State, that their whole number must be very great. For I do know, that here they crowd our prisons, our jails, our asylums, our poor-houses, and our work-shops; and that they may be found in our drawing-rooms, our halls of legislation, our halls of justice, our halls of science, and even—alas, that it should be so!—our temples of devotion!

Besides the loss of the intellectual resource, and the physical energy, and the sufferance of the indelible national disgrace, and the deep domestic misery, which this mighty army of drunkards occasion, they contribute, as has already been shown, more than any other cause,—nay, more than all other causes,—to augment our poor rates, to augment the expense for criminal arrests, for criminal prosecutions, and threaten ultimately to overthrow our civil institutions For, if their numbers shall increase hereafter as they have increased heretofore, the time will come, in this downward career, when revenues will be wanting to furnish bread for the poor, and build prisons for the guilty; because the time will come when the earnings of the sober and industrious few, will be inadequate to provide for the wants of the drunken and idle many, when intemperance itself, amid the common privation, will be restrained by the very destitution which intemperance has occasioned.

Be the number of drunkards in this republic what it may, that drunkenness exists, and that to a frightful extent, cannot be denied. And the question of chief concern is:

HOW CAN IT BE REMEDIED?

Can the axe be laid at the root of the tree? Or is the evil incurable? And must the process of destruction go on till all that is sublime in intellect, cheering in liberty, and holy in religion, fades and disappears before it? Must the eye as it glances onward through the vista of futurity, instead of meeting with the bright and joyous scenes of progressive improvement, until it reaches and rests on the predicted visions of millenial glory—instead of this, must it meet only with poverty, and crime, and decay, and desolation as exhibited in diminished trade, in less productive husbandry, in forsaken dwellings and augmented numbers of ragged, squalid wretches lounging in bar-rooms, hanging round the doors of dram-shops, staggering along the public avenues, or snoring in the gutters of those lanes and by-paths, which lead, not to the bread, but to the beer and rum-selling grocery? Must this be so by any necessity of nature? Or is there yet a remedy? There is—here, as elsewhere—REMOVE THE CAUSE, AND THE EFFECT CEASES.

But we cannot now discuss, at length, the remedy. That must remain for a future opportunity. In conclusion, therefore, we have only briefly to say, that if we would rid ourselves of the curse of the drunkard's drunkenness, we must rid ourselves of the use of the drunkard's drink. There is no alternative, the prevailing usage of society must be annulled or provision made, and made by us, for its future maintenance—a frightful provision; a provision of muscle, and of mind, as well as of money!

I repeat it, there is no alternative; this whole existing system of moderate drinking must be abolished, or the expense of sustaining it provided for by us, and by those who shall live after us; as it has hitherto been, by those who lived before us. Yes, as the years roll round, we must consent to the decimation of our families, and the families of our friends and neighbors, that we may furnish therefrom victims for the dispepsia, the dropsy, the delirium tremens; and inmates for the poor-house—the house of correction—and the house of silence! More than this, having furnished the victims of destruction, we must furnish also the elements of destruction, and the ministers of destruction.

We must pay for the growing of the grapes and the grain; then for the manufacture of the whiskey and the wine, and then for the distribution of both, by those privileged vendors, whose exclusive right it is to dispense among the people from their licensed stalls, these elements of death.

Frightful system! What a wreck of life: what a waste of money its continuance must occasion.

Britain pays, as appears from a late parliamentary report, annually, fifty millions sterling,* for the mere articles out of which intoxicating drinks are fabricated. Besides which, she loses annually fifty millions* by fires and wrecks occasioned by the drunkenness which those fabricated drinks produce. In like manner, she loses seventy millions by the productive industry thus paralyzed and rendered profitless; together with the product of one-seventh of her soil, which is appropriated to the raising of articles for the brew-house and the still.

If such be the ascertained expense of sustaining the usage of moderate drinking in Britain, what must it be in the United States? What in this State? What in this city? Were the inhabitants of which assembled, or could my voice reach them, dispersed as they are, I would say to the heads of every family apart: Though you cannot ascertain how much the State expends for intoxicating liquors, annually, you can ascertain how much you expend yourself. Will you ascertain this?—and having done so, distribute under appropriate heads, according to your best judgment, the entire amount.

Say, so much for furnishing victims to disease—so much for depriving men of their property—so much for depriving men of their reason—and so much for peopling the grave yard—so much for corrupting the morals of the youth—so much for aggravating the miseries of age—so much for disturbing

* $200,000,000.

the peace of families—so much for embittering the cup of connubial joy—and so much for mingling humiliation with the exercise of filial piety.

If you will do this, you will know, not only how much money you have paid away, but you will know also what you have paid that money for.

LECTURE No. II.

THE REMEDY.

Intoxicating liquors useful, but not as a beverage in health — Those who use intoxicating liquors, and live to be old, live not in consequence, but in spite of drinking — Intoxicating liquors analogous to exhilirating gas — The number of deaths by the use of intoxicating liquors very great — The waste of life by intoxicating liquors supplied from the ranks of temperate drinkers — Deleterious effects of distilled liquors, of beer and of bad wine.

HAVING glanced, in the preceding lecture, at the frightful evils of drunkenness, we come now to inquire,

Whether these evils are endured by any necessity of nature, or whether they are evils for which a remedy exists?

The latter doubtless. Here, as elsewhere, remove the cause and the effect ceases. What then is the cause of drunkenness? It is drinking. But be it observed, that it is not the drinking, or even the excessive drinking of water, the beverage which nature supplies for the allaying of thirst, or of milk, or of various other nutritive and healthful beverages, but the drinking of intoxicating liquors only, which produces these frightful results.

Why then should the drinking of those liquors be continued? Why? Methinks I hear the objector ask: Deserves this question even a reply?—would any one but a fanatic propose it? Are not intoxicating liquors among the good creatures of God, that their use as a beverage must be relinquished? Doubtless they are among the good creatures of God; and should therefore be received with gratitude, and may be used with innocence.

Far be it from me to speak irreverently of any of the bounties of Providence. Intoxicating liquors have doubtless their appropriate use, and may therefore be used whenever and wherever their use is appropriate; that is to say, they may be used in the arts, in sickness, in great physical exhaustion; and, in one word, on all those occasions and for all those purposes for which intended by the Creator. But does it follow from this that they were intended by him to be used as we use them, habitually and as a beverage in health? And if not so intended by him, then not rightfully so used by us; and such usage, by whomsoever indulged, will be productive of ultimate misery. It is vain to seek happiness where God forbids it, and the search, by whatever arguments defended, and however long continued, will end in disappointment.

But some, it is affirmed, have used intoxicating liquors—even distilled liquors—through a long life with entire impunity. And some too, it is also affirmed, have used arsenic, and even prussic acid, with a like impunity. And were it even so, could any general inference be drawn from this? Or should there be, and should arsenic and prussic acid, in consequence, be introduced into common use? What would be thought of the man who, standing amid the dying and the dead, occasioned by their introduction, should still point to the few solitary cases of seeming exemption, in evidence of the harmless and even healthful tendency of these destructive agents? What would be thought of him? Precisely what ought to be thought of the man who reasons in the same manner about intoxicating liquors, that however honest his convictions may be, the conclusions arrived at are not the less erroneous on that account.

But is it quite certain that any have used intoxicating liquors, as a common beverage, through a long life, with entire impunity? That such use of those liquors has been ruinous to multitudes is undeniable. And yet so gradual has the approach of their ruin been, that years have passed away before they have been convinced of such approach. Nor have they generally been convinced of it till it was too late to profit by the conviction. And who knows but those hoary headed veterans, who having outlived their generation, still drink and live; who knows but they still live in spite, not in consequence of drinking? Who knows but each treacherous sip, which even these men of years have taken from the poisoned chalice, may not, in place of adding, have taken some pulsations from a heart created to beat so often, some moments from a life granted to endure so long? so that even these iron constitutions of power to withstand so much, in place of owing anything to alcohol, may have been only impaired and enervated by its influence.* But who so well knows whether

* Dr. A. S. Pierson, of Salem, in his testimony before the committee of the Legislature of Massachusetts, said he had been a practitioner of medicine for twenty-two years, and had had frequent opportunities to notice the effects of alcohol on the physical system. He described the immediate and remote effect which was produced by alcohol. When introduced into the stomach, a morbid action is produced approximating to inflammation. This was greater or less in proportion to the quantity used. It then ascends into the brain, and materially affects the action of that delicate organ, interfering with and embarrassing the intellectual operations. It also causes a quickened motion of the heart, the action of which organ is thereby increased — being an exemplification of the saying that "a man lives too fast." This excitement is succeeded by a corresponding degree of languor. The free use of alcohol is often the cause of apoplexy, and congestion of the brain.

The remote effects produced by the use of alcoholic liquors as a drink, are more extensive. It is often the cause of disease in the stomach, occasioning an induration or thickening of the lining of that organ — or producing ulceration. The pylorus, or outlet of the stomach is particularly liable to be affected. It also produces a morbid effect on the brain, tending to apoplexy. Also on the heart, and through the blood by means of the capillary vessels to the farthest parts of the system, causing dropsy, &c.

It affects the breathing organs — distending the capillaries of the lungs, and creates tubercles, which is the proximate cause of consumption. It also often causes diseases of the liver.

The habitual use of alcohol renders the whole system morbid, and makes ordinary diseases more obstinate and difficult to be cured. It aggravates various diseases, and conduces to various diseases. Although the effect of cold on the system, while under the immediate excitement of ardent spirits may be diminished, yet in a short time the system becomes weak and languid, and more susceptible to cold than when no ardent spirit has been used. Hence when a man is found frozen to death, an empty rum bottle is almost always found

the habitual use of intoxicating liquors is beneficial, as those who use such liquors habitually; and why

---

by his side. The use of alcohol, although it may for a time increase action, does not increase power.

It is a mistaken notion that ardent spirit aids a man in enduring fatigue. It causes him to exert himself more for a brief period, but at the expense of his constitution. A man who pursues this course, merely silences the monitor which tells him he has labored enough. He disregards the voice of his physical conscience by using alcoholic drinks, and thus injures his physical system.

In the cross-examination of Dr. Pierson, the following facts were brought out in relation to the habits and age of the late Dr. Holyoke, of Salem.

Mr. Hallet.— How long may a person use ardent spirits moderately, without any perceptible injury to health?

Dr. Pierson.— In very small quantities a long time. A man may use poison of any sort, in very small quantities, and yet be preserved by the conservative principle implanted in the human system as a defence.

Mr. Hallet.— Were you acquainted with the late Dr. Holyoke, of Salem?

Dr. Pierson.— Yes. I had the honor of being his biographer.

Mr. Hallet.— How long did he live?

Dr. Pierson.— One hundred years.

Mr. Hallet.— What were his habits?

Dr. Pierson.— He was in the habit of being temperate in all things. He was a man of most remarkable character — never tempted to excess. He used to live without much care — without thinking whether he would do himself harm or not. He was very cheerful, and of a very benevolent heart and easy conscience, and patient of little injuries. He was in the habit of using intoxicating drinks in small quantities. He had a preparation which consisted of one table spoonful of Jamaica rum and one table spoonful of cider, diluted with water, which he used after dinner while smoking his pipe; I would mention in connection with this habit, that he did not die of old age. I examined the body myself with very great care and attention. The heart and organs which are apt to be diseased in aged persons, and to become hardened like stone, were as soft as an

on this mere question of fact is not their testimony decisive? Because these liquors act on the mind as

---

infant's; and for aught that appeared, might have gone another hundred years. And so of the other organs. The liver and brain were in a healthy state. He died of the disease which is most commonly produced by the use of ardent spirits and tobacco, an *internal cancer*. There was a band three or four inches broad around the stomach, which was schirrous or thickened. I am far from wishing to say anything to the discredit of the late Dr. Holyoke, who was my personal friend. But if his great age is to be made an argument for the moderate use of spirits, I desire that his schirrous stomach should be put along side of it.—*Temperance Journal for* 1839, *p.* 67.

Dr. Gordon, of the London Hospital, stated before the committee of the House of Commons in Great Britain, "that seventy-five cases of disease out of every hundred could be traced to drinking."

He also declared "that most of the bodies of moderate drinkers, which, when at Edingburgh he had opened, were found diseased in the liver; and that those symptoms appeared also in the bodies of temperate people, which he had examined in the West Indies. He more than once says that the bodies whose livers he had found diseased were those of moral and religious people."

That human life shall be very greatly prolonged beyond its present limits, is one of the plain declarations of prophecy. The following is Dr. Lowth's translation of the 65th chap. of Isaiah, verse 20, 23:

"No more shall there be an infant short lived,
Nor an old man who hath not fulfilled his days;
For he that dieth a hundred years old shall die a boy,
And the sinner that shall die at a hundred years
Shall be deemed accursed.

"And they shall build houses and inhabit them;
And they shall plant vineyards and *eat* the fruit of them;
They shall not build and another inhabit;
They shall not plant and another eat.

"For as the days of a tree shall be the days of my people,
And they shall wear out the works of their own hands.
My chosen shall not labor in vain,
Neither shall they generate a short lived race."

well as the body. Hence all who use them become excited; some less, some more; some even to mad-

---

In the tables of mortality for England and Wales, commencing at 1813, and ending with 1830, being a period of eighteen years, we find that from the age of eighty-one to that of one hundred and twenty-four, upwards of two hundred and forty-five thousand persons were buried. Of these eleven thousand one hundred and seventy-three lived to the age of ninety, and seven hundred and seven lived to the age of one hundred years; eighteen lived to one hundred and ten; three died at one hundred and twenty, and one man lived to be one hundred and twenty-four.

The following well authenticated instances of longevity, are copied from Baker's Curse of Britain, page 24, second edition:

Names.		Years.	Names.		Years.
Eleanor Aymar	lived	103	John Gordon	lived	132
Ellen Pritchard	"	103	John Taylor	"	133
Her Sisters	"	{ 104	Catharine Lopez	"	134
		108 }	Margaret Forster	"	136
Paul the Hermit	"	113	John Mount	"	136
James the Hermit	"	104	Margaret Patten	"	137
St. John the Silent	"	104	Juan Morroygota	"	138
St. Theodosius	"	105	Rebecca Parry	"	140
Thomas Davis	"	106	Dumitor Radaloy	"	140
His wife	"	105	Countess of Desmond	"	140
Ann Parker	"	108	Mr. Ecleston	"	143
St. Anthony	"	105	Solomon Nibel	"	143
Simon Stylites	"	109	William Evans	"	145
Mrs. Ann Wall	"	111	Joseph Bam	"	146
St. Epiphanius	"	115	Col. Thomas Winsloe	"	146
Arsenius	"	120	Slywark Hen	"	150
Romualdus	"	120	Judith Crawford	"	150
Apollonius of Tyana	"	130	Catharine Hyatt	"	150
Margaret Darly	"	130	Francis Consist	"	152
Francis Peat	"	130	James Bowels	"	152
William Ellis	"	130	Thomas Parr	"	152
Damberger	"	130	Thomas Dama	"	154
Peter Garden	"	131	Robert Lynch	"	160

ness. Indeed it may be questioned whether our perceptions are not always more clear, and our judgment more correct, without than with these feverish excitements. I do not pretend to have had any peculiar advantages for observing the effects of alco-

---

Names.		Years.	Names.		Years.
Mrs. Letitia Cox	lived	160	Peter Portin	lived	185
Sarah Rovin	"	164	Mongate	"	185
Henry Jenkins	"	169	Petratsch Czarten	"	185
John Rovin	"	172	Thomas Caen	"	207

From the Statistics of Russia, it appears that in 1838 there were in that country the following instances of longevity:

850	persons	had reached	from	100	to	105	years.
120	"		"	110	"	115	"
121	"		"	121	"	125	"
3	"		"	126	"	130	"
5	"		"	131	"	140	"
1	"		"	145			
3	"		"	150	to	155	years.
1	"		"	160			
1	"		"	165			

Herodotus tells us that the average life of the Macrobians was one hundred and twenty years, and that they never drank anything stronger than milk.

Speaking of the New Zealanders, Hawkenworth says: "Water is their universal and only liquor, and in all our visits to their towns, we never saw a single person who appeared to have any bodily complaint."

A further proof of health, is the facility with which wounds heal, and a still further, is the great number of old men we saw; many of whom by the loss of their hair and teeth, appeared to be very ancient, yet none were decrepit; and though not equal to the young in muscular strength, were not a whit behind them in cheerfulness and vivacity.—*Bacchus*, *p.* 115.

holic stimulants; but I have often witnessed the operation of a kindred influence.

It is usual for lecturers on chemistry to administer to certain of their hearers a gas, called in common parlance, exhilirating gas; why this is done I know not, unless it be to show how much like madmen individuals previously sane, may, by artificial stimulus, be made to act; a purpose, if indeed such be the purpose, which is answered most effectually.

Now to breathe this gas too long is death; this, those who are about to breathe it know; and yet knowing this, no sooner do they commence the breathing of this gas, than they severally persist in continuing to breathe it; and they would persist in continuing to breathe it even to the death if not forcibly prevented.

The case of the inebriate seems to be analogous. For, having once acquired the taste for intoxicating liquor, though he foresees the consequence, he clings with a death grasp to the chalice in which it is contained, and from which he can only be disengaged by violence.

But though, (not like exhilirating gas, which always kills if continued,) intoxicating liquor were innocuous to certain individuals, since, who they are can only be known by an experiment which must prove fatal to most of those who try it, can it be a question whether such experiment ought to be from age to age repeated?

Terrible as drunkenness is, it is not only computed, as has been shown, that there are five hundred thousand drunkards in this republic, but it has also been computed, that of our entire population, one in twenty-six die drunkards. If one-half of that population practice total abstinence, and including women and children, this is probably the case, then, of all who drink, one in thirteen die drunkards.

Now the life of drunkards by way of eminence, is short. Generations of them are swept away with a rapidity that amazes. And yet their frightful number is not diminished.

Whence do the successive columns of this unbroken and mighty army of inebriates come? How are its perpetually thinned ranks, perpetually filled up? Where is the exhaustless fountain that sends forth this everlasting stream of life, to replenish those mighty wastes which death by drunkenness occasions? Where? In the bosom of moderate drinking families; often intelligent, amiable and even educated moderate drinking families.

Who does not know that this class of community furnished all the raw material, the muscle and sinew, the intellect and virtue, in one word all the bodies and souls of men to be operated on. Nay, that they perform the operation; unintentionally, I admit, still that they perform the operation, by which that frightful transformation of moderate into immoderate drinkers is effected.

Yes, those interesting little groups of moderate drinking families, where everything is so tasteful and orderly; where so many moralities are practiced, so many sympathies cherished, and so many charities dispensed; those groups are the primary assemblies, whence most of the drunkards, which infest and disgrace community, are sent abroad. Nay, they are the elementary schools in which the first principles of inebriation are practically taught.

In these families, and in those larger social circles in which they meet, temptation in a thousand covert and alluring forms is every day presented; and under a thousand plausible pretences, usages are maintained, that go to create the taste, to confirm the habit, and carry forward, through all its humiliating stages, that downward process, by which one generation of temperate drinkers after another are gradually transformed into intemperate drinkers, and thus qualified to take, in their turn, the place of those confirmed drunkards who are constantly making their way, through the poor-house and the prison-house and every other avenue of death, down to the charnel-house.

And if, as has been computed by Chipman, one in thirteen of all who drink, die drunkards, and if, as has also been computed, the drunkard's life is shorter than the lives of other men; and if the perpetually thinned ranks of drunkards are wholly filled up from the ranks of moderate drinkers, how long, even though there were no other cause of mortality: How long, to speak in the language of political economists, would it take at the present rate of demand and supply, to remove from the world, by intemperance alone, the entire moderate drinking moiety of the human family?

In how many, think you, among those who now appear entirely sane and healthful, are the seeds of future disease and dissolution sown?

In how many will the secret malady begin to be developed this year, in how many the next, and in how many the year thereafter?

Were an inquest held by some minister from Heaven for separating from the congregation of moderate drinkers all infected persons, as the leprous were separated from the congregations of Israel, what think you would be the discoveries of such an inquest?

Could we, looking round on our families and kindred and neighbors, see their real condition as God sees it, might it not be said of one and another not now suspected, "That in this and this individual the infection has taken, and the process of death begun?" So much more time, and so many additional demijohns of wine or barrels of beer or jugs of rum, is all that is wanting to ripen into maturity the inflamed eye, the bloated countenance, the demented look, the disgusting hiccough, and even the frightful delirium tremens.

This is not history. I know it is not, but I also know that to many a temperate drinking family, within my hearing, unless they change their habits, or nature her laws, it will one day become history!

Considering the hazard that attends even the moderate habitual use of intoxicating liquors, who can say of any living man, that so uses those liquors, that he is safe?

Or, though this might be said of some, is it certain that it can be said of you? You have tasted of that chalice, sparingly I admit—still you have tasted of it, often tasted of it; and who knows whether the disease it so often generates may not, though latent have been already generated.

A disease destined hereafter to impair your reason, to impair your constitution, and bring down your manly frame prematurely and with dishonor to the grave.

But though you were safe, is it certain that your children and your children's children who surround your table, and have access to your sideboard, where temptation in so many forms is from day to day presented—is it certain that all these are safe also? Is it certain that *that* son of thine, wise above his years, that daughter, lovely beyond her sex, may not even now be under the inceptive, undiscovered, unsuspected, influence of a malady, often insidious and lingering indeed, but always progressive, and as inexorable as death?

But in reply to this, it will be said in certain quarters, "Though we and ours make use of intoxicating liquors, they are fermented, not distilled liquors: rum, gin, brandy, and those other noxious products of the still, have long since been relinquished; and *surely, mere malt liquor, when used in moderation, cannot injure any one; and as to wine, the Bible sanctioned its use in Palestine, and still sanctions its use.*"

It is well to have relinquished the use of rum, gin, brandy and those other noxious products of the still.

And it were well for any who have not yet relinquished their use to inquire into their nature, and their effects upon the human organism, that they too may be the better prepared to decide whether it be not wise in them also to relinquish their use.

Alcohol (which is the sole intoxicating principle in these liquors, when unadulterated), "pure alcohol coagulates all the animal fluids except the urine, and hardens the solid parts. It instantly contracts the extremities of the nerves it touches, and deprives them of sense and motion. If received into the stomach, it produces the same effects. If the quantity be considerable, a palsy or apoplexy follows, ending in death." Alcohol used constantly, and in less quantities, causes inflammation in this delicate organ: "The disease is insidious, and invariably advances, thickening and indurating the walls of the stomach, and producing sometimes schirrous and sometimes cancer; the orifices become occasionally indurated and contracted, and when this is the case, death soon puts an end to the sufferings of the wretched victims."

It should seem that such an article, an article not contained in rye, or barley, or grapes, or apples; not the product of the vineyard, or the orchard, or the harvest-field, as is usually supposed, but the product of putrefaction; it should seem that such an article, an article at once the product of death and the element of death; it should seem that such an article contained enough of vengeance in it to satisfy the avarice of dealers and the appetite of drinkers, without the addition of other and more deadly ingredients.

But so is not the fact!

Chemistry, which revealed the process by which alcohol is obtained, has also revealed the further process by which it may be adulterated, and cheaper as well as more deadly poisons furnished. By such a revelation avarice has not failed to profit; and as the knowledge of that further process has gradually been extended, the use of alcohol has gradually diminished, and intenser poisons been substituted in its place, till death has come to be more certainly than formerly dispensed in the inebriating cup, whether poured out by the hand of the landlord or the grocer! * So much for distilled liquors. More might

---

* In Dubrunfant and Jones, translated by Sheridan, 4th ed., London, 1830, it is asserted in reference to French brandies, page 132: "They are designedly imitated. Dulcified nitre is used for that purpose." Page 140: "Many distillers substitute caustic alkalies; in fact, almost every distiller has some secret nostrum for rectifying his spirits. They may be all reduced to three; by fixing alkaline salts; by acid spirits mixed with saline salts; and by saline bodies and flavoring additions."

Page 145: "Malt spirit is usually sold by weight to rectifying distillers, who distil it over again, combining it with certain materials, with a view of making it into gin, brandy, rum," &c.

Page 158, speaking of the various methods used for the "sophistication" of brandy, &c., he says of one of them: "this brandy recedes from those distilled spirits reckoned safe and wholesome." Of another method: "This brandy is more depraved than the first, as it comes over the still nearly as so much ardent spirits (malt) mixed with brandy, and it will of course exert its noxious qualities upon those who drink it."

indeed be said; but more is not necessary. They who believe not Moses and the Prophets, would not believe, though one were to rise from the dead.

" The most general mode of adulterating is, by putting a counterfeit kind to the genuine. This counterfeit brandy is made of malt spirits, dulcified by a re-distillation of acids."

Page 159: " Lapis infernalis, (infernal stone), made of lime, pearlash, potash, &c., is used for keeping down the *feints*, has a great effect upon the wholesomeness of the liquors. The acid used in the preparation of counterfeit brandy, is, aquafortis. When combined with rectified spirits, it raises a flavor and taste much resembling those of brandy; but if a certain proportion of water be mixed with such brandy, a separation of the ardent spirits and acid immediately follows."

The noxious effects of these on the health of those who drink such brandy are often melancholy in the extreme.

Page 161: He mentions that various simple additions are made to weak spirits to give a heat.

Page 193: " Pearl ashes, potash, ashes, soaper's ley water, oil of almonds, oil of vitrol, &c., to make *artificial proof.*" So convinced was he of the danger of this, that he says: "Notwithstanding I have given it, I do not recommend any to use it."

Page 194: " Vitriolic liquor, composed of spirits of wine, oil of vitriol, and the stronger caustics, &c., used to dissolve and to keep in solution the poisonous oils in liquor, and to prevent waste."

Page 197: " Dulcified spirits of nitre, made of spirits of wine and nitrous acid; to make counterfeit French brandy."

Page 205: " Oil of wormwood."

Page 210: " Kernels of apricots, nectarines, peaches, and bitter almonds."

Page 212: " Oil or essence of ambergris."

Page 214: " Alum."

Page 221: " Logwood."

Page 256: " Pepper."

Page 486: " Potashes, alkalis, salt worts, and lime."

Page 202: " Spirits of nitre, either strong or dulcified, used to give vinosity to spirits."

As to mere malt liquor, not now to agitate the question whether it be harmless; nor the question

---

Page 235: "Carbonic acid gas for wines, to *conceal* their acidity by certain substances, and if this cannot be longer done, to turn them into vinegar."

Page 475: "Acids used to give sharpness to liquors, &c."

Page 463: "The essential oil, or empyreuma, acrid, and caustic."

Page 468: "This oil is so energetic that a few drops are sufficient to give an obnoxious taste to a whole pipe. It is most difficult to succeed in separating this oil from distilled spirits. The distillers use other ingredients to *mask* their qualities."

Page 469: "Grain and potatoes, when distilled, have an essential oil, from certain causes, much worse than that furnished by those vegetables. This oil is acrid and extremely caustic. Distillers endeavor to disguise its flavor."

Page 507: "The oil in the spirits of lees is so penetrating and acrid, that six drops are sufficient to infect a whole pipe."

Page 508: "It is certain that lees and spirits contain a peculiar oil, odorous and very acrid, altering their qualities very much."

Extracts from the Wine and Spirit Merchants' Companion.
J. Hartley, London, 1835.

Page 13: "Beading for brandy, rum, &c. Oil of sweet almonds, oil of vitrol, &c."

Page 15: "Clearings for wine. The size of a walnut of sugar of lead, with sal-eruxum."

Page 25: "Finings for gin. Roach alum."

Page 20: "To make gin. Oils of juniper, bitter almonds, cassia, oil of vitrol."

Page 31: "Twenty gallons of water may be added, as the ingredients (30) will give ten gallons more apparent strength."

Page 32: "To clear tainted gin. American potash, roach alum, salts of tarter, &c."

Page 35: "Rum reduced with strong beer and water, which is sold for rum."

Page 41: "To make brandy imitate the French. Oil of cassia, bitter almonds, tincture of isponia, venella, &c."

Page 83: "To make spirits over proof. Soap and potashes."

whether impure water be or be not used in brewing;* and though it were conceded that such liquor were

---

Page 127: "To imitate port wine. Cider brandy and a little port made rough with certain ingredients, &c."

Page 144: *To sweeten casks.* "Boil fresh cow dung, and soak the casks with it."

Page 151: *To strengthen gin.* "Be particular in the quantity used. The spirits will appear stronger than they really are by five per cent. Blue stone, oil of vitrol, oil of almonds, &c."

Page 154: *Cordial Gin.* "Oil of bitter almonds, oil of vitrol, and oil of turpentine, &c."

From a "treatise on brewing and distilling," by Shannon, page 167. "It is a custom among retailing distillers, which I have not taken notice of in this directory, to put one-third or one-fourth part of proof molasses brandy, proportionably to what rum they dispose of; which cannot be distinguished except by an extraordinary palate, and does not at all lessen the body or quality of the goods, but makes them about two shillings a gallon cheaper, and must be well mixed and incorporated together in your retailing cask; but you should keep some of the best rum, not adulterated, to please some customers whose judgment and palate must be humored."

* Not that no reason for the agitation of these questions exists, for to use the words of a brewer, who, when asked, "Do you know what filthy water they use in brewing?" replied, "Oh yes, I know all about it, and the more filthy the water the better. In the great brewery in which for years I have been employed, the pipes which drew the water from the river came in just at the place which received the drainings from the horse stables; and there is no such beer in the world as was made from it." "But is not fermentation a purifying process, and does it not remove from the beer whatever is hurtful, filthy, or disgusting?" This question has received, from one competent to reply, the following answer: "The tartaric acid which may cause the *gout* in wine, the poisonous qualities of the hop, the henbane, the cocculus indicus, nux vomica, grains of paradise, copperas, or opium used, are not removed by fermentation from beer, nor is the foul matter of *animal substances* put in to promote the fermentation and vegetation of the malt by any means fully removed."—*Journal A. T. U. for* 1837, *p.* 103.

good, very good for everybody; still there are other things, to wit, henbane, nux vomica, cocculus indicus, sulphuric acid, and numerous other abominations which are not a whit the less hurtful on that account.

This is not mere declamation, but known and established truth.* But enough of mere malt liquor. And as to wine—although the Bible did authorize

---

* In S. Child's Practical Treatise on Brewery, 11th edition, after enumerating the numerous ingredients for brewing porter, p. 7, he says: "However much they may surprise, however disagreeable or pernicious they may appear, he has always found them requisite in brewing porter, and he thinks they must be invariably used by those who wish to continue the taste, flavor and appearance of the beer."

Page 16: "Though acts have been passed to prevent porter brewers from using many of them, yet the author can affirm from experience that he could never produce the present flavored porter without them."

Again page 16: "The intoxicating qualities of porter are to be ascribed to the various drugs intermixed with it. It is evident that some porter is more heady than others, and it arises from the greater or less quantity of stupefying ingredients. Malt, to produce intoxication, must be used in such large quantities as would very much diminish, if not totally exclude, the brewer's profit."

The ingredients mentioned by Child, and also by Maurice, and by the author of the "Home and Country Brewer," are various narcotics for producing stupefaction.

Alum, hops, calamus, cocculus indicus, coriander, capsicum, caraway seed, ginger, gentian, grains of paradise, nux vomica, quassia, salt, copperas, tobacco, opium, lime, soda, &c.

"Jackson, an English chemist, of notorious memory, first fell upon the plan of brewing from various drugs; and from that time to this there have been various written directions, and receipt books for using these preparations. And agents are to be found in England who sell the article manufactured for brewers only."—*Accum on Poisons*, 117.

the use in Palestine, of certain kinds of wine, there were even in Palestine, certain other kinds of wine, of which it did not authorize the use.

"To give beer a cauliflower head, beer heading is used, composed of green vitriol, alum, and salt. Alum gives likewise a smack of age to beer, and is penetrating to the palate."—*J. Childs.*

Page 23: "To make new beer older, use oil of vitriol."—*J. Childs.*

Page 163: "Hops. The intense bitter some hops afford, act very injuriously on the stomach; it is a fact noticed by ancients and moderns, that those persons who accustom themselves to intense bitters generally die suddenly."—*Journal A. T. U., pp.* 18 *and* 19, *for* 1838.

Accum or Culinary Poisons, Philadelphia, 1820, p. 113, says: "Malt liquor, and particularly porter, is among those articles in the manufacture of which the greatest frauds are committed."

Page 115: "Unwholesome ingredients are used by fraudulent brewers, and very deleterious substances are also vended both to brewers and retailers for adulterating beer."

Page 116: "The fraud of imparting to beer and ale an intoxicating quality by narcotic substances, appears to have flourished in 1806. And during the French war more cocculus indicus was imported in five years than had been before in the course of twelve years."

Page 134: "Quassia chips are used as a substitute for hops. Vast quantities of the shavings of this wood are sold in a half torrified and ground state, to disguise its obvious character, and to prevent its being recognized among the waste materials of the brewers."

Page 132: "Wormwood has likewise been used by fraudulent brewers."

Page 131: "Green vitriol, alum, and salt are used to give a head to beer. And the retailers frequently adulterate with isinglass, molasses, gentian root, and mixing beer and porter together."

Page 135: "Capsicum and grains of paradise, two highly acrid substances, are employed to give a pungent taste to weak, insipid beer. Ginger root, coriander seeds, orange peel, &c. It will be noticed that while some of the sophistications are comparatively harmless, others are effected by substances deleterious to health.

But we cannot enter on the discussion of this topic now. It must remain for a future opportunity.

In the meantime let us reflect on what has already been said, and so far as truth has been made apparent reduce the same to practice.

(But all are used for fraudulent purposes to deceive the people and cheat them out of their money)."

Page 148: After mentioning many ways of sophistication, he says: "To make the beer entire, or old, the brewers now need none of these, for by an admixture of sulphuric acid, it is done in an instant."

Page 149: "Alkaline earth, or alkali oyster shell powder, and sub-carbonate of potash, are used to make sour, stale beer, into mild."

Page 150: "To increase the intoxicating qualities of beer, cocculus indicus, opium, nux vomica, and extract of poppies are used."—*Journal A. T. U.* 1838, *p.* 50.

The effect of beer drinking corresponds to the nature of the article drank. Says Dr. Gordon, in his examination before alluded to: "The mortality among the coal whippers who are brought to the London hospital is frightful. The moment these beer drinkers are attacked with any acute disease they are unable to bear depletion and die directly." "Medical men," says Dr. Gordon, "are familiar with the fact that confirmed beer drinkers in London can scarcely scratch their finger without risk of their lives. A copious London beer drinker is all one vital part. He wears his heart on his sleeve, bare to a death wound even from a rusty nail or the claw of a cat. Sir Astley Cooper, on one occasion, was called to a drayman (the draymen have the unlimited privilege of the brewer's cellar), who had suffered an injury in his finger from a small splinter of a stave. Suppuration had taken place; this distinguished surgeon opened the small abscess with his lancet. Upon retiring he found he had forgotten his lancet case; on returning therefor he found his patient in a dying state. Every medical man in London," concludes this writer, "dreads above all things a beer drinker for his patient."

LECTURE No. III.

THE BIBLE.

The kind of wine in question — The authority of Scripture — Wine of different kinds, good and bad — Spoken of by sacred writers — Grape juice called wine — Good wine — Better than after fermentation — If not wine, but grape juice out of which wine is made, and called wine figuratively — Then is wine not commended, but grape juice merely — The wine of the press and vat in Palestine slightly fermented — What is meant by unfermented wine as here used.

HAVING urged, in the preceding lecture, the discontinuance of the use of all intoxicating liquors as a beverage, on account of the danger which attends such use, we adverted to the following reply:

"*Though we and ours make use of intoxicating liquors, they are fermented, not distilled liquors. Rum, Gin, Brandy, and those other noxious products of the still, have long since been relinquished. And surely, mere malt liquor, when used in moderation, cannot injure any one; and as to wine, the Bible sanctioned its use in Palestine, and still sanctions its use.*"

The pertinence and sufficiency of this reply in relation to distilled liquors, and in relation to fermented liquors, so far as malt liquors are concerned, have already been considered. And as to the assumption concerning wine, we have said:

That although the Bible did authorize the use of certain wines in Palestine, there were even in Palestine, certain other wines of which it did not authorize the use; and this position is what now remains to be explained and verified.

Far be it from me to promulgate or defend opinions contrary to the announcements of the Bible. The Bible is at once the unerring standard of faith, as well as the authoritative rule of life. I am aware that there are those who read, nay, who study the Bible, who are, notwithstanding, not learners, but teachers of both faith and practice. Men who bring their wit and learning and taste to bear authoritatively on that sacred volume, and who sit, and dare to sit in judgment on its doctrines and on its precepts. Not so the true disciple. He comes to the Bible, as to an authoritative and unerring teacher, and he brings along with him an enlightened faith, and a subdued understanding, and he sits down to his prescribed task with the docility of a child, and the engagedness of a learner. He pretends not to know, beforehand, what will be its counsel; much less does he pretend to prescribe what it ought to be. On the contrary, he attends to its several announcements as so many oracles from heaven, and surrendering all his pride and all his prepossessions says from the bottom of his heart, as he turns its hallowed pages: "Speak Lord, for thy servant heareth."

We may err in our interpretations of the language of the Bible, but the Bible itself never errs; and in nothing, as is believed, has its import been more misapprehended than in the countenance it has sometimes been supposed to give to the use of intoxicating liquors as a beverage. This supposed license has arrayed many good men on the side of the moderate use of intoxicating drinks, but against total abstinence; because total abstinence, as sometimes taught, has appeared to them not in accordance with the teachings of the Bible, for which they entertain so profound and so becoming a reverence—a reverence too seldom met with, and which cannot be too highly commended—a reverence to be regarded as favorable, and not adverse to the ultimate and abiding triumph of the temperance reformation. For those men who, having carried forward this reformation on the acknowledged principles of the Bible, up to the limit believed by them to be prescribed by the Bible, refuse to advance beyond that limit, are the men on whom, during the fluctuation of a fickle and changeful public opinion, reliance may most confidently be placed for the permanent maintenance of total abstinence, if it shall eventually be made to appear that the Bible sanctions such abstinence—as made to appear it will be—if, indeed, it does sanction it.

Truth is mighty, and where free discussion is allowed, will, despite even of the errors of its advocates, ultimately prevail. Nor has anything hitherto contributed so much to alarm the fears and combine the influence of these revered and wakeful conservators of the moralities of our religion, as the occasional enforcement of total abstinence, on principles rather infidel than christian, and with an apparent design to compel acquiescence, whether the Bible should be found to sanction such abstinence or not.

But if the ultimate appeal for the decision of the question is to the Bible, how can it be considered any longer an open question; for in that case what room is there even for debate?

Is it to be denied that wine is spoken of in the Bible, in terms of commendation; that it is employed as a symbol of mercy; that it was offered in sacrifice; that it was distributed to the guests at the passover; at the supper of our Lord, and at the marriage in Cana of Galilee? No, this is not to be denied. As little, however, is it to be denied, that it is also spoken of in terms of reprobation; that it is employed as a symbol of wrath, forbidden to Nazarites, forbidden to Kings: that to look upon it, even, is forbidden, and that it is declared that they who are deceived thereby are not wise.

What shall we say to this? Can the same thing in the same state be good and bad, a symbol of wrath, a symbol of mercy, a thing to be sought after, and a thing to be avoided? Certainly not!

And is the Bible then inconsistent with itself? No, it is not, and this seeming inconsistency will vanish, and the Bible will be not only, but will appear to be in harmony with itself, in harmony with history, with science, and with the providence of God, if, on examination, it shall be found that the kinds or states of vinous beverage referred to, under the name of wine, were as unlike in their nature or effects, as were those mercies and judgments for which the same were respectively employed as symbols, or as were those terms of praise or dispraise by which the same were respectively indicated.

No less than nine words are employed in the Hebrew Bible to express the different kinds of vinous beverage formerly in use; all of which kinds of beverage are expressed in our English version by the single term "WINE," or by that term in connection with some other term expressive of quality.*

The term wine, therefore, as used in our English Bible, is to be regarded as a generic term; comprehending different kinds of beverage, and of very different qualities; some of which kinds were good, some bad; some to be used frequently and freely, some seldom and sparingly; and some to be utterly and at all times avoided.

By a mere comparison of the passages in which the term wine occurs, this will be rendered probable.

---

* These terms are, *Yayin*, a generic term, comprehending wine of all kinds. *Tirosh*, also a generic term, denoting the fruit of the vine in the cluster, the press and the vat, either in the solid form of grapes, or of grape-juice expressed, (i. e.) new wine. *Ausis*, the fresh juice of the grape, and even of other fruit. *Sobhe*, inspissated wine, corresponding to the Latin *sapa*, or the Greek *sireaum* and *hepsema*. *Hamar*, unmingled wine, wine red, thick, turbid. *Mesech*, mixed wine; whether with water or with drugs. *Shemarin*, lees of wine, and sometimes preserves or jellies. *Eshisha*, cooked wine, or grape cake. *Shechar*, sweet drink, from the palm or other trees, but not from the vine.

For it were difficult to believe that the wine by which Noah was dishonored; by which Lot was defiled; the wine which caused prophets to err in judgment, and priests to stumble and fall; the wine which occasions wo and sorrow, and wounds without cause; wine of which he who is deceived thereby, is not wise; wine which Solomon styles a mocker, and which is alluded to by One who is greater than Solomon, as a symbol of wrath; it were difficult to believe that this wine—the wine mingled by harlots, and sought by libertines, was THE VERY WINE which wisdom mingles; to which wisdom invites; wine which priests offered in sacrifice; evangelists dispensed at communion-tables, and which, making glad the heart of man, was a fit emblem of the mercies of God.

There is a wine of some sort spoken of very frequently in the Bible, with express disapprobation, or in connection with drunken feasts, or as an emblem of temporal and eternal judgment. And there is also a wine spoken of perhaps as frequently with express approbation, or in connection with religious festivals, or as an emblem of temporal and eternal blessings.

That wines of such different qualities, and presented in such different aspects and even in such frequent and frightful contrast, were one and the same article, in one and the same state, would seem, even though history, both sacred and profane, had been silent, quite incredible. How much more so now, that in place of silence, history, both sacred and profane, hath spoken; and spoken, not of their identity, but known and marked dissimilarity.

It is not to be denied that the Bible makes a distinction in the kinds of wine of which it speaks. I allude not to wine as medicine, but as beverage. Wine as beverage, was, in the language of the Bible, either good or bad.

By good wine, I mean wine that in the use is beneficial to the bodies or the souls of men. By bad wine, I mean wine which is injurious to the one or the other, or both. Wine which (when used, not excessively, but moderately as beverage) is injurious either to the physical, intellectual or moral constitution of man, is bad wine. It is with this distinction between wines that this discussion is concerned—a distinction, recognized in those terms of praise or dispraise in which the Bible speaks of or alludes to different kinds of wine, as either actually existing in the concrete, or as assumed to exist in the abstract. The truth of this will be apparent, by a comparison (in the subjoined schedule) of a few out of many passages that might have been selected.

TEXTS IN WHICH GOOD WINE IS SPOKEN OF, OR ALLUDED TO.

Gen., xxvii., 28: "Therefore God give thee of the dew of heaven, and the fatness of the earth, and plenty of corn, and (*tirosh*) wine."

Num., xxviii., 12: "All the best of the oil, and all the best of the (*tirosh*) wine, and of the wheat, first fruits of them which they shall offer unto the Lord, them have I given thee."

Deut., xiv., 24, 25, 26: "And if the way be too long for thee, then thou shalt turn it into money, and thou shalt bestow that money for whatsoever thy soul lusteth after, for oxen, or for sheep, or for (*yayin*) wine."

Psalm civ., 15: "And (*yayin*) wine that maketh glad the heart of man, and oil to make his face to shine, and bread which strengtheneth man's heart."

Zech., ix., 17: "Corn shall make the young men cheerful, and (*tirosh*) new wine the maids."

Prov., ix., 1, 4, 5: "Wisdom hath killed her beasts; she hath mingled her wine (*yayin*); she saith, come eat of my bread, and drink of the (*yayin*) wine I have mingled."

Cant. v., 1: "I have drunk my (*yayin*) wine with my milk; eat O friends; drink; yea, drink abundantly, O beloved."

Isaiah, xxvii., 2: "In that day sing you unto her, a vineyard of red (*yayin*) wine. I, the Lord, do keep it. I will water it every moment, lest any hurt it. I will keep it night and day."

Gen., xlix., 11: "He washeth his garments in (*yayin*) wine, and his clothes in the blood of grapes.

Gen., xlviii., 33: "I have caused (*yayin*) to fall from the wine press, none shall tread with shouting."

Deut., vii., 13: "He will love thee and bless thee; and bless the fruit of thy land; thy corn and thy (*tirosh*) wine."

Luke, xxii., 18: "For I say unto you, I will not drink of the fruit of the vine, till the kingdom of God shall come."

Mark, xiv., 25: "Verily I say unto you, I will drink no more of the fruit of the vine, until that day that I shall drink it new in the kingdom of God."

1 Cor., x., 16: The cup of blessing which we bless, is it not the communion of the blood of Christ?"

Isaiah, lxv., 8: "Thus saith the Lord, as the (*tirosh*) new wine is found in the cluster, and one saith, destroy it not, for a blessing is in it, so will I do for my servants."

TEXTS IN WHICH BAD WINE IS SPOKEN OF, OR ALLUDED TO.

Deut., xxxii., 33: "For their vine is the vine of Sodom, and of the fields of Gomorrah. Their (*yayin*) wine is the poison of dragons, and the cruel venom of asps."

Amos, ii., 6, 8: "Thus saith the Lord, for three transgressions of Israel, and for four, I will not turn away the punishment thereof. Because, * * * they lay themselves down upon clothes laid to pledge upon every altar, and drink the (*yayin*) wine of the condemned in the house of their God."

Mark, xv., 23: "And they gave him to drink (*oinon*) wine mingled with myrrh; but he received it not."

Prov., xxiii., 20, 30, 31, 32: "Who hath woe; who hath sorrow; who hath contention; who hath babbling; who hath wounds without cause; who hath redness of eyes? They that tarry long at the (*yayin*) wine; they that go to seek (*mesech*) mixed wine; look not thou upon the (*yayin*) wine when it is red; when it giveth his color in the cup; when it moveth itself aright. At the last, it biteth like a serpent, and stingeth like an adder."

Isaiah, v., 22: "Woe unto them that are mighty to drink (*yayin*) wine, and men of strength to mingle strong drink."

Prov., xxiii., 30: "Look thou not upon the (*yayin*) wine when it is red; when it giveth his color in the cup, when it moveth itself aright."

Psalm lxxv., 8: "In the hand of the Lord there is a cup, and the (*yayin*) wine is red; it is full of mixture, and he poureth out the same, but the dregs thereof, all the wicked of the earth shall wring them out, and drink them."

Psalm lx., 3: "Thou hast showed thy people hard things; thou hast made us drink the (*yayin*) wine of astonishment."

Jer., li., 7: "The nations have drunk of her (*yayin*) wine, therefore the nations are mad."

Rev., xiv., 10: "The same shall drink of the (*oinon*) wine of the wrath of God, which is poured out without mixture into the cup of his indignation."

Jer., xxv., 15: "For thus saith the Lord * * take the (*yayin*) wine cup of this fury at my hand, and cause all the nations to whom I send thee, to drink it."

Prov., xx., 1: "(*Yayin*) wine is a mocker, (*shechar*) strong drink is raging, and whosoever is deceived thereby is not wise."

The above are samples merely of passages (which might if necessary be extended) in which wines are distinguished, according to their qualities, among which are good and bad; wine, that is a blessing, and wine, a curse; wine, to be presented at sacrifice, and wine, that might not be drank in the house of the Lord; wine, occasioning joy and gladness, and wine, occasioning woe and sorrow; wine, of which guests were to drink abundantly, and wine, not to be drank at all; wine, the emblem of heavenly joy, and wine, the symbol of endless misery; red wine, the especial care of the Almighty; and red wine, that might not be looked upon; wine, signifying the blood of Christ, and wine, a mocker.

In the view of these texts, and texts like these, though ignorant of the fact that different kinds of wine exist now, who could doubt of their existence formerly, or question whether wines presented in such frequent and fearful contrast, or referred to respectively in such marked terms of praise or dispraise, were not, after all, one and the same article, in the same state?

Here then, on this broad distinction between good and bad wine, recognized in the sacred writings, we take our stand. And be it remembered, it is not against the moderate use (in ordinary times) of good, healthful wine, which the Bible sanctions and employs as an emblem of mercy, but against the use of bad, deleterious wine which the Bible reprobates and employs as an emblem of wrath, that we array ourselves.

The wine, and the only wine that we abjure, is wine abjured by the Bible, abjured by reason; wine, which in the use as a beverage, enervates and diseases the body, depraves and crazes the mind, and exerts over the whole man a morbid and a mortal influence; in one word, wine containing POISON not only, but containing it in sufficient quantity, also, when used as beverage, to disturb the healthy action of the system: and such are the wines generally in use in this country. Nor is it material to the question now at issue whether that poison be generated in the juice of the grape by fermentation, or superadded by drugging.

Wine in which poison is contained in the quantity and intensity indicated, no matter how generated or whence derived, will be found to receive as little advocacy from revelation as reason; nor will the drinker of such wine (as the light of truth advances) be able ultimately to find protection under the mere shelter of a name.

That the term wine is always used, either by sacred or profane writers, to indicate the same beverage or to indicate the beverage for which we now use it, is an error which cannot fail, on full examination, to be corrected.

Pliny, who was cotemporary with the apostles, says (Lib. xiv., chap. 22), as we have already seen, "that the ingenuity of man had produced ninety-five different kinds of wine; and if the species of these genera were enumerated, they would amount to almost double that number."

Virgil, who lived about the same time, having enumerated several kinds of wine then in use, sums up what he had to say, by declaring the residue innumerable. Nor does the fact in question depend on the testimony of Pliny and Virgil only. Horace, Cato, Columella, Plutarch, and many other ancient writers, have confirmed what Pliny and Virgil stated. They enumerated a great variety of wines, and even furnish recipes for making very many of the varieties enumerated. Among which varieties are wine made from millet, dates, and the lotus tree; from figs, beans, pears, all sorts of apples, mulberries, pineapples; the leaves, berries and twigs of myrtle; from rue, asparagus, savory, &c. Spiced and aromatic wines, made from a composition of spices, from myrrh, Celtic nard, bitumen. (Pliny, chap. 16, book xiv.)

Of the different kinds of wine formerly in use, some were medicinal, nutritive; some refreshing, exhilirating; some stupefactive, and some intoxicating.

By intoxicating wine, as used in this discussion, is meant not merely wine containing poison, but containing it in sufficient quantity and intensity, when used as beverage, to poison those who use it.

By poison, I mean anything which injures the organism, interrupts its healthy action, producing local or general derangement in the system, and which, if taken in quantities sufficiently large, or in smaller quantities sufficiently long, will impair the reason, impair the health, and even extinguish life itself.

All this intoxicating liquors will do: what more can be said of arsenic, or even prussic acid?

Not to mention remote effects, intoxicating liquors operate with sudden and mighty energy on the whole vascular and nervous system, and especially on the brain, exciting usually to folly, often to madness, sometimes even to death.

The poison contained in intoxicating liquors is either generated in the liquors by fermentation, or superadded by drugging.

FERMENTATION is a chemical process, of which there are several kinds, to wit: the vinous, the acetous, and the putrefactive.

The elements of fermentation are saccharine matter, barm or yeast.

The conditions of fermentation are contact, fluidity and temperature. The degree of temperature requisite for vinous fermentation is from sixty to seventy or seventy-five degrees Fahrenheit.

If the temperature be increased, acetous fermentation follows the vinous.

Grapes and apples, as well as certain other vegetable productions, contain the elements of fermentation in the requisite proportion to secure the process, provided the requisite fluidity, contact and temperature exist.

The vinous fermentation, with which this discussion is principally concerned, generates alcohol, one of the most virulent poisons, and a poison contained in many if not most, of the intoxicating liquors now in use.

DISTILLATION is a modern art, and the difference between fermented and distilled liquors consists in this: that in the former, a portion, though a very small portion, of solid vegetable matter is held in solution in the alcohol and water; whereas in the latter alcohol and water exist alone.

Alcohol, however, is not the only poison contained in intoxicating liquors; others are added by drugging.

DRUGGING is an artificial process, by which foreign ingredients of any kind and in any quantity are added to liquors at pleasure.

Pliny affirms that calamus and ground oak, together with numerous other ingredients, were added to the juice of the grape, to render it aromatic, medicinal, or stupefying. (Book xiv., chap. 16.)

Homer, who lived long before the Christian era, frequently mentions the potent drugs mingled with wine in those early times.

The potion which Helen prepared for Telemachus and his companions was at once soothing and stupefactive. To impart these qualities, he says "she mingled in her wine delirious drugs of power to assuage grief, to allay rage, and to become the oblivious antidote of misfortune." Elsewhere he says, that Ulysses took in his boat "a goat-skin of sweet black wine, a divine drink, which Maron, Apollo's priest, had given him, a beverage that was as sweet as honey, that was imperishable, that when drank was diluted with twenty parts water, and that from it a sweet and divine odor exhaled."

Says Pliny (Lib. xiv., chap. 5), "Androcydes, a physician renowned for wisdom, addressing Alexander, said, 'O King! remember that when you are about to drink the blood of the earth, hemlock is poison to man, and wine is hemlock.'"

Nor was this process of drugging confined to ancient Pagan nations. Says Bishop Lowth, on Isaiah, i, 22: "the Hebrews generally, by mixed wine, mean wine made inebriating by the adoption of higher and more powerful ingredients, such as spices, myrrh, mandragora, opiates, and other strong drugs. Such were the exhilirating or rather stupefying ingredients which Helen mixed in the bowl together with the wine for her guests, oppressed with grief, to raise their spirits, the composition of which she had learned from Egypt."

Thus the drunkard is described, as one who seeks "mixed wine," and is "mighty to mingle strong drink."

And hence the Psalmist took the highly poetical and sublime image of the cup of God's wrath, called by Isaiah "the cup of trembling," causing intoxication and stupefaction, containing, as St. John (Rev., xiv., 10,) expresses in Greek, the Hebrew idea with the utmost precision, though with a seeming contradiction in the terms "*kekerasmenon akraton*," mixed, unmixed wine. "In the hand of Jehovah," saith the Psalmist, Psalm lxxv., 8, "there is a cup, the wine is turbid, it is full of mixed liquor, he poureth out of it. Verily the dregs thereof (the thickest sediment of the strong ingredients merged in it), all the ungodly of the earth shall wring them out and drink them."

Stupefying wines were given by the ancients to condemned criminals, to render them less sensible to the agonies of death. Of such wine, it was not allowable for Israelites in their solemn assemblies to drink; an offence with which they are reproached. Amos, ii, 8: "they lay themselves down upon clothes laid to pledge by every altar, and they drink the wine of the condemned in the house of their God."

Dr. A. Clark, in his commentary, says: "Inebriating drinks were given to condemned prisoners, to render them less sensible to the torture they endured when dying." This custom is alluded to in Proverbs, xxxi., 6: "Give strong drink to him that is ready to perish," i. e., who is condemned to death, "and wine to him who is bitter of soul, because he is just going to suffer the punishment of death;" and thus the Rabbins understand it.

It is asserted in the Talmud that this drink consisted of wine mixed with frankincense, and was given to criminals immediately before execution. It is moreover recorded of our Savior, that "they gave him to drink wine mingled with myrrh, but he received it not." Allusion is made to these mixed wines in Lam., iii., 15: "He hath filled me with bitterness, he hath made me drunken with wormwood." In Psalm lxxv., 8, it is said that "In the hand of the Lord is a cup, and the wine is red, it is full of mixture." Isaiah speaks of "a cup of trembling and giddiness." In Proverbs we read of "*mixed wine*," of soporific wines, of which kings might not drink, lest they should "forget the law;" the same to be given, as above stated, to those of a heavy heart, that they might forget their sorrows.

Thus apparent is it that foreign ingredients were formerly added to wines to render them intoxicating, many of which were the most potent poisons. And it is also apparent that these were wines disapproved of by the Bible, and in reference to which, not temperance, but abstinence, total, perpetual abstinence, was enjoined.

Now, were these wines repudiated because they were mixed, or because they were bad, soporific, oblivious, stupefactive? Not the former, surely, for there were mixed wines deemed worthy of commendation, and such were wines mingled by wisdom for her guests. And if the latter, then deleterious wine, irrespective of the manner in which it has been rendered deleterious, is in effect repudiated by the Bible. But wine containing poison in sufficient quantity to produce intoxication, when used as beverage, is deleterious wine, and ought not, therefore, on Bible principles, to be so used.

However becoming and even obligatory total abstinence from all vinous beverage, at a time like the present, and in a country where its use and the use of kindred stimulants has been carried to such criminal excess, it is not to be understood that, under other circumstances, in other times, good nutritious unintoxicating wine might not be temperately drank with innocence.

But is there any such wine? There is; for such is ever the fruit of the vine in its original state.

THAT THE FRUIT OF THE VINE, IN THE FORM OF GRAPE JUICE AS EXPRESSED FROM THE CLUSTER, HAS BEEN FROM REMOTE ANTIQUITY AND STILL IS USED AS A BEVERAGE, IS ABUNDANTLY IN PROOF.

Of Gaal and his brethren, it is said (Judges, ix., 27) that "they went out into the field and gathered in their *grapes*, and did eat and drink." Of what did Gaal and his brethren eat and drink? Doubtless, as the text intimates, of the grapes which they had gathered. For, be it remembered, grapes furnish to those who cultivate them, both food and drink.

In connection with the blessings conferred on Jacob (among which are honey, oil, butter, milk, &c.), it is said (Deut., xxxii., 14,) that he drank ("*dham gnenabh hhamer*") *the pure blood of the grape.* In the Vulgate this is translated ("*et sanguinem uvæ bibisti merum,*" in the Septuaguint "*oinon*") "and the blood of the grape thou didst drink wine;" and Dr. A. Clarke says that "blood," as used here, is synonymous with "*juice.*" The allusion probably was to the simple must of red grapes—the most approved grapes. Among the principal things enumerated as needful to man, are "water, flour, honey, milk, and the *blood of the grape,*" meaning, in the language of the ancients, *grape-juice.* That the ancients thus understood the terms, there can be no doubt. In the Apocrypha (1 Mac., vi., 34) it is written: "and to the end that they might provoke the elephants to fight, they showed them the blood of grapes and mulberries;" and in Ecclesiasticus (xv.), "and finishing the service of the altar, that he (high priest) might adorn the offering of the Most High, he stretched out his hand to the cup and poured of the blood of the grape."

It is a recorded fact that, in remote antiquity, grapes were brought to the table and the juice there

expressed for immediate use. An instance occurs in Pharaoh's cup-bearer; the recently exhumed Bacchus, holding a bunch of grapes in his hand and pressing the juice into the vase, standing on a pedestal, is in evidence of the existence of such a usage.*

In keeping with the office here asssigned to the reputed inventor of wine, is a scene described between him and a Tyrian shepherd (Achilles Tatius, lib. xi., chap. ii). Bacchus having been hospitably entertained by this shepherd with food and water, presented him in return with a cup filled with fresh grape juice; on tasting which, the shepherd exclaimed, "Whence, my guest, have you this purple water, or where in the world have you so sweet a blood? It surely is not from that which flows through the land! Water affects (goes into) the breast with little pleasure; this, however, applied to the mouth, gratifies the nostrils, and though it be cold to the touch, yet when it is imbibed, it raises throughout an agreeable warmth." Bacchus replied, "This autumnal water (alluding to the period when grapes were ripe) and *blood* flows out of branches;" and having led the shepherd to a vine (and pointed to the pendent clusters), he said, "this is the water, but these are the fountains."

"Grapes" (says Sir Edward Barry, speaking of the ancients), "became at first a usual article of their aliment, and the recently expressed juice of the grape a cooling drink."

The Pylean king who lived to so great an age, is spoken of by Juvenal (lib. x., line 250) as one "*Quive novum toties mustum bibit;*" "who so often drank fresh

* Lib. Useful Knowledge, Pompeii, vol. xi., p. 213.

must." And it is recorded of the noble Venetian Cornaro, who lived to so great an age, that he found by experience, that as soon as he could procure fresh grape juice, it presently restored him to the health he had lost while drinking old wine.

Columella says (book iii., chap. 2), "the vine is planted either for food to eat, or liquor to drink." Mahomet says in the Koran, "of grapes ye obtain an inebriating liquor, and also good nourishment."

From a quotation in *Com. Michaelis*, it appears that the Mahomedans of Arabia press the juice of the grape through a linen cloth, pour it into a cup and drink it as Pharaoh did; and Captain Charles Stewart says "that the unfermented juice of the grape and palm tree are a delightful beverage, in India, Persia, Palestine, and other adjacent countries."

To this use of grape juice, Milton alludes in the following words:

> " For drink, the grape
> She crushes — inoffensive must."

And in Gray we meet with a similar allusion—

> " Scent the new fragrance of the breathing rose,
> And quaff the pendant vintage as it grows."

It were easy to multiply authorities—but it is unnecessary. That the fruit of the vine, as expressed from the cluster, in the form of fresh grape juice, has been from remote antiquity used as beverage, is not to be denied.

BUT IS SUCH GRAPE JUICE WINE?

That is the question—a question which must be answered in the affirmative, if either Moses or the prophets are to be accredited.

Among the blessings granted to Jacob, it is recorded, as we have seen, that he "drank the pure blood of the grape;" that by the "pure blood of the grape," was meant wine, is admitted by Dr. Adam Clarke and other distinguished commentators. The passage, as we have also seen, is even rendered in the Vulgate, "*Et sanguinem uvæ bibisti* MERUM"—that is, *and of the blood of the grape thou didst drink* (*oinon*, Septuagint,) *wine.*

Now, if the beverage of which Jacob drank, and which is so often referred to among enumerated blessings, was not wine, then the translators of the Septuagint, and also of the Vulgate, as well as of the English Bible, were mistaken; and if they were, and if this blood of the grape, declared to be wine by patriarchs and prophets; declared to be wine by their translators and their commentators; by men belonging to different nations, speaking different languages, and living in different ages; if this blood of the grape, after all, be not truly wine, and if some other and further process be necessary to convert it into wine, what was that process, when or where did it take place; how long did it occupy, or by which of the sacred writers has the fact been recorded? By none of them. In relation to each and all these particulars the Bible is silent, or rather it speaks only to give assurance that none of them were requisite.

Here we are not left to inference. The sacred writers are explicit: This fruit of the vine, in its natural state IS, AND IT IS DECLARED TO BE, "TIROSH," TO BE "YAYIN," TO BE "AUSIS," AND, TO ADD NO MORE, TO BE "HHEMER;" all terms rendered OINIS IN

GREEK, VINUM OR MERUM IN LATIN, AND WINE IN ENGLISH.

Here there can be no mistake. The blood of the grape, that is, grape juice in its natural state, is, in the judgment of these high authorities, WINE; and it is declared to be so; declared TO BE WINE, AS EXPRESSED IN THE VAT; TO BE WINE IN THE PRESS, BY WHICH IT IS EXPRESSED; WINE IN THE CLUSTER FROM WHICH IT IS EXPRESSED; WINE IN THE VINEYARD WHERE THE CLUSTER RIPENED, AND WHEN IT WAS GATHERED; AND TO CROWN THE EVIDENCE, DECLARED TO BE SWEET WINE, NEW WINE, AND WINE in the season thereof.

THE FRUIT OF THE VINE IS DECLARED TO BE (*tirosh*) WINE, AS EXPRESSED IN THE VAT.

Joel, ii., 24: "And the floors shall be full of wheat, and the vats shall overflow with (in Hebrew, '*tirosh*;' in Greek, '*oinon*;' in Latin, '*vino*;'* and in English) wine."

IT IS DECLARED TO BE (*tirosh*) WINE, IN THE PRESS BY WHICH IT WAS EXPRESSED.

Proverbs, iii., 10: "So shall thy barns be filled with plenty, and thy presses burst out with (*tirosh*, *oinon*, *vino*) new wine."

---

* The Hebrew, Greek and Latin terms in this and the following quotations are transferred from the Hebrew Bible, the Septaugint and the Vulgate, as they exist there, in the corresponding passages, without change of case.

Hosea, ix., 2: "The floor and the wine press shall not feed them, and the (*tirosh, oinos, vinum*) new wine shall fail in her."

IT IS DECLARED TO BE (*tirosh*) WINE IN THE CLUSTER FROM WHICH IT WAS EXPRESSED.

Isaiah, lxv., 8: "Thus saith the Lord, as the (*tirosh*) new wine is found in the cluster and one saith, destroy it not, for a blessing is in it; so will I do for my servants' sakes, that I may not destroy them all."

IT IS DECLARED TO BE (*tirosh*) WINE IN THE VINEYARD, WHERE THE CLUSTER IS RIPENED.

Judges, ix., 13: "And the vine said unto them, should I leave my (*tirosh, oinon, vinum*) wine, which cheereth God and man, and go to be promoted over the trees?"

Psalms, iv., 7: "Thou hast put gladness in my heart, more than in the time that their corn and (*tirosh, oinou, vini*) wine increased."

Joel, i., 10: "The field is wasted, the land mourneth, for the corn is wasted; the (*tirosh, oinos, vinum*) new wine is dried up, the oil languisheth."

IT IS DECLARED TO BE (*tirosh*) SWEET WINE, NEW WINE, AND WINE IN THE SEASON THEREOF.

Micah, vi., 15: "Thou shalt sow but thou shalt not reap; thou shalt tread the olives, but thou shalt not anoint thee with oil; and (*tirosh, oinou*) sweet wine, but shalt not drink (*yayin, vinum*) wine."

Isaiah, xxiv., 7: "The (*tirosh, oinos*) new wine mourneth, the vine languisheth, all the merry-hearted do sigh."

Haggai, i., 11: "And I called for a drought upon the land, and upon the mountains and upon the corn, and upon the (*tirosh, oinou, vinum*) new wine, and upon the oil, and upon that which the ground bringeth forth, and upon men, and upon cattle, and upon all the labor of the hands."

Zech., ix., 17: "For how great is his goodness, and how great is his beauty! corn shall make the young men cheerful, and (*tirosh, oinos, vinum*) new wine the maids."

Neh., xiii., 5: "And he had prepared for him a great chamber, where aforetime they laid the meat offerings, the frankincense and the vessels, and the tithes of the corn, the (*tirosh, oinou, vini*) new wine, and the oil, which was commanded to be given to the Levites, and the singers, and the porters, and the offerings of the priests."

Neh., xiii., 12: "Then brought all Judah the tithe of the corn, and the (*tirosh, oinou, vini*) new wine, and the oil unto the treasuries."

Finally, the fruit of the vine in its natural state is DECLARED TO BE (*tirosh*) WINE, AS ASSOCIATED WITH CORN AND OIL, AND OTHER PRODUCTS OF THE FOLD, AND OF THE FIELD, AND EXISTING ALMOST, IF NOT ALWAYS, NOT IN AN ARTIFICIAL, BUT IN THE NATURAL STATE; AND THUS ASSOCIATED WITH CORN AND OTHER NATURAL PRODUCTIONS, AS A BLESSING—AS FIRST FRUITS—AS TITHES—AS OFFERINGS—AS INCREASING AND LAN-

GUISHING IN THE FIELD — AS IN ITS SEASON — AS GATHERED FROM THE FIELD — AND WITH CORN AND (*yayin*) WINE.

IT IS DECLARED TO BE WINE WHEN ASSOCIATED WITH CORN AND OTHER PRODUCTS, IN THEIR NATURAL STATE CONSIDERED A BLESSING.

Gen., xxvii., 28: "Therefore God give thee of the dew of Heaven, and the fatness of the earth, and plenty of corn and (*tirosh, oinou, vini*) wine."

Gen., xxvii., 37: "And Isaac answered and said unto Esau, behold I have made him thy lord, and all his brethren have I given to him for servants; and with corn and (*tirosh, oino, vino*) wine have I sustained him; and what shall I do now unto thee, my son?"

Deut., vii., 13: "And he will love thee * * * he will bless the fruit of thy land, thy corn, and thy (*tirosh, oinon*) wine, and thine oil," &c.

Deut., xxviii., 51: "Which also shall not leave thee either corn (*tirosh, oinon, vinum*), wine, or oil," &c., "until he have destroyed thee."

Deut., xxxiii., 28: "The fountain of Jacob shall be upon a land of corn and (*tirosh, oino, vini*) wine, also his heavens shall drop down dew."

Hosea, ii., 8: "For she did not know that I gave her corn and (*tirosh, oinon, vinum*) wine, and oil, and multipled her silver and gold, which they prepared for Baal."

Hosea, ii., 22: "And the earth shall bear the corn, and the (*tirosh, oinon, vinum*) wine, and the oil," &c.

Joel, ii., 19: "Behold I will send you corn and (*tirosh, oinou, vinum*) wine, and oil, and ye shall be satisfied therewith."

2 Kings, xviii., 32: "Until I come and take you away to a land like your own land, a land of corn and (*tirosh, oinou, vini*) wine, a land of bread and vineyards, a land of oil-olive and of honey," &c.

Isaiah, xxxvi., 17: "Until I come and take you away to a land like your own land, a land of corn and (*tirosh, oinou, vini*) wine, a land of bread and vineyards."

Isaiah, lxii., 8: "Surely I will no more give thy corn to be meat for thine enemies; and the sons of the stranger shall not drink the (*tirosh, oinon, vinum*) wine for the which thou hast labored."

Jer., xxxi., 12: "Therefore they shall come and sing in the height of Zion, and shall flow together to the goodness of the Lord—for wheat, and for (*tirosh, oinou, vino*) wine, and for oil," &c.

Neh., v., 11: "Restore, I pray you, to them, even this day, their lands, their vineyards, also the hundredth part of the money * * * and of the corn, the (*tirosh, oinon, vini*) wine, and the oil, that ye exact from them.

IT IS DECLARED TO BE WINE WHEN ASSOCIATED WITH CORN AS FIRST FRUITS.

Deut., xii., 17: "Thou mayest not eat within thy gates the tithe of thy corn, or of thy (*tirosh, oinou, vini*) wine, or of thy oil," &c.

Deut., xiv., 23: "And thou shalt eat before the Lord thy God in the place which he shall choose to place his name there, the tithe of thy corn, of thy (*tirosh*, *oinou*, *vini*) wine, and of thine oil," &c.

IT IS DECLARED TO BE WINE WHEN ASSOCIATED WITH CORN, ETC., AS OFFERINGS.

Neh., x., 39: "For the children of Israel, and the children of Levi shall bring the offering of the corn, of the (*tirosh*, *oinou*, *vini*) new wine, and the oil, unto the chambers."

IT IS DECLARED TO BE WINE WHEN ASSOCIATED WITH CORN, ETC., AS INCREASING OR LANGUISHING IN THE FIELD.

Deut., xxxiii., 28: "The fountain of Jacob shall be upon a land of corn and (*tirosh*, *oino*, *vini*) wine, also his heavens shall drop down dew."

2 Chron., xxxi., 5: "The children of Israel brought in abundance the first fruits of corn (*tirosh*, *oinou*, *vini*), wine, and oil, and honey, and of all the increase of the field," &c.

Psalms, iv., 7: "Thou hast put gladness in my heart, more than in the time that their corn and their (*tirosh*, *oinou*, *vini*) wine increased."

Joel. i., 10: "The field is wasted, the land mourneth, for the corn is wasted; the (*tirosh*, *oinos*, *vinum*) new wine is dried up, the oil languisheth."

IT IS DECLARED TO BE WINE WHEN ASSOCIATED WITH CORN IN ITS SEASON.

Hosea, ii., 9: "Therefore will I return and take away my corn in the time thereof, and my (*tirosh*, *oinon, vinum*) wine in the season thereof, and will recover my wool and my flax," &c.

IT IS DECLARED TO BE WINE WHEN ASSOCIATED WITH CORN AS GATHERED FROM THE FIELD.

Deut., xi., 14: "That I will give you the rain of your land in his due season, the first rain and the latter rain, that thou mayest gather in thy corn, and thy (*tirosh, onion, vinum*) wine and thy oil."

IT IS DECLARED TO BE WINE WHEN ASSOCIATED WITH CORN, ALSO WITH (*yayin*) WINE.

Hosea, vii., 14: "They assemble themselves for corn and (*tirosh oino, vinum*) wine, and they rebel against me."

Hosea, iv., 11: "Whoredom and (*yayin, oinon, vinum*) wine, and (*tirosh*) new wine take away the heart."

THE FRUIT OF THE VINE IN ITS NATURAL STATE IS DECLARED TO BE (*ausis*) NEW WINE.

Joel, i., 5: "Awaye, ye drunkards, and weep; and howl all ye drinkers of (*yayin, oinou, vinum in dulcedine*) wine, because of the (*ausis*) new wine, for it is cut off from your mouth."

Joel, iii., 18. "And it shall come to pass in that day, that the mountains shall drop down (*ausis, glukasmon, dulcedinum*) new wine, and the hills shall flow with milk, and all the rivers shall flow with waters, and a fountain shall come forth of the house of the Lord, and shall water the valley of Shittim.'

Amos, ix., 13: "Behold the days come, saith the Lord, that the ploughman shall overtake the reaper, and the treader of grapes, him that soweth seed; and the mountains shall drop (*ausis*, *glukasmon*, *dulcedinum*) sweet wine, and all the hills shall melt."

IT IS DECLARED TO BE (*yayin*) WINE IN THE PRESS.

Neh., xiii., 15: "In those days saw I in Judah some treading wine presses on the Sabbath, and bringing in sheaves, * * * as also (*yayin*, *oino*, *vinum*) wine, grapes and figs."

Isaiah, xvi., 10: "And gladness is taken away, and joy out of the plentiful fields, and in the vineyards there shall be no singing, neither shall there be shoutings; the treaders shall tread out no (*yayin*, *oinon*, *vinum*) wine in their presses; I have made their vintage shouting to cease."

Jer., xlviii., 33: "And joy and gladness is taken from the plentiful field, and from the land of Moab, and I have caused (*yayin*, *oinos*, *vinum*) wine to fail from the wine presses; none shall tread with shoutings; their shoutings shall be no shouting."

IT IS DECLARED TO BE (*yayin*) WINE IN THE VINEYARD.

1 Chron., xxvii., 27: "And over the vineyards was Shimei, the Ramathite, over the increase of the vineyards, for the (*yayin*, *oinou*, *vinariis*) wine-sellers was Zabdi, the Shiphmite."

Amos, v., 11: "For as much therefore, as your treading is upon the poor, * * * ye have planted pleasant vineyards, but ye shall not drink (*yayin, oinon, vinum*) wine in them."

Amos, ix., 14: "And I will bring again the captivity of my people Israel, * * * and they shall plant vineyards, and drink the (*yayin, oinon, vinum*) wine thereof; they shall also make gardens and eat the fruit of them."

Zeph., i., 13: "Therefore their goods shall become a booty, and their houses a desolation; they shall also build houses but not inhabit them; and they shall plant vineyards, but not drink the (*yayin, oinon, vinum*) wine thereof."

Isaiah, xxvii., 2: "In that day sing ye to her, (*hhemer, vinea meri*) a vineyard of red wine."

Gen., xlix., 11: "Binding his foal unto the vine, and his ass's colt unto the choice vine, he washed his garments in (*yayin, oino, vino*) wine, and his clothes in the blood of grapes."

Deut., xxviii., 39: "Thou shalt plant vineyards and dress them, but shalt neither drink of the (*yayin, oinon, vinum*) wine, nor gather the grapes, for the worms shall eat them."

2 Kings, xviii., 32: "Until I come and take you away to a land like your own land, a land of corn (*tirosh, oinou, vini*) wine, a land of bread and vineyards, a land of oil-olive, and of honey, that ye may live and not die."

Isaiah, xxxvi., 17: "Until I come and take you away to a land like your own land, a land of corn and (*tirosh, oinou, vini*) wine, a land of bread and vineyards."

Jer., xl., 10: "But ye, gather ye (*yayin*, *oinon*, *vindemiam*) wine and summer fruits, and oil, and put them in your vessels, and dwell in your cities that you have taken."

Joel, i., 5: "Awake, ye drunkards, and weep; and howl all ye drinkers of (*yayin*, *oinon*, *vinum*) wine, because of the (*ausis*) new wine, for it is cut off from your mouth."

FINALLY THE FRUIT OF THE VINE, IN ITS NATURAL STATE, IS DECLARED TO BE (*hhemer*) RED WINE IN THE VINEYARD.

Isaiah, xxvii., 2: "In that day sing ye to her (*hhemer*) a vineyard of red wine."

Thus apparent is it, that in the opinion of the translators of our English Bible, the fruit of the vine, in its natural and unintoxicating, as well as in its artificial and intoxicating state, was called by Moses and the Prophets, WINE.

Nor in the opinion of the translators of our English Bible only, but in the opinion also of the translators of the Septuagint, and the Vulgate also. These all, as has been shown, render the terms by which the fruit of the vine in its natural state is designated, by the same terms which designate it in its artificial state.

Had there been but a single undisputed text in which the fruit of the vine in its natural unintoxicating state was called WINE, that single text ought to be deemed conclusive. How much more so, when there are so many texts in which it is so called by different writers, and during so many ages.

What the terms were which the sacred writers actually employed to denote the fruit of the vine in the press, the vat, the cluster, and the vineyard, admits of no debate. They called the fruit of the vine in this state *tirosh*, *ausis*, *hhemer*, *yayin*, rendered over and over again, *oinos* in Greek, *vinum* or *merum* in Latin, and *wine* in English.

By the name wine, and by no other name, this article has always been known to the reader of the English Bible. There it is always called wine, as every reader of the Bible can assure himself. And whether it is rightly called wine there; and rightly called *oinos* in the Sept., and *vinum* in the Vulgate, has never (it is believed) till of late been called in question.

Be this, however, as it may, that the unfermented fruit of the vine in the form of grape juice was called wine, is as apparent as it is that it was used as a beverage. More than this, it was not only called wine, but it was also accounted to be good wine.

WINE OF SUPERIOR QUALITY, for it was employed by way of distinction as a symbol of mercy, enumerated among other blessings, and declared to be itself a blessing.

TIROSH, always used by the sacred writers to denote the fruit of the vine in its natural, and not in its artificial state, occurs but thirty-eight times in the Hebrew Bible: In thirty-six of which it is clearly used in a good sense and with approbation. It is used once (Hosea, vii., 14) in a doubtful sense; and once and only once (Hosea, iv., 11) in a bad sense or with disapprobation, and then in connection with *yayin;* but not on account of any imputed inebriating qualities, but as contributing to take away the heart.*

YAYIN is a generic term, and when not restricted in its meaning by some word or circumstance, comprehends vinous beverage of every sort, however produced, and whether the fruit of the vine or not. It is, however, as we have seen, often restricted to the fruit of the vine in its natural and unintoxicating state. But when so restricted, we have in no instance found it used in a bad sense, or with disapprobation. Yayin is also frequently restricted to the fruit of the vine in its artificial or intoxicating state, in which state it is usually, if not uniformly, used in a bad sense or with disapprobation.

In most, if not all the following passages, *yayin* is clearly used for the fruit of the vine in an artificial and intoxicating state, and with disapprobation, expressed or implied.

Yayin, used as causing, or in connection with drunkenness, or drinking, to wit:

With the drunkenness of Noah,	Gen., ix., 21, 24.
" " of Lot,	Gen., xix., 32, 33, 34, 35.
" " of Nabal (supposed),	1 Sam., xxv., 37.
" " of Ammon,	2 Sam. xiii., 28.
" " of priests and prophets,	Isaiah xxviii., 1.
" " of kings and people,	Jer. xiii., 13, 14.
As causing drunkenness, to prophets,	Jer., xxiii., 9.
" " to priests and prophets,	Isaiah, xxviii., 7.
With woe to those inflamed by it,	Isaiah, v., 11, 12, 22.

* See Appendix.

With woe to the drunkards of Ephraim,................	Isaiah, xxviii., 1.
As an illustration of drunkenness,......................	Isaiah, xxix., 9.
As a symbol of drunkenness,............................	Isaiah, li., 21.
With weeping of drunkards,............................	Joel, i., 5.
With dissoluteness,....................................	Joel, iii., 3.
also	Hosea, iv., 11.
With treachery,..	Gen., xxvii., 25.
With the poison of dragons,............................	Deut, xxxii., 33.
With idolatry,...	Deut., xxxii., 38.
With fury,...	Jer., xxv., 15.
With astonishment,.....................................	Psalms, lx., 3.
With drugs,..	Psalms, lxxv., 8.
With violence,...	Prov., iv., 17.
With falsehood,..	Micah, ii., 11.
With the mocker,.......................................	Prov., xx., 1.
With woe and sorrow,...................................	Prov., xxiii., 29, 31, 32, 33
With profaneness,......................................	Amos, ii., 8.
With voluptuousness,...................................	Eccles., ii., 3.
With festivity and merriment,..........................	Eccles., x., 19
also	Amos, vi., 6.
With sensuality,.......................................	Isaiah, v., 11, 12, 22. Isaiah, xxii, 13. Isaiah, lvi., 12.
With transgression,....................................	Hab., ii., 5.
With woe,..	Isaiah, xxviii., 1, also 7.
With prohibition to Nazarites,.........................	Num., vi., 3.
" " to the mother of Sampson,.............	Jud., xiii., 4, 7, 14.
" " to the mother of Samuel,..............	1 Sam., i., 14, 15.
" " to the Rechabites,....................	Jer., xxxv., 6, 7, 8.
" " to the priests,.......................	Lev., x., 9.
also	Ezekiel, xliv., 21.
With reproof to kings,.................................	Prov., xxxi., 4.
With temptations to Nazarites,.........................	Amos, ii., 12.
With temptation to Rechabites,.........................	Jer., xxxv ,2, 5.
With refusal by Rechabites,............................	Jer., xxxv., 6, 8, 16
With refusal by Daniel,................................	Danl, i., 5, 8, 16.
also	Danl., x., 3.
With punishment,.......................................	Psalms, lxxv., 8.
With madness,..	Jer., xli., 7.

In most if not all the following passages, *yayin* is used to denote the fruit of the vine in its natural and unintoxicating state, and in none of them is it used with disapprobation, either expressed or implied; nor is it elsewhere ever so used when employed to denote the fruit of the vine in its natural and unintoxicating state:

Gen., xliv., 11: Used for new wine or the blood of the grape.

Deut., xxviii., 30: For the same in connection with grapes.

2 Kings, xviii., 32: For the same in connection with corn and vineyards.

Psalms, civ., 15: In connection with oil and bread.

Isaiah, xvi., 10: In connection with wine presses and the treading of grapes.

Isaiah, xxxvi., 15: With corn and vineyards.

Isaiah, lv., 1: With milk.

Jer., xl., 10: As a blessing in connection with summer fruits.

Jer., xl., 12: Same.

Jer., xlviii., 33: With wine presses and the treading of grapes.

Lam., ii., 12: With corn.

Amos, v., 11: With vineyards.

Amos, ix., 14: With vineyards.

Neh., xiii., 15: With wine presses.

Zeph., i., 13: With vineyards.

Cant., vii., 9: With sweetness.

Cant., v., 1: With milk.

Besides the foregoing, there are passages in which *yayin* is used, where there is nothing in the immediate connection to indicate whether it be used for the fruit of the vine in its natural or artificial state; that is, whether it is in the state in which it exists in the vineyard and the vat, or in the state in which it exists after being removed therefrom and subjected to further fermentation.

SHECHAR, sweet or saccharine beverage, from the sap of the palm, or the sap or fruit of other trees, except the vine, is rendered σικερα in the Sept. (from the Hebrew verb shachar); and with a single exception, strong drink in the English Bible, that exception is Exod., xxix., 40, where it is rendered strong wine; by Theoderet and Chrysostom, both natives of Syria, it is called palm wine. That it is rightly so called, is confirmed by the testimony of Doctor Shaw, as well as of the modern Arabs.

It occurs but twenty-three times. It is usually associated with yayin. One or the other, or both of these terms, are used in connection with drunkenness or drunken feasts, or are spoken of with disapprobation, upwards of seventy times, and in twenty-one instances are employed to express temporal or eternal judgment. Whereas tirosh, expressive of the fruit of the vine in its natural state, is never once used in such connection, nor employed for such a purpose; nor, with the single exception before alluded to, is it ever spoken of with disapprobation of any sort. And here it may not be impertinent to remark, that whenever wine is denounced in the Bible, the denunciation is never against tirosh, ausis, hhemer or sobe, but always against yayin. And that whenever any other word expressive of vinous beverage is associated with shechar in speaking of drunkenness and drunken feasts, that other word is never tirosh, or ausis, or sobe, or hhemer, but always yayin.

So many and such repeated commendations of the fruit of the vine in its natural and unfermented state, and so many and such repeated condemnations of it in its artificial and fermented state, cannot have been left upon record without design; and if that design, to say the least, be not to encourage the use of the fruit of the vine in the former state, and to discourage the use of it in the latter, it would be difficult to divine what it was.

The difference existing in the kinds of vinous beverage formerly in use, and which is so distinctly marked in the Hebrew text, is for the most part concealed from the reader of the English Bible by the uniform manner in which the several terms expressive of that difference are translated wine. But for which uniformity, the fact of the existence of such difference, it is believed, would not now be made a question; and notwithstanding that uniformity, it is reasonable to suppose (especially considering the poverty of the Hebrew language) that seven different words have been employed by patriarchs and prophets to express the same identical beverage in the same state.

In the preceding analysis we have found, as it might have been expected we should, one generic term (YAYIN) expressive of vinous beverage of every sort. We have also found a term (TIROSH) expressive of the fruit of the vine as it exists in the cluster in the vineyard, or press, or vat; a term (AUSIS) expressive of it as it exists dropping or expressed fresh from the cluster; a term (SOBHE) expressive of it as inspissated or boiled; a term (HHEMER) expressive of it when unmingled with other ingredients, and a term (MESCH) expressive of it when mingled; whether with water or with drugs.*

That the fruit of the vine in all these states is called wine, there can be no doubt. The proof of this is palpable and abundant, and if rightly so called, then different kinds of wine formerly existed, and unfermented as well as fermented grape juice is truly wine.

But it may be said, though the fruit of the vine in its natural and unfermented state is called wine, it is not really so, and is only so called by a well known figure of speech, the applying of the name of the product to the material from which it is produced.

It is readily admitted that in poetry and in other imaginative writings this often occurs, and sometimes, even though rarely, in mere prose. But were this admitted in many, nay in most, nay in all the passages quoted (which it is believed no scholar will claim to be the case); but were this admitted, it is not perceived that the admission would change the issue made, or in the least weaken the arguments adduced.

The fruit of the vine in its natural state is either wine before fermentation or it is not. Be it then that

---

* See Appendix.

before fermentation, though often called wine, it is not so; but merely something else out of which wine is made. This admitted, then all the commendations of the fruit of the vine, previous to fermentation, with which the Bible abounds, are not commendations of wine at all, but merely commendations of that out of which wine is made; and all the condemnations of wine with which the Bible also abounds, are condemations of the fruit of the vine, not before but after fermentation, and are therefore condemnations, not of that out of which wine is made, but condemnations of the veritable article made, WINE ITSELF.

And if the numerous commendations of the fruit of the vine, before fermentation, with which the Bible abounds, be laid out of the account, it will be very difficult to find any clear and unequivocal commendations of wine in the Bible at all. For it is before and not after fermentation that the possession of the fruit of the vine is spoken of as a national blessing, its loss as a national curse. And it is after and not before fermentation that the fruit is styled a mocker, associated with crime, and employed itself as a symbol of wrath.

To test the truth of this, let any reader of the Bible collect and arrange in one column all the passages in which wine is spoken of with approbation, either expressly or by implication; and let him also collect and arrange in another column all the passages in which wine is spoken of with disapprobation, either expressly or by implication, and if he does not discover in the sequel that the approbation expressed in the passages selected is usually, if not always, approbation of the fruit of the vine before fermentation, and that the disapprobation expressed is disapprobation of the fruit of the vine after fermentation, he will have succeeded in collecting (and arranging in separate columns) a series of texts which have been overlooked in this inquiry.

If wine be commended at all in the Bible, and there is no doubt it is, its commendation will be found, it is believed, chiefly if not wholly in the commendation of the so-called wine of the vineyard, the cluster, the press and the vat. Grapes and grape juice, then, before fermentation (whether wine or not), are articles which God appoves and commends—whereas grape juice after fermentation, though truly wine, and the only article by supposition rightly so called, is an article often repudiated and abundantly spoken against—and, if its nature has not changed, not without reason was it spoken against. For it is now what it was said to be then, "a mocker;" and now as then it causes woe and sorrow and redness of eyes and wounds without cause; and now as then it is armed with the serpent's bite and the adder's sting.

To conclude: That the fruit of the vine, in its natural state, was not only called wine, but was accounted by the sacred writers a better article, being more frequently commended and less frequently spoken against than the fruit of the vine in its artificial state, would seem sufficiently apparent from the authorities already quoted.

Whether the fruit of the vine in the former state might not possibly be procured and preserved at so low a temperature as wholly to prevent the formation of alcohol, by preventing fermentation, it is not, in so far as this discussion is concerned, needful to inquire; since it is readily admitted that in the climate of Judea this could not ordinarily if ever be the case.

BY UNFERMENTED WINE, therefore, as used in this discussion, is meant wine that has undergone no artificial or other or further fermentation than what ordinarily takes place in the vat and the press, and sometimes perhaps even in the cluster. Such wine, though not entirely free from alcohol, contains but little of that element, and that little so modified by the remaining saccharine matter, with which it exists in admixture, as to prevent its producing intoxication, even though used freely and to the extent required for common beverage. Nor would it, even if used to excess (though it might produce sickness), produce intoxication; and it may, therefore, in distinction from the more fully fermented fruit of the vine, be fitly called, as we have called it, UNINTOXICATING WINE. Whether profane writers have made the same distinction as the sacred writers have made, in the states in which the fruit of the vine exists, and whether, when in its natural state, they call it wine, and in what estimation it was formerly and is still held by them in this state, will be made the subject of inquiry in our next lecture.

LECTURE No. IV.

INQUIRY EXTENDED TO PROFANE WRITERS.

The wine question continued — Grape juice spoken of as a beverage by profane writers — Called wine — Pronounced good wine — better before than after fermentation — The formation of alcohol intentionally prevented by arresting fermentation — dissipated when formed by the filter, or counteracted by dilution —The question at issue a question of degree, not of totality — The question of sin *per se* considered — Perfect purity not attainable — Wine placed on the same footing as other articles of food.

WE have attempted, in the preceding lecture, to show that sacred writers make a distinction between the fruit of the vine in its natural (that is, its unfermented and unintoxicating) state, and its artificial (that is, its fermented and intoxicating) state; that in both these states it is called in the Hebrew text *yayin*, in the Greek version *oinon*, in the Latin *vinum*, and in the English *wine;* that the fruit of the vine, in its natural state, was not only called wine, but was accounted better wine, being more highly com mended, and less frequently and severely spoken against, than the fruit of the vine in its artificial and intoxicating state.

Now, though this were peculiar to the sacred writers, it would be decisive of the question at issue. It is what Moses and Samuel and David and Isaiah and Jeremiah and other sacred writers, and not what Aristotle and Plato and Columella and other profane writers say, that we are chiefly concerned to know. But whether this be peculiar to the sacred writers, or common to them and to profane writers, we are now prepared to inquire.

That the profane writers made the same distinction between the fruit of the vine in its natural and artificial state, as the sacred writers made; that the fruit of the vine in its natural state was used as a beverage, and that in both states it was called wine, would seem apparent from the following testimony:

Cato the elder, in his work on "Rural Affairs," has a chapter concerning PENDANT WINE. "*Lex vini pendentis*," is the heading of this chapter. It is the cxlvii.

The regulation concerning the hanging or ungathered wine is as follows: "*Hac lege vinum pendens venire oportet. Vinaceos illutos et fæces relinquito. Locus vinis ad kalendas Octobris primas dabitur; si non ante ea exportaveris, dominus vino quod volet faciet.*" "According to this regulation, the hanging wine ought to be sold. You are to leave the husks unwatered, and the dregs. A place shall be set apart for the wine, down to the first kalends of October; if you have not carried them clear off before, the proprietor shall do whatever he pleases with the wine." That Cato used the term *vinum*, for wine in the cluster, is apparent from the next chapter, in which he treats of *vinum in doliis*—the wine in the casks.

Livy, who flourished in the golden age of Roman literature, when accounting for the settlement in the plains of Italy of the Clusii (one of the barbarous tribes of ancient Gaul), says (lib. v., chap. 33): "*Eam gentem (scil. Clusinum) traditur fama dulcedine frugum, maximeque vini, nova tum uoluptate, captam, Alpes transisse, agrosque ab Etruscis ante cultos possedisse: et invexisse in Galliam vinum inliciendæ gentis causa Aruntem Clusinum,*" *&c.* "There is a traditionary report that that nation (the Clusii), captivated by the lusciousness of the fruits, and especially of the (*vinum*) wine, crossed over the Alps, and took possession of the inclosed lands, hitherto cultivated by the Eturians; and that Aruns, the Clusian, for the purpose of alluring his people, imported (*vinum*) wine into Gaul."

Ovid applies the Latin *merum*, wine, in the same manner: "*Vixque merum capiunt grana, quod intus habent.*" "And scarce the grapes contain the *wine* within."

Calmet says: "The ancients had the secret of preserving wine sweet throughout the year;" and Plutarch affirms, that "before the time of Psammeticus, the Egyptians neither drank fermented wine, nor offered it in sacrifice."

According to Plautus, who lived about two hundred years before Christ, the Latin *mustum* signified "both wine and sweet juice."*

---

* Leigh's Critica Sacra, p. 58.

Says Nicander: "Οἰνευς δ'ἐν κοιλοιδιν ἀποθλιψας δεπαεσσιν, οἰνον ἐκλησε." "And Œnus having squeezed the juice of the grapes, into hollow cups, called it wine (οἰνον)." Thus the Greeks, as well as the Hebrews, called fresh grape juice wine.

Says Tibullus, in his fifth Elegy: "*Illa deo sciet agricolæ pro vitibus uvam, pro segete spicas grege ferre dapem.*"

> "With pious care, will load each rural shrine,
> For *ripened crops a golden sheaf assign,*
> Cates for my fold, *rich clusters for my wine.*" *

"A white sweet liquor distils from the Palm," which, Prof. Kid says, "is used extensively in India, under the name of Palm wine." †

(*Yayin*,) "Wine which is made by squeezing the grapes—the expressed juice of grapes." ‡

"Pressed wine is that which is squeezed with a press from the grapes; sweet wine is that which has not yet fermented." §

"Must, the wine or liquor in the vat." ||

"The modern Turks carry the unfermented wine along with them in their journeys." ¶

That profane writers, both Greek and Latin, have not only made the distinction between the fruit of the vine in its natural and its artificial state, and spoke of the former as beverage, and called it wine —BUT THAT THEY HAVE ALSO SPOKEN OF IT AS GOOD

---

* Grainger.

† Bridgewater's Treatise, p. 214.

‡ Parkhurst.

§ Rees' Encyclopedia.

|| Dr. Sanders.

¶ Sir Edward Barry.

WINE, AND SPOKEN OF OTHER WINE AS GOOD, WHICH, ON ACCOUNT OF ITS UNINTOXICATING NATURE, RESEMBLED THE FRUIT OF THE VINE IN ITS NATURAL STATE, WILL BE APPARENT FROM THE FOLLOWING AUTHORITIES.

Whatever may be the decision of those whose taste has been depraved by the fabricated wines of commerce and the drinking usages of the moderns, there cannot be a doubt that the wise and good men among the ancients, as well uninspired as inspired, appreciated wines of every kind the higher, the less alcohol and the more saccharine matter they severally contained; and the contained alcohol, other things being equal, depended on the extent to which fermentation was carried.

Even Horace was evidently aware of the distinction between intoxicating and unintoxicating wine:

"Aufidius forti miscebat mella Falerno
Mendose; quoniam vacuis committere venis
Nil nisi lene decet, leni præcordia *mulso*
Prolueris melius."*

"*Aufidius* first, most injudicious, quaffed
Strong wine and honey for his morning draught;
With lenient beverage fill your empty *veins*,
For lenient *must* will better cleanse the reins."

Elsewhere the same poet says:

'Hic innocentis pocula Lesbii,
Duces sub umbra; nec Semelius
Cum Marte confundet Thyoneus
Prælia."

* Horace, Sat. 4, 24.

He tells his friend Mecænas, that he might drink a "hundred glasses of this innocent Lesbian," without any danger to his head or senses. In the Delphian edition of Horace, we are told that "Lesbian wine could injure no one; that, as it would neither affect the head nor inflame the passions, there was no fear that those who drank it would become quarrelsome." It is added, that "there is no wine sweeter to drink than Lesbian; that it was like nectar, and more resembled ambrosia than wine; that it was perfectly harmless, and would not produce intoxication."

Athenæus (as translated by Baccius) says, that *Surrentinum pingue et valde debile*," "Surrentine wine was fat and very weak;" which is in keeping with the words of Pliny: "*Surrentina vina caput non tenent.*" "Surrentine wine does not affect the head." As are also the words of Persius, iii., 93:

"Lenia loturo sibi Surrentina rogavit."
"He has asked for himself, about to bathe, mild Surrentine."

Columella (book iii., cap. 2), alluding to the weak wines of Greece, says: "Those small Greek wines, as the Mareotic, Thasian, Psythian, Sophortian, though they have a tolerable good taste, yet, in our climate, they yield but little wine, from the thinness of their clusters, and the smallness of their berries. Nevertheless, the black *Inerticula* (the sluggish vine), which some Greeks call *Amethyston,* may be placed, as it were, in the second tribe, because it both yields a good wine, and is harmless—from which, also, it took its name—because it is reckoned dull, and not to have spirit enough to affect the nerves, though it is not dull and flat to the taste."

Speaking of sweet wine, Aristotle says (Meteor., lib. iv., cap. 9): "οἶνος δ', ὁ μεν γλυκυς, διὸ και οὐ μεθυσκει," "that sweet wine would not intoxicate."

There was a Spanish wine, says Pliny (lib. xiv., cap. 2), called "*inerticulam justius sobrium, viribus innoxium, siquidem temulentiam sola non facit*," "a wine which would not intoxicate."

Pliny and Varro speak of a wine called *murrina*, "a wine not mixed with myrrh, but a very sweet aromatic drink, much approved of by Roman ladies, and conceded to them because it would not inebriate." "*Dulcis nec inebriens*," are the words of Varro. Of this wine Pliny also says (lib. xiv., cap. 3), that it would not intoxicate.

Athenæus speaks of the "innocent Chian," and the "unintoxicating Biblinum," and Plautus of the "toothless Thanium and Coan;" all of which vinous beverages are comprehended under the term *oinos*, each of which is designated by that term; and even when different kinds of wine are indicated, the same name is applied to more than one kind. It is not sufficient, therefore, to say, "He drank Crete wine," for as Baccius affirms, "*Duplex meminit vinosum et* DULCE *quod passum dicit*." It is needful, in judging ancient wines, to attend to the quality as well as the name: "*quia* VINUM *non temetum, sed* PASSUM DULCE, *permittitur mulieribus; dulce vero non inebriens*." Thus the *vinosum temetum*, or strong intoxicating wine, is exhibited in contrast with the *weak* unintoxicating wine. The one class is spoken of as "*potens vinum*," powerful wine; the other, as having "*nihil vinosum*," nothing vinous.

"All Italy," says Andreas Baccius, "naturally, at this time, abounds in wines and delights throughout in sweet wines, and not less in black wines; but these are altogether different from the ancient wines, both in their preparation and in their treatment, as well as their quality, for our sweet, as well as the white and black, intoxicate."

There were wines which, without being subjected to any special treatment, would, on account of their excess of saccharine matter, remain without fermenting, in their natural and unintoxicating state, for a great length of time; such, especially, were the wines of Tenedos.

Says Dr. E. Clark, in his travels: "Perhaps there is no part of the world where the vine yields such redundant and luscious fruit; the juice of the Cyprian grape resembles a concentrated essence. The wine of this island is so famous all over the Levant, that, in the hyperbolical language of the Greeks, it is said to have the power of restoring youth to age, and animation to those who are at the point of death. Englishmen, however, do not consider it as a favorite beverage; it requires near a century of age to deprive it of that sickly sweetness which renders it repugnant to their palates."

"When it has remained in bottles for ten or twelve years, it acquires *a slight* degree of fermentation upon exposure to the air; and this, added to its sweetness and high color, causes it to resemble Tokay more than any other wine; but the Cypriots do not drink it in this state; it is preserved by them in casks to which the air has constantly access, and will keep in this manner for any number of years. After it has withstood the vicissitudes of the seasons for a single year, it is supposed to have passed the requisite proof, and then it sells for three Turkish piastres a goose (about twenty-one pints). Afterwards the price augments in proportion to its age. We tasted some of the Commanderia, which they said was forty years old, although still in the cask. After this period it is considered as a balm, and reserved on the account of its supposed restorative and healing quality for the sick and dying. A greater proof of its *strength* cannot be given, than by relating the manner in which it is kept—in casks neither filled nor closed. A piece of sheet lead is merely laid over the bung hole, and this is removed every day when customers visit their cellars to taste the different sorts of wine proposed for sale."

Even in wines expressed from less luscious grapes, wine could be, and often was produced, that would remain permanently sweet and unintoxicating.

Calmet informs us, that "the ancients had the secret of preserving wine sweet throughout the year;" and Plutarch records, that "before the time of Psammetticus, the Egyptians neither drank fermented wine, nor used it in their offerings." And there are writers who inform us how the preservation of wine sweet throughout the year might be effected.

Says Columella (lib. xii., chap. 27): "*De vino dulci faciendo*:" "Gather the grapes, and expose them for three days to the sun; on the fourth, at midday, tread them; take the *mustum lixivium*, that is, the juice which flows into the lake before you use the press, and when it has cooled, add one ounce of pounded iris, strain the wine from its fæces, and pour it into a vessel. This wine will be sweet, firm or durable, and healthful to the body."

Says Didymus (lib. vii., cap. 18): "In Bythinia, some persons thus make sweet wine: Thirty days before the vintage, they twist the twigs which bear the clusters, and strip off the foliage, so that (the rays of) the sun striking down, may dry up the moisture (sap), and make the wine sweet, just as we do by boiling. They twist the twigs for this reason, (viz.): that they may withdraw the clusters from the sap and nourishment of the vine, so that they may no longer receive any moisture (sap) from it. Some persons, after they have bared the bunches from the leaves, and the grapes begin to wrinkle, gather them together in the clusters, and expose them to the sun, until they have all become *uvæ passæ* (rasins). Lastly, they take them up when the sun is at the hottest point, carry them to the upper press, and leave them there the rest of the day, and the whole of the following night, and about daylight they tread them."

Suidas calls "γλευκος," which is said to be *mustum, vinum, et succus dulcis*, must, wine and a sweet juice, "το ἀποσταγμα τῆς σταφυλῆς πρὶν πατηθη," the wine "that dropped from the grape before it was trodden."

Mr. Buckingham says that wine in Smyrna is called "the droppings of the wine press," and "virgin wine."

According to Pliny, Protropum was "*mustum quod sponte profluit antequam uvæ calcentur*," the "must which flows spontaneously from the grapes before they have been trodden."

These rich, slightly fermented, unintoxicating wines were not only held in peculiar estimation among the ancients, but by them various expedients were adopted, not to increase, but to diminish the production of alcohol, by arresting the process of fermentation in their other and less luscious wines, among which expedients were the EXCLUSION OF AIR, AND THE REDUCTION OF TEMPERATURE, THE EVAPORATION OF CONTAINED WATER, AND THE ABSORPTION OF THE CONTAINED OXYGEN.

1*st.* THE EXCLUSION OF AIR, AND THE REDUCTION OF TEMPERATURE, FOR THE PURPOSE OF PREVENTING THE PRODUCTION OF ALCOHOL, BY ARRESTING THE PROCESS OF FERMENTATION.

It was a well known fact that air and a certain degree of heat were requisite to fermentation, and it was also a well known fact that wines were less liable to run into the vinous fermentation, after they had been kept a considerable length of time in an unfermented state.

Hence the Romans were accustomed to put the new wine into jars, which, being well stopped, new ones being preferred, were then immersed for several weeks in a cistern or pond; in fact, as the wine was made about September and October, they were sometimes allowed to remain immersed during the whole of the winter, until, as Pliny naively observes, "the wine had acquired the habit of being cold." Sometimes the same object was effected by the cask being buried deep under ground.*

Says Columella (lib. xii., cap. 29), "*quemadmodum mustum semper dulce tanquam recens permaneat*:" "that your must may be always as sweet as it is new, thus proceed: before you apply the press to the fruit, take the newest must from the lake, put it into a new amphora, bung it up, and cover it very carefully with pitch, lest any water should enter; then immerse it in a cistern or pond of pure cold water, and allow no part of the amphora to remain above the surface. After forty days, take it out, and it will remain sweet for a year."

2*d*. THE EVAPORATION OF THE CONTAINED WATER FOR THE PURPOSE OF PREVENTING THE PRODUCTION OF ALCOHOL, BY ARRESTING THE PROCESS OF FERMENTATION.

It is conceded by modern chemists generally, it is believed, that the ancients were correct in the opinion, that a certain degree of fluidity is essential to fermentation.

When grape juice is very weak and watery, boiling may indeed, by increasing the relative proportion

* Pliny's Natural History, lib. xiv., chap. 9.

of the saccharine matter, facilitate the process of fermentation. But where the requisite fluidity, and the requisite proportions between the barm or yeast and the saccharine matter already exist, boiling will obstruct or prevent fermentation.

Says Boerhaave: "By boiling, the juice of the richest grapes loses all its aptitude for fermentation, and may afterwards be preserved for years without undergoing any further change."

Says Newman: "It is observable, that when thick juices are boiled down to a thick consistence, they not only do not ferment in that state, but are not easily brought into fermentation when diluted with as much water as they had lost in the evaporation, or even with the very individual water that had exhaled from them. Thus sundry sweet liquors are preserved for a length of time by boiling. From these considerations, it is probable that the qualities for which the Romans and Greeks valued their wines were very different from those sought after in the present day; and that they contained much saccharine matter and but little alcohol."

Says Aristotle: "The wine of Arcadia was so thick that it was necessary to scrape it from the skin bottles in which it was contained, and to dissolve the scrapings in water."

Says Democritus: "The Lacedæmonians, εἰς το πυρ ἑῶσι τον οἶνον, ἕως ἀν το πεμπτον μερος αφεψηθη και μετα τεσσαρα ἐτη χρῶνται, were accustomed to boil their wine upon the fire until the fifth part had been consumed. It was drunk after a period of four years had elapsed."

Says Pliny: "*musto usque ad tertiam partem mensuræ decocto; quod ubi factum ad dimidiam est, defrutum vocamus.*" *

The practice of boiling wine was and still is prevalent among the Asiatics. To the existence and prevalence of this practice, Dr. Bowring bears testimony. Among the boiled wines spoken of by the ancient writers, are *Sapa*, *Defrutum*, *Siræum* and *Hepsima*.

These wines are very similar, and the chief difference between them appears to consist in the degree to which they were severally reduced. The derivation of *sapa* may have been, perhaps, from the Hebrew *sobhe*, as *siræum* may have been from the Hebrew *syr*, caldron, in which the process of boiling was performed.

Fabbroni, an Italian writer, treating of Jewish husbandry, says: "The palm trees, also, which especially abounded in the neighborhood of Jericho and Engaddi, served to make a very sweet wine, which is made all over the East, being called '*palm wine*' by the Latins, and '*syra*' in India, from the Persian *shir*, which means 'luscious liquor or drink.'"

These preparations are all distinctly included under the class οἶνος, wines. In deciding, therefore, concerning ancient wines, it is necessary to consider the quality, as well as the name, because, as Baccius informs us, "*duplex meminit et dulce quod passum dicit;*" and hence as another ancient writer says: "*Quia*

* Pliny's Natural History, cap. ix.

vinum non TEMETUM *sed passum dulce permittitur mulieribus*—DULCE VERO NON INEBRIANS."

3*d*. ABSORPTION OF THE CONTAINED OXYGEN, FOR THE PURPOSE OF PREVENTING THE FORMATION OF ALCOHOL, BY ARRESTING THE PROCESS OF FERMENTATION.

Says C. Reading in his history and description of modern wines, p. 41: "Its object (sulphurization) is to impart to wine clearness and the principle of preservation, and to prevent fermentation."

Says Dr. Ure: "Fermentation may be tempered or stopped by those means which render the yeast inoperative, particularly by the oils that contain sulphur, as oil of mustard; as also by the sulphurous and sulphuric acids. The operation of sulphurous acid, in obstructing the fermentation of must, consists partly, no doubt, in its absorbing oxygen, whereby the elimination of the yeasty particles is prevented. The sulphurous acid, moreover, acts more powerfully upon fermenting liquors that contain tartar, as grape juice, than sulphuric acid. This acid decomposes the tartaric salts; combining with their bases, sets the vegetable acids free, which does not interfere with the fermentation, but the sulpurous acid operates directly upon the yeast."

In the London Encyclopedia, "stum" is termed an unfermented wine; to prevent it from fermenting, the casks are matched, or have brimstone burnt in them. Sulphur is placed among the antiferments mentioned by Donovan.

Says Count Dandolo, on the art of making and preserving of the wines of Italy, first published at Milan, 1812: "The last process in wine making is sulphurization; its object is to secure the most long continued preservation of all wines, even of the very commonest sort. The classifications (spoken of in a former section) tend to assist this keeping of wines; but sulphurization, or the application of sulphur (sulphurous acid) to the wine, is that process which more directly attacks that pernicious fermenting principle, in the very bowels of the wine itself (if such an expression may be allowed), and destroys its power of mischief. The action of this vapor of sulphur not only neutralizes, changes and destroys the fermenting principle existing as yet undeveloped in the must fresh pressed from the grape, leaving untouched the saccharine part, but it operates equally upon the quantity of ferment remaining in the wine which has already undergone fermentation." "This process shows the effect of sulphurization to annihilate entirely the power of the fermenting principle in the wine, and even in the must, without ever changing the sugary substance in the must, or the alcohol in the wine." By this means, a sound wine, though on the very point of changing, and a wine which could not be carried twenty miles without becoming muddy, or being spoiled, after clarification or sulphurization, is in a state for keeping a hundred years, and will bear the motion of a long journey.

And not only is it the rich and generous wines, such as the well known ones of Bordeaux, which by sulphurization can be rendered capable of long keeping and bearing a journey, but even the very lightest wines, like those of Burgundy, are equally influenced by it, and become fit for exportation or removal to distant places.

Sulphurization, then, not only leaves untouched the alcohol which may be already existing, and the aromatic principles of the wine, but when a wine that has been sulphurized contains any sugary matter not decomposed, that sugary matter continues perfectly untouched, in consequence of the ferment (which would have converted it into spirit) being neutralized by the sulphurization.

The ancients were aware that the process of fermentation could thus be arrested, and hence both the interior and exterior of the vessels in which the new wine was contained, were said to have been covered with gypsum.

THE ANCIENTS USED MEANS, AS WELL TO DISSIPATE OR NEUTRALIZE THE ALCOHOL, WHEN GENERATED, IN THEIR WINES, AS TO PREVENT ITS GENERATION.

1*st.* THE YEAST WAS NOT ONLY SEPARATED FROM THE SACCHARINE MATTER BY SUBSIDENCE, BUT THE WINE ITSELF WAS PASSED THROUGH THE FILTER.

Says Pliny: "*Ut plus capiamus sacco franguntur vires; et alia irritamenta excogitantur; ac bibendi causa etiam venena conficiuntur.*" "That we may be able to drink a greater quantity of wine, we break, or deprive it of its strength, &c., by the filter, and various incentives to thirst are invented."

Says Horace: "*Liques vina,*" Car. lib. i., Ode 11. On these words the Delphin notes are as follows: "Be careful to prepare for yourself wine percolated, and defœcated by the filter, and thus rendered sweet and more in accordance to nature and a female taste. Certainly the ancients strained and defœcated their must through the filter repeatedly before they could have fermented; and, by this process, taking away the fœces that nourish and increase the strength of the wine, they rendered them more liquid, weaker, lighter and sweeter, and more pleasant to drink."

2d. WHERE THE ALCOHOL GENERATED BY FERMENTATION WAS NOT SUFFICIENTLY DISSIPATED BY THE FILTER OR OTHERWISE, ITS INFLUENCE WAS COUNTERACTED BY THE ADDITION OF WATER.

Hippocrates informs us that the wines of the ancients were divided into ὀλιγοφοροι and πολυφοροι, such as did and such as did not require dilution by water.

Plutarch mentions three dilutions. Hesiod prescribed, during the summer months, three parts of water to one of wine.

Athenæus has treated of the manner in which the ancients mingled their wines. He represents Archippus as inquiring: "Who of you has mingled an equal quantity of water with wine? It is far better to use one part of wine and four of water."

Nichocates considers one part of wine to five of water as the most desirable proportion.

According to Homer, Pramnian and Maronian wines required twenty parts of water to one of wine; and

Hippocrates considered twenty parts of water and one of Thasian wine to be a proper beverage.

Pliny declares that Maronian wine, celebrated by Homer, had maintained its character; for during the time of Mutianus, their consul, each pint was mingled with eighty parts of water.

In the receipt for making Cato's family wine, the vinegar and sea-water greatly exceeded the sapa; and to the grape juice was to be added five times its quantity of pure water; and from the whole the air was to be excluded ten days. Thus a celebrated wine was produced, that would keep till the following summer solstice. What the strength of such a wine must have been, and how it would be appreciated by wine-drinkers of our day, can readily be imagined.

The ancient Greeks, like the ancient Romans, heathens though they were, furnished, by their exemplary abstemiousness, a severe rebuke to modern christians. Their festivals were schools of temperance and sobriety. The wines used on these occasions were invariably mixed with water. None other were allowed. Indeed, in reputable society, the practice of mingling their wine with water was universal.

Those ancient authors, who treat upon domestic manners, abound with allusions to this usage. Hot water, tepid water, or cold water, was used for the dilution of wines, according to the season.

The process was common, and reduced to system. "Sometimes they were so luxurious as to mix their wine with hot water, so as to secure perfect combination, and then cool it down with ice or snow. In Italy the habit was so universally diffused, that there was an establishment at Rome for the public sale of water for mixing it with wine.

It was called Thermopolium, and, from the accounts left of it, was upon a large scale. The remains of several have been discovered among the ruins of Pompeii. Cold, warm and tepid water was procurable at these establishments, as well as wine; and the inhabitants resorted there for the purpose of drinking, and also sent their servants for the water. The fact of the practice being interwoven with the daily habits of the Greeks, may be judged from the circumstance of the Greek term for bowl or goblet: κρατηρ (quasi κερατηρ)—literally implying "a mingler," being derived from a verb signifying "to mingle." Each nation, as already shown, had its peculiar terms for inspissated wines which required mingling, as *sapa*, *carænum*, *siræum*, and *hepsema;* each, too, had its peculiar term to denote wine not yet mingled, as the Greek ακρατον, the Latin *merum*—(*tirosh lo yayin.*)

Nor was it peculiar to pagans to mingle water with wine for beverage and at feasts; nor to profane writers to record the fact. It is written of wisdom, not only, that she had killed her fat things, but also that she had mingled her wine; and so written by an inspired penman.

But what gives the greater weight to the inference to be drawn from these usages of the ancients is, that they not only resorted to expedients to prevent the generation of alcohol, and to dissipate it when generated:·

But that THEY ALSO PRONOUNCED THAT THE BETTER WINE IN WHICH THE GENERATION OF ALCOHOL HAD BEEN THE MOST EFFECTUALLY PREVENTED—OR HAVING BEEN GENERATED, WHERE IT HAD BEEN MOST EFFECTUALLY DISSIPATED, OR ITS POTENCY OTHERWISE COUNTERACTED OR DESTROYED.

Says Pliny: "*Utilissimum oinum omnibus sacco viribus fractis.*" The most useful wine is that which has its strength broken or destroyed by the filter, "*inveterari vina saccisque castrari,*" and again, "*Minus infestat nervos quod vetustate dulcescit.*" "Wines which become sweet by age are less injurious to the nerves." "Wines were rendered old, and deprived of their vigor by filtering." lib. xxiii., chap. 1.

The same author mentions, (lib. xiv., chap. 2) a wine called *inerticulam, justus sobriam, viribus innoxiam, siquidem temulentiam sola non facit;* a wine which would not intoxicate, *iners*, without spirit, more properly termed, "sober wine," harmless, "and which alone would not inebriate."

Columella speaks (lib. iii., chap. 2) of a wine called "Amethyston," unintoxicating. He adds, that it was "a good wine—harmless"—and called "*iners*"—weak—and would not affect the nerves.

"Be careful," says the Delphin Notes on Horace's 11th Ode, "to prepare for yourself wine percolated, and defœcated by the filter, and thus rendered sweet, and more in accordance to nature—and a female taste."

Theophrastus called wine that had been "*castratum*," deprived of its strength, "ἠθικου," "moral wine." Nor Theophrastus only. The ancients, when speaking of wine deprived of its potency, use the terms, "*eunuchum*," "*effæminatum*," "*castratum*." The corresponding Hebrew word is even used by Isaiah, i., 22, when speaking of wine reduced by water.

Polybius, in a fragment of his 6th book, states: "Among the Romans the women were forbidden to drink wine; they drank a wine which is called passum (*Latine, Passum*), and this was made from dried grapes or raisins. As a drink, it very much resembled *Ægosthenian* and *Cretan* (γλευκος), sweet wine, and which is used for the purpose of allaying thirst."

Both Pliny and Varro treat of wine which was conceded to Roman ladies, because it did not inebriate.

Says Plutarch (in his Sympos): "Wine is rendered old or feeble in strength when it is frequently filtered; this percolation makes it more pleasant to the palate; the strength of the wine is thus taken away, without any injury to its pleasing flavor. The strength being thus withdrawn or excluded, the wine neither inflames the head nor infests the mind and the passions, but is much more pleasant to drink. Doubtless defœcation takes away the spirit of potency that torments the head of the drinker; and this being removed, the wine is reduced to a state both mild, salubrious and wholesome."

That unintoxicating as well as intoxicating wines existed from remote antiquity, and that the former were held in higher estimation than the latter, by the wise and good, there can, I think, be no reasonable doubt. The evidence is unequivocal and plenary. Not indeed that the wines in use in Syria or the Holy Land were universally or even generally unintoxicating. We have demonstrative evidence that they are not so now, and presumptive evidence that they were not so formerly. We know that then, as now, inebriety existed; and then, as now, the taste for inebriating wines may have been the prevalent taste; and intoxicating wines the prevalent wines. Still, unintoxicating wines existed, and there were men who preferred such wines, and who have left on record the avowal of that preference. That these men were comparatively few in number, and that the wines they recommended were not generally in request, does not surely render it the less probable that they were wines deserving commendation. It might then as now, and, in reference to this as well as other questions of right and duty, be said:

> " Broad is the road that leads to death,
> And thousands walk together there;
> While wisdom shows a narrow path,
> With here and there a traveler."

From the foregoing examination, it is apparent that the fruit of the vine, in the state it exists in the vat, the vineyard and the cluster, is called in the original by the sacred writers of the Old Testament, *tirosh*, *yayin*, *ausis*, *hhemer*, &c., that in the Greek translation of these terms by the Seventy, it is called *oinon*, in the Latin translation, *vinum*, and in the English, *wine*. And it is further apparent that the fruit of the vine, in the same state, is called by the same name by profane writers; hence we meet in Aristotle with (*oinon*), wine of the vat; in Livy, with (*vinum*), wine of the field; and in Cato as well as Isaiah, with (*vinum pendens*), wine of the cluster; and hence, also, when we do so meet with these terms, though the presumption will be that they refer to the fruit of the vine in some state, it can only be determined in which by considering the attendant circumstances; and for the obvious reason, that the terms *yayin*, *oinos*, and *vinum*, are generic terms, and embrace in their comprehensive meaning the fruit of the vine or pure blood of the grape, in all of the states in which it exists.

But whatever question may be raised about the quality of other kinds of wine, there can be no question about this pendent wine of Cato; for it is the wine of the cluster of Isaiah. This wine must be good wine, for it is wine approved of God; and there was, as we have seen, a time when it was approved of man also; and however it may now be spoken against, we believe it still to be not the less worthy of commendation on that account, because we believe it still to be what it then was (in the sense in which we use the terms), *unintoxicating wine*. Not that we affirm the pure blood of the grape, as expressed from the ripened cluster, to have been always absolutely unaffected by fermentation, but only slightly and insensibly affected by it.* In olden time, wine, as we believe, was appreciated not as now, according to its strength, but according to its weakness.

---

* The admission in Dr. Nott's Lectures, that there may perhaps be a very slight degree of alcohol, even in the wine allowed and pronounced good by the Bible, gave offence to many sincere friends of temperance, when they were first published; and several able and esteemed advocates of the cause felt it their duty to repudiate and condemn it as a needless and injurious concession. This matter has been referred to the author, with reference to the publication of this new edition of his Lectures, and we learn that after carefully and candidly examining the whole of this criticism, he still does not feel it to be his duty to suppress or alter the text. And certainly no such liberties would be warrantable in the Editor. He will have discharged his duty, after advertising the reader that this is debatable ground, on which equally honest advocates of temperance truth maintain conflicting opinions.

There is a question of science, involved in this discussion, which is still an unsettled one. It is well settled, indeed, that of the three stages of fermentation (vinous, acetous and putrefactive), alcohol is the product of the first. But *when* it has reached that stage, and therefore when alcohol enters into the expressed juice of the grape, is still undecided. One chemist has said that if the must is exposed to the air, for a few seconds only, it absorbs oxygen, and fermentation takes place. Others have given the opinion that a much longer time must elapse before the composition and quality of the liquid can be said to be tinged by the admission of alcohol. One of the latest writers, the author of the "Chemistry of Common Life" (see Vol. I., p. 262), would seem to hold that no "sensible quantity of alcohol" had been found in the body of the liquid until the lapse of "three hours" of ordinary summer weather. But we do not understand that either of these views are advanced as matured scientific opinions, and the result of actual experiments. We regard the point in hand, therefore, to be still an open question of science, to be hereafter determined by scientific men.

The most accurate writers and speakers on Temperance, when they reason from the Bible, in connection with wines (the products of

I am aware that there are those who consider the question of fermentation in wine A QUESTION NOT OF DEGREE BUT OF TOTALITY.

---

the brew-house and distillery are inventions sought out by man since the canon of Scripture closed), recognize this as a question still in dispute. They do not speak of the good and bad wine of the Bible, as alcoholic and non-alcoholic, nor as fermented and unfermented, but as *intoxicating* and *unintoxicating;* the unintoxicating being clearly the good wine of the Bible, and the intoxicating being clearly the bad.

As this point is an unsettled question in the science of temperance, so we regard these views in Dr. Nott's Lectures as among the disputed questions in its ethics and philosophy, which are to be cleared up by future inquiry and discussion.

But let it be observed, even by those who regard this admission by the author as gratuitous, and unfortunate, that his Lectures elsewhere contend for abstinence, not only from intoxicating, alcoholic and fermented wine, but also from the freshly expressed juice of the grape. So that, if the author here is in error, he has not left the reader entirely without an antidote. In the closing paragraph of the fourth lecture, he says:

"Still it does not follow that *even the pure blood of the grape* should now be used by us as a beverage The circumstances of society (since the grant to Jacob) have changed; distillation has been discovered; chemistry has mixed new poisons with the wine cup; and, to save the church and the world from ruin, it has become necessary, and it is, therefore, as we have already said, incumbent on us, in the spirit of the first law of Christian love, *wholly to abstain from the use of vinous beverage of every sort.*"

Whatever fault may be found, therefore, with these particular passages in Dr. Nott's Lectures, their general tenor, it will be seen, teaches temperance doctrine which is sufficiently comprehensive and severe. And it is supported by an argument so authoritative and conclusive, that it must ever silence all cavillers at Abstinence, who are not bold enough also to question the inspiration of Scripture: "*It is good neither to eat flesh,* NOR TO DRINK WINE, *nor anything whereby thy brother stumbleth, or is offended, or is made weak.*" —Romans, xiv., 21.

Pure alcohol, say they, is poison; and because it is so, every beverage in which alcohol is contained, how minute soever the quantity, must be poison also. This, though plausable, is not conclusive; and were it so, the water we drink, nay, the very air we breathe, would be poison; for oxygen and nitrogen, of which it is composed, are so; and so is every mixture of the two in any other proportions than the proportion in which the God of nature has united them in the vital air; and yet, when so united, they are breathed not only with impunity, but of necessity, as an essential element of life. In like manner, though alcohol be poison, and though every mixture of it in any greater proportion than that in which God has united it with those other elements in the "*pure blood of the grape*," may also be poison, it does not follow, if so united, it must be so.

On the contrary, the beverage thus formed may be not only innocuous, but nutritious and renovating, as the noble Canaro found it when he drank the fresh new wine of the recent vintage; and yet this same beverage, so bland and healthful, while its original

---

Nature and Science unite, with a thousand tongues, to plead for and enforce the doctrines of Total Abstinence. But if, through lack of sufficient knowledge or the imperfections of human reason, the principle is ever for a moment involved in doubt, we have only to fall back upon this sublime saying of the Apostle Paul, and which is accepted by the whole Christian world. Here, at least, our author plants his feet on ground which is incontestable, and as firm as the everlasting hills. Nay, it is easier for heaven and earth to pass away than one tittle of the law to fail.—[EDITOR.]

elemental proportions are maintained, may increase in potency, as its contained alcohol is increased by progressive fermentation, till, changed in its nature, it becomes what the Bible significantly calls it, a "*mocker*;" executing on those who drink it a vengeance which the Bible no less significantly describes, by comparing it to the bite of the serpent and the sting of the adder.

It is urged, I am aware, that these terms, and terms like these, when applied to wine of some sort, are to be understood not as conveying counsel to refrain from the use of bad wine, but merely to avoid excess in the use of good. But according to what principle of interpretation is this urged? Is wine, in distinction from all the other bounties of Providence, always of good quality, that wine of bad quality should never have been spoken against by any writer, either sacred or profane? And, as if this were proven to be the case, are we bound, contrary to experience, contrary to reason, contrary to express declarations of Scripture, when we meet with passages in which wine is spoken of in terms of reprobation, and as a base article and an article to be avoided; are we bound in such cases, in disregard both of the spirit and the letter of the text, to understand the terms employed, not as implying the avoidance of a bad article, but merely as a caution against the abuse of a good one?

Or, if bad wine as well as good wine exists, then it may be asked whether good wine, among all the good creatures of God, is alone liable to abuse, that it should on that account be singled out and spoken against as a vile thing, and to be avoided? Are not corn, and oil, and milk, and honey, as well as wine, abused? Or, is the abuse of these not sinful, that neither of them on that account is ever styled the "mocker?" employed as a symbol of wrath, said to occasion woe and sorrow, that neither of these is forbidden to kings, forbidden to be brought into the house of the Lord, forbidden to be looked upon, or said to bite like a serpent or sting like an adder?

If because good wine can be abused, such wine deserves to be styled a "mocker," and can fitly be employed in the same state, and in allusion to the same attributes as a symbol of wrath, as well as of mercy, why may not sunlight and Sabbaths, and even the visitation of the Holy Spirit, be spoken of in the same manner; for all these (good and glorious in themselves) are, as well as wine, liable to abuse, and the abuse of these, as well as the abuse of wine, is sinful; and yet no such array of texts against these, or either of these, can be found in either Testament, as meets the eye against wine in both.

The fact that good wine may be abused, but ill accounts for the application to such wine of those terms of reprobation applied to wine of some sort so often in the Bible. To justify such an application of such terms, in such frequency, it should seem that not only good wine, which in the use might be abused, must have existed, but bad wine, and wine therefore unfit for use, must also have existed.

Since good and bad wine both exist now, why should they not have existed then? And if both existed then (as the Bible assures us they did), why should it be doubted when wine is commended, that the commendation respects the former kind of wine; and when wine is condemned, that the condemnation respects the latter kind? Does either the honor of religion or the analogy of faith require that it should be otherwise?

When commending wine, if, in place of commending the weak, nutritious, unintoxicating wines of nature, the Bible commends the strong, innutritious, intoxicating wines of art, it does so in contravention of the will of God, as everywhere else expressed; and the doing of this, *here* stands forth an isolated fact, at variance with all the other facts recorded in the Scriptures, a fact unexplained and unexplainable.

All the other articles recommended as food or beverage, are not only pronounced good, but are practically found to be so. Elsewhere, in reference to articles of diet, the word and providence of God are in harmony; here only at variance; for, however bland, refreshing and life-sustaining the nutritious, unintoxicating wines of nature may be, the strong, exciting, intoxicating wines of art are, and have ever proved themselves to be, both life and soul-destroying.

Against the use of such wines, God hath not left himself without a witness in his Providence. From the chalice that contains it, is audibly breathed out the serpent's hiss, and visibly darted forth the adder's sting. Around this chalice ruins are strewed

—strewed by the mocker—in which ruins there is a voice that speaks, and it speaks for God, and its language is, *Touch not, taste not, handle not.* Here there can be no mistake. That woe, and sorrow, and crime, and disease, flow from this inebriating chalice, none can deny; nor can any sophistry shelter its bewildering, crime-producing contents from deserved reprobation, or bring its use as a beverage, within the sanction of the sanctuary.

The books of nature and revelation were written by the same unerring hand. The former is more full and explicit in relation to the physical, the latter in relation to the moral laws of our nature; still, however, where both touch on the same subject, they will ever be found, when rightly interpreted, to be in harmony.

There was a time when the Copernican system, the truth of which was stamped on the phases of the planets, and proclaimed in the revolution of the stars, was pronounced a heresy, because it was believed to be irreconcilable with the language of the Bible. Councils decreed that the earth stood still, and that the sun and stars revolved around it. Regardless of that decree, the sun and stars maintained their unalterable position, and the earth, unawed, moved onward in its orbit, and revolved on its axis; and it has continued to do so, till mankind, familiarized to its movements, see no longer any contradiction between those movements and the language in which they were formerly spoken of by patriarchs and prophets.

Nature and revelation are as little at variance on the wine question as on other questions, and when rightly consulted, they will be found to be so. It is not in the text, but in the interpretation, that men have felt straitened in their consciences; and though this feeling should continue, unless the providence of God changes, it will not alter the facts of the case.

In vain will sophists teach, or councils decree, that intoxicating wine, wine the mocker, is good wine, and fit for beverage, so long as God in his providence proclaims that it is not. In despite of the teachings of sophists and the decrees of councils, the purpose of God will stand, and human arrogance continue to be rebuked, till it shall be felt that the laws of nature are sacred, and that it is as fatal to resist, as idle to reason, against the will of Him who ordained them.

To condemn as sin, *per se*, all use of intoxicating wine on the one hand, and to vindicate its use as a common beverage on the other, appears equally erroneous.

The wine of the condemned was doubtless an intoxicating wine, disallowed to worshippers in the house of the Lord, disallowed to kings, rejected by the Savior, and yet it might be given to the sad of heart, as strong drink might to those ready to perish.

Doubtless other intoxicating wines follow the same rule. None of them were made in vain; each has its appropriate use, and may be used whenever the use is beneficial, and to the extent it is beneficial;

and each is to be avoided when its use would be injurious, as experience shows it to be, when used as custom sanctions its use as a beverage.

It is true that wine, as well as flesh and herbs, and bread and milk and honey, is contained in the original grant of good things to man, but this implies no sanction of bad wine, any more than of any other bad article.

Because flesh is contained in the same grant, no one feels called upon to defend the use of the flesh of horses, or of dogs, or of reptiles; nay, not even the flesh of kine, when diseased or rendered noxious by putrescence or otherwise. Neither does any one, because herbs are contained in that grant, feel called upon to defend the use of henbane or deadly nightshade, or even of garden herbs, after having become wilted, and especially after having become deleterious by decay.

As little, because wine is contained in that grant, can the wines of Sodom be defended; nay, nor even wine from the vines of Eschol, or of Lebanon, after they shall have been rendered deleterious by the process of fermentation, or any other process through which it may have passed, before reaching ultimate, utter putrefaction.

Who ever thought, because bread and milk are sanctioned in the Bible, that therefore bread must be eaten after it had become mouldy by age, or milk, after it had become sour by fermentation?

From the moment the animal is slain, the herb gathered, or the cluster of the vine plucked, the process of decay commences, which, unless arrested, will continue in each, till all alike are rendered unfit for use, by progressive fermentation.

With wines, as with herbs and meats, some were originally comparatively good, and some comparatively bad; and some which were originally good became bad through mistaken treatment, the progressive process of fermentation, or some other incidental process through which they may have passed.

Meats recently slaughtered, herbs recently gathered, and wines recently expressed from the cluster, are usually the most healthful, nutritious and refreshing. And though wine perfectly free from alcohol may not be obtainable, and though its most perfect state be the state in which it is expressed from the cluster, still it may be more or less objectionable, as it deviates more or less from that state till it becomes positively deleterious and intoxicating.

Though God's grant to man covers wine among other good things, it designates no particular kind, it gives no directions as to the mode of preparation, or the time when it is most fit for use. These and similar instructions are to be looked for, not in the book of revelation, but of nature.

Man is a rational creature, and God treats him as such. The great store-house of nature is flung open before him, and permission is given him to slay or gather and eat; not indeed inconsiderately and indiscriminately, but of such and only such as are suited to his nature, and as are good for food.

In the selection and preparation of the articles, reason is to be exercised, experience consulted, the good distinguished from the bad, the precious from the vile.

That Patriarchs and Prophets drank wine, and that the Scriptural right to drink it still remains unimpaired, there can be no doubt; still, in making the selection, other directions than what the Bible contains must be followed. Here, as we have said, reason must be exercised, and experience consulted. Who, in the selection of herbs, or milk, or meat, would venture to take a contrary course; or who, having taken it, would not find in the sequel his temerity rebuked?

How often, in the course of events, have herbs, or meat, or milk, proved poisonous, and produced disease or death? In cases of this sort, how unavailing to declare that these articles, because included in the original grant, were not poisonous, when God declared in His providence that they were. Herbs, and meat, and milk, stand on the same footing as wine, and we only insist that the same discrimination should be exercised in relation to the latter that is exercised in relation to the former. The question, so far as good wine is concerned, is a question of expediency, and only of expediency, and abstinence becomes a duty only when indulgence would be injurious.

But abstinence from bad wine is always a duty; and whether intoxicating wine, wine that enervates the reason, defiles the conscience, destroys the constitution, and peoples the prison-house with criminals and the graveyard with victims, be not bad wine, will hardly, where prejudice is not indulged and appetite consulted, at this late day, be made a question.

Perfect purity nowhere exists on this crime-curst planet. Earth supplies neither air, or food, or beverage, suited to immortal natures. Even the well, at the entrance of which Jesus Christ revealed to the woman of Samaria his Messiahship, contained not the water of life. Jacob, who drank at that well, was dead; the Patriarchs who drank at it were dead. Were perfect purity insisted on, man could neither eat, or drink, or breathe. This insisted on, would exclude the mechanic from the workshop, the husbandman from the harvest field, and the worshipper from the temple of his God. But it is not insisted on—at least not elsewhere—why then should it be insisted on here?

It is enough, if wine be placed on the same footing as other articles of diet, with respect to each of which, the question in relation to deleterious qualities is a question of degree, not of totality.

If we procure the best articles in our power, it is all that can be required of us; and it is only those articles which contain deleterious ingredients in such quantity or such proportion as produce disease of body or mind, the use of which is to be avoided. Here, not temperance, but abstinence, is a duty. The evil to be apprehended in the use of deleterious ingredients often depends less on quantity than intensity. A single *drop of pure alcohol* may inflame some point in the mucus membrane of the stomach, with which it comes in contact, and thus produce the inception of a disease which may afterwards diffuse itself over the entire surface of that vital organ, which drop might have been innocuous, or at least have produced no appreciable injury, had it been diluted to a certain extent by water.

In estimating the effect of other agencies than poison, intensity as well as quantity must be taken into the account. There is a temperature conducive to life and health, and there is a temperature above and below which life becomes extinct. The rays of solar light and heat, so grateful to the eye and the body under certain circumstances, become as distressful as destructive when their intensity is increased, as it may be by the intervention of a burning glass.

Although the heat concentrated in a spark of fire or a drop of boiling water might blister some small and delicate portion of the human cuticle with which it might chance to come in contact, still the effect of that same heat, if imparted to a volume of water sufficient for the immersion of the body, if appreciable at all, might be only bland and genial.

In diet as in respiration, the action of one element may neutralize that of another; or its own action may depend, as in the case of light and heat, less on quantity than concentration.

Hence, wine in which its (*entire*) saccharine matter has been converted by continuous fermentation into alcohol, may be highly exciting and deleterious; and, at the same time, wine in which the process of fermentation is inceptive merely, and in which but a small portion of its saccharine matter has been so converted, may be both nutritious and healthful; and the more so, when the proportion in which these elements exist in the cask, is the proportion in which they existed in the cluster or the vat; as that proportion may be the proportion best suited to the constitution of man, for whose use, in this state, wine has been from the beginning spontaneously furnished by the Creator himself.

Still it does not follow that even the pure blood of the grape should now be used by us as a beverage. The circumstances of society (since the grant to Jacob) have changed; distillation has been discovered; chemistry has mingled new poisons in the wine cup; and to save the church and the world from ruin, it has become necessary, and it is therefore, as we have already said, incumbent on us, in the spirit of the great law of Christian love, wholly to abstain from the use of vinous beverage of every sort. Even as medicine, intoxicating liquors will seldom be required; other and safer remedies exist. As an element at the Lord's Supper, the use of wine will indeed be perpetual. This, its sacramental use, will be considered in the next lecture. To the consideration of which, the distinction in wines and the principle governing the selection hinted at in this, may be considered as preliminary. On all these several questions, research and caution are necessary, for all the circumstances that bear on such must be taken into account if we would arrive at the true result.

LECTURE No. V.

WINE—ITS SACRAMENTAL USE.

The wine made use of at the Paschal Supper, at the wedding at Cana of Galilee—and the wine recommended to Timothy.

In the preceding lecture we have shown that different kinds of wine existed, and were known to exist from remote antiquity, some of which were salubrious, sober wines, and some deleterious and intoxicating.

Since these things are so, since different kinds of wine exist, and are known to have existed from remote antiquity—to ascertain which of these, whether salubrious and sober, or insalubrious and intoxicating wine was used by our Lord in the sacramental supper, it will be of use first to ascertain which of these kinds of wine was used at the paschal supper.

And here it is obvious to remark that the fruit of the vine in none of its forms constituted any part of the original institution, as will appear from the thirteenth chapter of Exodus. On the contrary, on the fourteenth of Nisan, a lamb without blemish, was by each family to be eaten, with bitter herbs; eaten standing with their loins girded, their shoes on their feet, their staves in their hands, and eaten in haste.

In whatever form the fruit of the vine was subse quently used, it was probably introduced after the settlement in Canaan—when the guests, in place of standing (as appears from John, xii., 23), reclined on their left arm on couches placed round the table—a posture which, according to the writers in the Talmud, was an emblem of that rest and freedom which God had granted to his people.

But at whatever time wine was introduced at the paschal supper, it might be presumed, in the absence of evidence to the contrary, that the kind selected would be in keeping with the nature of the ordinance. And this it should seem could not well be intoxicating wine, since this would but ill accord with a solemnity in which bitter herbs were to be eaten, and from which leaven was to be excluded. "Unleavened bread shall be eaten seven days; and there shall no leavened bread be seen with thee, neither shall there be leaven seen with thee in all thy quarters."

Gesenius declares that the Hebrew word which the English translators have rendered *leaven*, applies to wine as well as bread.

"The word chomets," says Mr. Herschell, a converted Jew, "has a wider signification than that which is generally attached to 'leaven,' by which it is rendered in the English Bible, and applies to the fermentation of corn in any form, to beer, and to all fermented liquors."

The Rev. C. F. Frey says, "that during the passover Jews dare not drink any liquor made from grain, nor any that has passed through the process of fermentation."

The testimony of Mr Frey is corroborated by another Hebrew writer, who declares "that their drink during the time of the feast is either pure water or raisin wine prepared by themselves, but no kind of leaven must be mixed therein."

And M. M. Noah, Esq., says in a recent publication: "unfermented liquor or wine free from alcohol was alone used in those times, as it is used at the present day at the passover."

But not to insist on this. Whatever the kind of wine made use of at the paschal supper, it was always, if the writers in the Talmud or even the Christian fathers are to be credited, diluted with water.*

---

* Dr. Lightfoot (I quote from Horne's introduction to the Practical Study of the Scriptures) Dr. Lightfoot has collected from the Talmud a variety of passages relative to the Jewish mode of celebrating the passover; from which we have abridged the following particulars calculated to illustrate the history of our Lord's last passover:

1. The guests being seated around the table, they mingled a cup of wine with water, over which the master of the family gave thanks and then drank it off. The thanksgiving for the wine was, "Blessed be thou, O Lord, who hast created the fruit of the vine. Blessed be thou for this good day and for this convocation which thou hast given us for joy and rejoicing. Blessed be thou, O Lord, who hast sanctified Israel and the times."

2. After which they washed their hands and the table was furnished with the paschal lamb, bitter herbs and cakes of unleavened bread.

3. The person presiding took a leaf of salad, and having blessed God for creating the fruit of the ground, he ate it, as did the other guests; after which, the table being cleared, the children were

But if the wine made use of in the paschal supper was diluted with water, then probably the wine made use of at the supper of our Lord was also diluted.

For we are told that, having on the night before his passion retired to an inner chamber at Jerusalem and celebrated for the last time the paschal supper, he took bread and the cup, and having blessed and brake the one, and poured out the other, he gave both to his disciples in token of his love and as memorials

---

instructed in the nature of their feast. In like manner the Savior makes use of the Lord's Supper to declare the great mercy of God in our redemption, for it shows forth the Lord's death until he come.

4. Replacing the supper they explained the import of the bitter herbs and paschal lamb, repeating the 113th and 114th psalms, with an eucharistic prayer.

5. The hands were again washed, and the master, after an ejaculatory prayer, proceeded to break and bless a cake of unleavened bread, which he distributed, reserving a portion thereof for the last morsel; for the rule, after the destruction of the Temple, was to conclude by eating a small piece of unleavened bread.

In like manner our Lord, upon instituting the sacrament of the eucharist, which was prefigured by the passover, took bread, and having blessed it, brake it and gave it to his disciples, saying, take, eat, this is my body which is broken for you. This do in remembrance of me.

6. They then ate the remainder of the cake with bitter herbs, dipping the bread into the charoseth or sauce provided. To which practice the Evangelists Matthew and Mark allude; into which our Savior is supposed to have dipped the sop which he gave to Judas.

7. Next they ate the flesh of the peace offerings which had been sacrificed, and then the paschal lamb, which was followed by returning thanks to God.

of his death; which solemnity was thereafter to be repeated, that by its repetition his death might be showed forth until his second coming.

As our Lord in this latter ordinance, for aught that appears, made use of the elements previously prepared for the former ordinance, it may fairly be concluded, that if water was mingled in the wine contained in the cup made use of in the former, it was also mingled in the wine contained in the cup made use of in the latter.

---

8. A cup of wine was then filled, over which they blessed God, and hence it was called the cup of blessing. To which circumstance Paul alludes when he says: "The cup of blessing which we bless, is it not the communion of the body of Christ?" It was at this part of the paschal supper that the Lord took the cup and said: "This is the new testament in my blood which is shed for you and for many for the remission of sins."

9. The last cup was called the cup of hallel, over which they sang or recited the Psalms from the 115th to the 118th inclusive, and concluded.

In like manner our Lord and his disciples, when they had sung an hymn, departed to the Mount of Olives.

So much in relation to the wine of the passover.

Besides the passover, there was a mingling of wine with water at the feast of the tabernacle in the Temple, referred to by our Lord, John, vii., 37 and 38, and fully described by the Talmudists:

"When the fruits of sacrifice were laid on the altar, one of the priests with a golden tankard went to the fountain Siloion and there filled it with water. He returned back into the court of the Temple through the water gate. The trumpet sounded. On the altar stood two basins, one containing wine, and the other empty, into which the water was poured; and then they were poured into each other by way of oblation. The ceremony was in honor of God; and in gratitude for supplying water to the children of Israel in the wilderness."

And thus the Fathers of the church believed, and the early councils authoritatively ordered.* But if the wine made use of in these offices of religion was not *intoxicating, why was it diluted with water?* Does not its dilution prove that it was intoxicating wine? Cer-

---

* The Council of Trent decreed (ch. 7, the mass): "Further, the Holy Council reminds all men that the priests are commanded by the church to mix water in the wine in the cup, when they offer the sacrifice; partly because Christ the Lord is believed to have done the same, and partly because water together with blood flowed from his side, which sacrament is brought to remembrance by this mixture."

Says Cave, in his Primitive Christianity, speaking of the early Christians:

"Their sacramental wine was generally diluted and mixed with water, as is evident from Justin Martyr, Ireneus, Cyprian and others. Cyprian in a long epistle expressly pleads for it, as the only true and warrantable tradition, derived from Christ and his Apostles, and endeavors to find out many mystical significations intended by it, and seems to intimate as if he had been peculiarly warned of God so to observe it."

In like manner the sacramental wine was originally diluted in the Episcopal church; and among the changes made in the Book of Common Prayer, is expressly mentioned, "The omitting the rubric that ordered water to be mixed with the wine" used in the eucharist. Wheatly, in his apology for this omission, says that Dr. Lightfoot observes from the Babylonish Talmud that this ("the fruit of the vine") was a term the Jews used in their blessings for wine mixed with water. He admits that before the time of Origen the mixture was the general practice of the church. That F. Cyprian pleads strenuously for the mixture and urges it from the practice and example of our Lord. "And indeed," says he, "it must be confessed that the mixture has in all ages been the general practice, and for that reason was enjoined, as has been noted above, to be continued in our church by the first reformers."

Says Palmer, in his antiquities of the English ritual: "The custom of mingling water with the wine of the eucharist, is one which prevailed

tainly not. Other qualities apart from its contained alcohol may have rendered dilution necessary. The unintoxicating wines of antiquity were often thick and even ropy, and therefore required to be diluted to fit them for convenient and sometimes for healthful and pleasurable use.*

---

universally in the Christian church from the earliest ages. Justin Martyr of Syria, Ireneus of Gaul, Clemens of Alexandria, and Cyprian of Carthage, bear testimony to its prevalence in the second and third centuries. There is in fact no sort of reason to deny that the Apostles themselves had the same custom. It is even probable that the cup which our Savior blessed at the last supper contained water as well as wine, since it appears that it was generally the practice of the Jews to mix the paschal cup, which our Savior used in instituting the sacrament of his blood."

Bernard, in speaking of persons who thought water essential, adds: "The judgment of theologians is certain, that consecration is valid even if water be omitted, though he who omits it is guilty of a serious offence."

In the Church of England the wine of the eucharist was always no doubt mixed with water. In the canons of the Anglo-Saxon church, published in the time of King Edgar, it is enjoined that no priest shall celebrate the liturgy, unless he have all things that pertain to the holy eucharist, that is, a pure oblation, pure wine and pure water. In after ages we find no canons made to enforce the use of water, for it was an established custom: certainly none can be more canonical or more conformable to the practice of the primitive church.

* Pliny says it was common in Italy and Greece to boil their wines: thus the must was sometimes boiled down to one-half and sometimes to one-third part of its quantity. The wines of Arcadia, as we have seen, were declared by Aristotle to be so thick that they dried up in the goat skins; that it was the practice to scrape them off, and dissolve the scrapings in water. Very similar to the wines of Arcadia were the wines of Lebanon and Helbon, spoken of in Scripture. The wines of Syria, among the best of which are those of Lebanon,

Since then the unintoxicating wines of antiquity required dilution, and since the wines made use of in the offices of religion were actually diluted, the fact of their dilution increases rather than diminishes the presumption that the wines so made use of were unintoxicating wines.

On the whole, since the bread of the passover must be unleavened, that is unfermented; since the use, nay, even the possession of leaven was prohibited during this festival; since many of the modern Jews, who may be supposed to understand the usages of their fathers better than we do, refuse even now the use of fermented wine in the cup of blessing which they bless—to say the least, it is not improbable

---

are, says a modern traveler, "prepared by boiling immediately after they are expressed from the grape." There is reason to believe, says W. G. Brown, that this mode of boiling their wines was in general practice among the ancients. It is still retained in some parts of Provence, where it is called cooked wine. "The wines of Syria," says Mons. Volney, "are of three sorts, the red, the white and the yellow. The white, which are the most rare, are so bitter as to be disagreeable; the two others, on the contrary, are too sweet and sugary. This arises from their being boiled, which makes them resemble the baked wines of Provence. The general custom of the country is to reduce the must to two-thirds of its quantity.

"The yellow wine is much esteemed among our merchants, under the name of Golden Wine (Vin d'or), which has been given to it from its color. The most esteemed is produced from the hill sides of the Zouk, a village of Mazbeh, near Antoura. It is not necessary to heat it, but it is too sugary. Such are the wines of Lebanon, so boasted by the Grecian and Roman epicures. It is probable that the inhabitants of Lebanon have made no change in their ancient method of making wines, nor in the culture of their vines."—*Volney's Travels in Egypt and Syria, vol. ii., ch.* 29, *p.* 205, *ed.* 1788.

that unfermented wine as well as unfermented bread was made use of at the paschal supper, and if at the paschal supper, then probably at the supper of our Lord.

Nor let it be forgotten, that however much may of late have been said by the disciples about fermented, that is, intoxicating wine, the Master has said nothing of the use of wine of any kind in that solemnity. Nor is the term wine ever once employed by the sacred writers in connection with the sacramental supper. It was the "CUP" that Jesus Christ gave to his disciples; and *neither fermented nor unfermented wine*, but the "FRUIT OF THE VINE" are the terms by which the contents of that cup are, by him that poured it out, designated. And surely the pure blood of the grape, as it is expressed from the cluster, is quite as intelligible and striking an emblem of the blood of Christ, and quite as truly the fruit of the vine, as that same blood of the grape will be after continued fermentation shall have converted a nutritive and healthful into an intoxicating and deleterious beverage. And if it be so, then surely it may be used on sacramental occasions without scruple and without offence.

As to the dilution of the paschal and sacramental wine with water, the usage may be said to have been peculiarly pertinent and proper, if the wine itself was unfermented wine, because such wine often, if not usually, required dilution.

If these things are so — if the wine used in primitive times and on sacred occasions, and whether fermented or unfermented, was diluted with water—then how inconclusive the argument drawn from such usage, in favor of the use, as a common beverage, of fermented wine without dilution!

As to the wine at Cana of Galilee, if it be arrogant to assume that it was certainly not intoxicating, it is no less arrogant to assume that it certainly was intoxicating. All that the sacred text communicates is, that water was converted into wine; but the question as to the kind of wine, is left an open question; and the same, for aught asserted to the contrary, may have been the wine of Helbon or of Lebanon, or of any of those numerous kinds of wine alluded to by Pliny. Some of which wines were bitter, poisonous and stupefactive; some sweet, healthful and invigorating; and some acid, fragrant and refreshing. Amid this variety, which was selected as the most appropriate for manifesting the Savior's power and goodness in his first miracle, has not been told us, and can, therefore, only be inferred from the occasion, the person performing the miracle, and the circumstances under which it was performed.

What, then, was the occasion, who were the guests, who the person performing the miracle, and at what stage of the entertainment was it performed?

The occasion was the solemnization of an ordinance of God; the guests were grave, devout persons; Jesus, the mother and disciples of Jesus, were there; the person performing the miracle was Jesus himself; the time was near the close of the entertainment, when the guests, it would seem, had already well drank, and the original supply of wine provided was exhausted, and the additional supply furnished at this late hour was, in the judgment of the master of the festival, of the BEST QUALITY.

Had Pliny, Columella, Theophrastus, Plutarch, and other ancient sages, some of whom were cotemporary with the Apostles, presided at this festival, the question at issue as to the kind of wine miraculously supplied, would have been decided; for these men have sat in judgment on the quality of wines, and pronounced the weaker, unintoxicating winess the better wines.

But these men did not preside at this festival, and whether the master of the feast, who did, agreed with them in their opinion concerning the relative goodness of wines, we are not informed, and will not, therefore, presume authoritatively to decide; but, on the contrary, leave the question whether the Savior of the world miraculously supplied on this occasion deleterious, exciting, intoxicating wine, or sober, moral, unintoxicating wine, to be passed on by the enlightened reason and conscience of others.

For ourselves, however, we may be permittted to say, in view of all the circumstances of the case, we incline to the opinion that the wine declared by the master of the feast to be "good wine" was *good wine* —good in the sense that Pliny, Columella or Theophrastus would have used the term "good" when applied to wine; that is, good because nutritious and unintoxicating ; and of which the guests, even at such an hour, might drink freely and without apprehension, because it was wine which, though it would refresh and cheer, would not derange, demoralize or intoxicate.

But be this as it may, did not Paul expressly recommend the use of wine to Timothy? He did so. But it was but little, and that medicinally. His words are, "Drink no longer water, but use a little wine for thy stomach's sake, and thine often infirmities." Both the quantity and the quality of the wine recommended here are indicated.

Timothy at the time was an invalid, and Paul was prescribing for him as such. The quantity of wine prescribed was *small,* the kind *medicinal,* for it was prescribed for his stomach's sake and his many infirmities.

Though we do not know what all the infirmities of Timothy were, we do know that among them was a diseased or disordered stomach; and the wine prescribed, be the kind what it may, must by the apostle have been deemed good for such a stomach.

Now at the time this prescription was given, there was in use, as we have seen, wines, the pure juice or blood of the grape, in the state in which it was expressed—also wines containing a diminished quantity of saccharine matter and an increased quantity of alcohol, produced by converting the former into the latter by continued fermentation—as well as wines to which drugs had been added, most of which were intoxicating, and some of which, as Aristotle and Pliny both affirm, were deleterious, and "produced headaches, dropsy, madness, dysentery and stomach complaints;" and some of which, on the contrary, as the same authors affirm, were salubrious and medicinal, and particularly commended for enfeebled or "diseased stomachs."

Although we do not know the effect produced upon the human stomach, by all the poisons contained in ancient drugged wines, we do know the effect produced upon that delicate organ by Alcohol, the poison contained in fermented wine; for it has been made apparent from post mortem examinations. "Alcohol used frequently and in considerable quantities, causes inflammation of this delicate organ, which is generally of the chronic kind." This disease is insidious in its character and slow in its effects, but it invariably advances while the noxious cause is continually applied, until great induration, schirrous, and sometimes cancers and ulcers, are the deplorable consequences.

The pyloric and cardiac orifices become occasionally indurated and contracted, and when this is the case, death soon puts an end to the tantalizing suffering of the wretched victim.

But not from post mortem examinations alone are the effects of alcohol upon the human stomach made apparent.

By a singular providence, ocular demonstration of these effects, while in progress, has been furnished.

A young Canadian, St. Martin by name, was wounded by a cannon ball, which in its passage opened an orifice in his stomach, which, though the wound was healed, was never closed.

Hence it became necessary, in order to prevent the escape of food, to cover that orifice by a pad.

Dr. Beaumont, the army surgeon, who effected the cure, being impressed with a sense of the importance of the opportunity thus furnished for investigating the process of digestion, received the young man into his family, and instituted a series of experiments, which were continued two or three years.

During these experiments he found, that whenever St. Martin drank fermented liquor, "the mucus membrane of the stomach was covered with inflammatory and ulcerous patches, the secretions were vitiated, and the gastric juice diminished in quantity, and of an unnatural viscidity, and yet he described himself as perfectly well, and complained of nothing.

"Two days subsequent to this, the inner membrane of the stomach was unusually morbid, the inflammatory appearance more extensive, the spots more livid than usual; from the surface of some of them exuded small drops of grumous blood: the ulcerous patches were larger and more numerous; the mucus covering thicker than usual, and the gastric secretions much more vitiated. The gastric fluids extracted were mixed with a large proportion of thick ropy mucus, and a considerable mucopurulent discharge, slightly tinged with blood, resembling discharges from the bowels in some cases of dysentery. Notwithstanding this diseased appearace of the stomach, no very essential aberration of its functions was manifested. St. Martin complained of no symptoms indicating any general derangement of the system, except an uneasy sensation and tenderness at the pit of the stomach, and some vertigo with dimness and yellowness of vision on stooping down and raising up again." Dr. Beaumont further observed, that "the free use of ardent spirits, wine, beer, or any other intoxicating liquor, when continued for some days, has invariably produced these changes."

Now whatever may have been the other infirmities in question, is it probable that Paul recommended even a little of that kind of wine which produced such effects on the stomach, to be druuk by his young friend Timothy for his "stomach's sake?" Especially, is this probable, when there existed at the time other kinds of wine known to be harmless not only, but medicinal also; nay, even adapted especially to disordered or diseased stomachs?

If any, in view of so many probabilities to the contrary, shall, notwithstanding, be of this opinion, they will, it is to be hoped, since the question cannot be authoritatively and infallibly settled, admit that it is not altogether without color of reason, that the advocates of total abstinence from all that can intoxicate differ from them in opinion. But though the probability were much greater than it is believed to be, that the wine recommended by Paul to Timothy was intoxicating wine, still it would be obvious to remark, that it was recommended medicinally, and has therefore no bearing on the use of wine in health and as a common beverage. And it is also obvious to remark, that be the kind of wine in question what it may, up to the time this recommendation was given, Timothy was, in the fullest sense, a cold water drinker; and that an apostolic recommendation was necessary to induce him to take even a little wine, and that medicinally; and judge ye, what must have been the state of society, and the conviction of duty among Christians, at a time when such a license was requisite for such a purpose.

With all that tendency to ultraism said to prevail at present, it may be doubted whether evangelists might not even now be found who, though in health, would require no such license for such a liberty; and it may also be doubted, whether a mighty change does not yet remain to be effected in our manners, before our abstinence will equal the abstinence of primitive Christians, or come within those limits which the Bible prescribes.

Speaking of the exemplary and self-denying habits of those Christians, says Minutius Felix: "Our feasts are not only chaste but sober; we indulge not ourselves in banquets, nor make our feasts with wine, but temper our cheerfulness with gravity and seriousness." With these primitive habits, how will the habits of modern Christians compare? To say nothing of public festivals, how is it at ordinary meals and among those select and exemplary persons called, by way of eminence, *temperate drinkers?* Alas! that it should be so, but so it is, among such temperate drinkers, wines, even intoxicating wines, are drank habitually and freely and without dilution; a license this, which, among the more moral Pagans, was formerly deemed disreputable. The Greeks regard undiluted wine as the symbol of drunkenness, and as constituting the boundary between the sober and moral and the dissolute and drunken.

Laws were enacted, as we have shown, disallowing wine not mixed with water to be drank even at festivals.

Young men below thirty, and women all their lives, were forbidden to drink intoxicating wine at all as a common beverage.

And wine among the Romans, when drank on ordinary occasions, and by men of character, was always diluted with water.*

Whereas among us, wine, intoxicating wine, even brandied wine, is drank, and drank unmixed, as a common beverage, by men, women and children; and drank, too, without reproach, without scruple, and perhaps even occasionally on principle and for conscience sake.

It is impossible to have glanced, even as we have done in passing, at the opinions and practices of primitive times, without being struck with our manifest departure from that reserve and caution once observed in the use of liquors, the product even of the vineyard and the wine press.

---

* Potter's Antiquities.

LECTURE No. VI.

THINGS, NOT NAMES.

How wines called by the same name can be distinguished — Abstinence from wine urged on the ground of expediency.

If in primitive times, as has been attempted to be shown, distinct kinds of wine actually existed, some of which were pure, healthful, and a fit emblem of mercy; and some of which were impure, deleterious, and a fit emblem of wrath, it might naturally be expected, it is said, that products and preparations so distinct in their nature and opposite in their effects, would invariably have been designated by terms equally distinct; and some of the advocates of total abstinence may have unadvisedly assumed that such was actually the case.

I say unadvisedly, for though such an assumption would be verified by an appeal to the sacred text, in many cases, as we have shown, still it would not be uniformly and universally so verified, and the discovery that it would not, has by the opponents of total abstinence been hailed as a signal and decisive triumph.

With how much reason it has been so hailed, will, by an attention to THINGS, in place of NAMES, ultimately become apparent.

For however numerous and various and interchangeable the terms may be, which are used to denote those different kinds of vinous preparations of which the Bible speaks, all of which terms in our translation are rendered *wine*, the broad and notorious fact, that a marked and mighty difference existed between the different kinds of such preparations, is not a whit the less undeniable on that account.

Be the confusion of terms then what it may, there is no confusion of things; different kinds of wine actually existed, and are known to have existed, some of which were intoxicating, and some of which were not intoxicating.

The one kind usually safe and salutary, the other always dangerous, often hurtful, and sometimes even deadly.

By calling both by the same name, though they were uniformly so called, which they are not, would not alter the nature of either.*

---

* See the analysis of Scripture texts in Lecture Third, from which it will appear, that though *yayin* in Hebrew, like wine in English, is used for vinous beverage of every kind, *tirosh* is uniformly used for the unfermented fruit of the vine, as it exists in the cluster on the vine or in the vat, and never for the fermented fruit of the vine as it exists in the cask; and that *ausis* is used for the droppings of the juice from the cluster, or newly expressed in the vat, as *sobhe* seems to be for the same when inspissated, so that it is not the fact that in Hebrew no distinction is made between the different kinds of vinous beverage, called wine in English. (*See Appendix, A.*)

But if both kinds of wine are called by the same name, how can the two be distinguished? How? As other dissimilar things are distinguished by their distinctive attributes and effects.

When the fruit of the vine is spoken of at one time as the symbol of mercy, and at another time as the symbol of wrath, even though the same terms were used in both cases, would it follow that they were used in both in the same sense, and that in both the same kind of wine was in the contemplation of the prophet?

There is a kind of vinous preparation, pure, bland, cheering, a fit emblem of mercy; and there is also another kind of vinous preparation, impure, deleterious, demoralizing, maddening, a fit emblem of wrath.

And whatever may be the similarity, or even identity of terms employed in referring to these distinct kinds of preparation as emblems, who would be at a loss to divine which of these two kinds of preparation was referred to as an emblem of mercy, and which as an emblem of wrath?

If "teetotalers" cannot in all cases prove by verbal criticism, when wine is spoken of in terms of commendation, that unintoxicating wine is meant, because the terms employed are common to both intoxicating and unintoxicating wines, their opponents, be it remembered, cannot, for the same reason, prove the contrary.

What the truth is, however, is not the less discoverable on that account. For the real question at issue is not a question of words, but of facts.

Whether distinct kinds of vinous preparations, the one intoxicating and the other not, actually existed in the Holy Land, and whether the Bible recognizes their existence, and not whether they are always designated by different names, is what concerns us to know.

And the fact that such distinct kinds of wine did exist, the one intoxicating and the other not, and that the Bible does recognize their existence, are facts, and facts which denial cannot alter.

More than this the friends of total abstinence from all that intoxicates may not claim, and more than this the cause of total abstinence does not require.

Let us attempt an illustration by analogy.

What we call bread may either be made of the flour of wheat, of rye, of corn, of barley, of oats—or it may be made of the starch of the potato, or of various other farinaceous vegetables; it may be made even of bran, even of spurred rye, than which few poisons are more destructive to the health or fatal to the life of man. Moreover, the same may be fermented or unfermented—debased by the mixture of innutritious ingredients, and even of the most deadly poisons; but however made, or of whatever made, it is still called bread.

But because it is so called, are we to believe when bread is spoken of in terms of commendation, that that among all the kinds of bread which exist, the very vilest of them all is had in contemplation; or because the use of bread is sanctioned in the Bible, sanctioned habitually, sanctioned even at the communion table, are we to believe that the use of that sort of bread which is known to be destructive of health, and even of life, is therefore sanctioned?

And that although it might be well to partake sparingly of this bread of disease and death, still to abstain from its use altogether, since the use of bread is authorized by the Bible, would be both ultra and fanatical?

Who does not know that MIXED vinous beverages are sometimes spoken of in the Bible, in terms of commendation, and at other times in terms of condemnation? And who does not also know that a corresponding difference existed in the mixtures themselves?

Some being mixed with pure water or healthful medicaments, and some with deleterious drugs—the former by wisdom for her abstemious votaries, the latter by folly for her licentious guests.

And who, knowing this, will believe that because both preparations are called MIXED WINES, it cannot, therefore, be known, when these terms occur, which mixture is meant? And because it cannot, that all the commendations of "*mixed wines*" contained in the Bible may be legitimately claimed for those stupefying or maddening mixtures, prepared for idolators in their worship, for convicts at their executions, or even for the guests of harlots in their adulterous chambers?

Be the identity of the terms employed what it may, the distinctness of the mixtures indicated by their use, is not a whit the less real or intelligible on that account.

The same may be said, and with equal truth, of *unmixed* vinous beverages.

The good and the bad stand out in contrast on the sacred page; and not the less distinguishable because both are sometimes designated by one common name. Each kind being made apparent, notwithstanding this identity of name, by the manner of its use, the effects produced, or by the terms of praise or dispraise joined in the context.

Since then, there existed, and was known by the sacred writers to have existed in Palestine, different kinds of wine, distinct in their nature and opposite in their effects; the one safe and salutary, the other dangerous and sometimes deadly—the one the pure juice of the grape—the other the juice of the grape after having become deleterious, by a change wrought therein by continued fermentation or by drugging; since these two kinds of wine existed, and were known to exist, will it be pretended, when wine is spoken of, at one time as an emblem of mercy and at another as an emblem of wrath—that it cannot in either case be known which kind of wine was in the contemplation of the speaker? And if so, why?

Is it because it cannot be known which kind of wine, the good or the bad, is the fitter emblem of mercy, and which of wrath? or whether the bad and the good are not each equally fitted to become an emblem of either?

When Moses speaks of a wine that dishonored Noah, that polluted Lot—a wine that is the poison of dragons, and the cruel venom of asps—when Isaiah speaks of a wine that causes priests and even prophets to err in vision and stumble in judgment, so that it could be said in reference to its effects: "All tables are full of vomit and filthiness, and there is no place clean"—when Solomon speaks of a wine that is a mocker, that biteth like a serpent and stingeth like an adder—that causeth wounds and sorrow, and may not even be looked upon—when Asaph speaks of a wine of retribution, poured from a cup in the hand of God, the dregs whereof are to be wrung out and drank by the wicked; is it to be believed that the wine in question is the same kind of wine as that which wisdom mingles; to which wisdom invites—a wine fitly joined with bread and oil, and milk and honey, a wine that not only sustains the life but makes glad the heart of man? Is this to be believed, and believed in the face of so much evidence to the contrary, because vinous preparations, however distinct in their nature and opposite in their effects, are designated by the same name in the English Bible, and often even in the Greek and Hebrew?

But do not the very terms of the text alluded to, "And wine that maketh glad the heart of man," do not these terms show that the wine in the contemplation of the Psalmist was inebriating wine? Not in the judgment of "teetotalers," and why should they be thought to do this in the judgment of other men?

Is it because no joy ever arises in the bosom of the pious vine dresser, when, weary and exhausted, he reclines beneath the shadow of his vine, breathes the peculiar fragrance of its opening blossom, tastes the rich flavor of its ripened fruits, or allays his burning thirst with the delicious and refreshing beverage pressed fresh from its overhanging clusters?

Although the sensualist, insensible to the gratitude that ought to be called forth by these bounties of Providence, can perceive no gladness that could have been excited in the bosom of the Israelite by the contemplation of the vine, except that which springs from the intoxicating poison which its fermented juice contains, still there are those who can, and it is quite possible that the Psalmist did.

The wine commended by David was wine that causes joy and gladness; that is associated with oil that causes man's face to shine, and bread that strengtheneth man's heart. Whereas the wine condemned by Solomon was wine that causes "woe and sorrow," is associated with "redness of eyes and wounds without cause."

With what color of reason are wines producing such opposite effects believed to be one and the same article?

And yet for the latter intoxicating, dementing, soul destroying beverage, are claimed all the commendations of wine contained in the Bible, as confidently and exclusively as if IT were the only beverage that the vine produced, or that God when speaking of the vine regarded; as confidently and exclusively as if the vine dresser derived no joys from breathing the fragrance, or reclining beneath the shadow of his vine; as if the clusters that hung from its richly laden branches neither served to allay his hunger or quench his thirst; in one word, as confidently as if the eye of the prophet, as he delivered his eulogium, overlooking so many benefits and blessings, were like the eye of the wine bibber, fixed only on the treacherous, maddening contents of the intoxicating chalice.

And yet, had the process of producing intoxicating wine never been discovered, nor a drop of intoxicating wine produced, the commendations of the vine contained in the Bible would not have been a whit the less intelligible or pertinent or proper on that account.

And were that discovery lost, the fact of its existence forgotten, and the very law of God, by which it is produced, obliterated from the book of nature, no obliterations would in consequence be required from the book of revelation, except only the obliterations of the cautions therein contained in relation to the juice of the grape, in form of intoxicating wine; and except, also, the recorded condemnation of that drunkenness that springs from the use of such wine.

All else that had been written, and written in commendation of the grape and the vine, and the vineyard and the wine press, might remain untouched, and would not, I repeat it, be a whit the less intelligible or pertinent or proper than before.

That the voluntary transformation of the fruit of the vine or orchard, or the barley field, into intoxicating liquor by continuous fermentation is a profanation, I will not affirm; nor will I affirm that the article so produced in certain cases may not be useful and used with innocence—but I will affirm that for the wine bibber to claim for intoxicating wine the exclusive commendations pronounced by Moses and the Prophets in favor of the vine and the vineyards of the Holy Land, is as absurd as it would be for the cider drinker to claim in like manner for cider, the commendation of the apple tree by Solomon, or the beer drinker for beer, the commendation of barley by Jeremiah, or even the whiskey drinker for whiskey, those beautiful allusions of the Savior himself, to the husbandman, the harvest field and the reapers.*

---

* Says the Rev. Dr. Duff, "In these countries mantled with vineyards, one cannot help learning the true intent and use of the vine, in the scheme of Providence. In our own land wine has become so exclusively a mere luxury, or what is worse, by a species of manufacture, an intoxicating beverage, that many have wondered how the Bible speaks of wine, in conjunction with corn, and other such staple supports of animal life. Now, in passing through the region of vineyards in the east of France, one must at once perceive that the vine greatly flourishes on slopes and heights, where the soil is too poor and gravelly to maintain either corn for food or pasture for cattle. But what is the providential design in rendering this soil — favored by a genial atmosphere — so productive of the vine, if its fruits become solely either an article of luxury or an instrument of vice? The answer is, that Providence had no such design. Look at the peasant and his meals in vine bearing districts. Instead of milk, he has a basin of pure unadulterated 'blood of the grape.' In this, its native, original state, it is a plain, simple and wholesome liquid;

As healthful, sober, as well as deleterious intoxicating wines existed, and as the same terms are frequently applied indiscriminately to both, it is not and cannot be shown to be certain that deleterious intoxicating wine is even spoken of with approbation throughout the entire Bible.

But though it were otherwise, though the commendations of the vine in the Bible were merely commendations of intoxicating wine—and though it were admitted that the habitual use of such wine as a beverage were both safe and salutary in Palestine, it would not follow that such use of it would be either safe or salutary here.*

---

which, at every repast, becomes to the husbandman what milk is to the shepherd—not a luxury, but a necessary—not an intoxicating, but a nutritive beverage. Hence, to the vine dressing peasant of Auxerre, for example, an abundant vintage, as connected with his own immediate sustenance, is as important as an overflowing dairy to the pastoral peasant of Ayrshire. And hence, by such a view of the subject, are the language and the sense of the Scripture vindicated from the very appearance of favoring what is merely luxurious or positively noxious, when it so constantly magnifies a well replenished wine press, in a rocky' mountainous country, like that of Palestine, as one of the richest bounties of a generous Providence."

* Intoxicating wine here is not what it was in Palestine. Even Palm wine, the strong drink of Scripture, contained but very little alcohol.

The strongest native wine which the mere fruit of the vine produces, contains only about one-third of the alcoholic poisons contained in the stronger and more favorite alcoholic wines here in use.

In view of this fact, would it follow that because it was Scriptural to drink the alcoholic wines of Palestine, that it was also Scriptural to drink our intoxicating wines, in which so much intenser poisons

Here the use of wine, by moderate drinkers, creates the taste and prepares the way for the use of brandy, and, among reclaimed inebriates, reëstablishes the taste and reopens the way for a return to it again.

We are no longer what we once were, distinguished for sobriety.

In this one respect at least we have changed for the worse our social character, all classes of community having, previous to the late attempt at reformation, acquired the taste and become accustomed to the use, in some of its forms, of alcoholic stimulants ; so that, not without reason, a distinguished statesman not long since said that we were in danger of becoming a nation of drunkards—and it is well if this be not even still the case.

Long familiarized to the use of distilled liquors, and corrupted by that use, we cannot (however others might) safely indulge in the use of mere fermented liquors; so that could we obtain the fermented wines of Spain, France, Italy, or even of the Holy Land, no matter in what purity or abundance, with our present love of rum, gin, brandy, and even

---

are contained? And even though this absurdity would follow, the argument in favor of the use of wine by us, under existing circumstances, would still be inconclusive. We live in a different age. Our climate, our constitution, our habits, are different from those of the ancient dwellers in the Holy Land.

And besides, since the canon of scripture was completed, distillation has been invented, or at least, introduced into Europe. Hence, we have come into the possession of vastly intenser stimulants than the strongest wines in the Holy Land furnished.

whiskey, and our facilities for procuring them, even such wines and in such abundance, it is believed, would not prove a blessing but a curse; so that with our propensities and habits, the only alternative is abstinence or ruin.

I am aware that "teetotalism," as it is called, is smiled at by some as a weakness, ridiculed by others as a folly, and by others censured as a crime; and I am also aware that there is nothing imposing or exclusive in the use of water, that common beverage furnished by God himself in such abundance for the convenience and comfort of man; and that he who uses no other beverage, must remain a stranger to that transient and fitful joy, that alternates with a corresponding sorrow in the bosoms of those who indulge in the more fashionable use of intoxicating liquors. Still, in the view of that withered intellect, those blighted hopes, those unnatural crimes, and that undying misery, that the use of these liquors everywhere occasions, I put it to the candor of every ingenuous man who hears me, even among those who still indulge in that use, whether we who have abjured it, have not, under the existing state of things, a very intelligible and weighty reason for our conduct?

Will not the thought, as you return to your homes to-night and sit down amid a virtuous and beloved family, but a family familiarized to the use of intoxicating liquors in some of those forms which fashion sanctions—will not the thought that those same liquors, to the temperate use of which you are accustoming your household, must be to them the occasion of so much peril; perhaps of so much suffering; suffering in which, though they escape, so many other human beings must participate;—will not the thought of this mar the pleasure to be derived from that cup which is to be hereafter, as it has heretofore been to multitudes who drank of it, the cup of death?

Will not the thought of those uncounted thousands who have lived and died accursed on this planet, in consequence of intoxicating liquors; and those other and yet other thousands who will hereafter so live and die upon it, as long as the use of such liquors shall continue to be tolerated; and will not the thought of this wanton, gratuitous and unmeasured misery abate somewhat the displeasure you have felt, and soften the severity of the censures in which you have indulged against those who have combined to banish the use of those liquors as a beverage from the earth? More than this, will it not induce you, after all, to coöperate with us in consummating so humane and benevolent an enterprise?

Not now to question the healthfulness of the wines of Palestine and of other grape bearing countries, when obtained in purity and used in moderation; not now to question your ability so to obtain such wines, or your disposition so to use them when obtained; still, considering what multitudes there are who cannot so obtain those wines, and who would not so use them if they could; considering the taste that has already been created by other and stronger stimulants; considering the impossibility of correcting that taste and of reclaiming the drunken, or of preventing the drinker from hereafter becoming drunken, while custom everywhere pampers appetite, and fashion on every side invites her guests, her deluded guests, to partake of other banquets than those of wine: considering these things, is there not a cause for questioning the wisdom of existing habits, and making one great united effort to effect a change?

But why should we relinquish comforts because others abuse them? Why? Because it is great, and good, and God-like to do so. Needs it to be told in this assembly who it was that being rich, became poor for the sake of others, even for our sakes? Since the Son of God hath visited the earth on an errand of mercy, reason, conscience, religion, sanction self-denials, especially among that race he came to save, and on that planet where he submitted to his privations, endured his sufferings and planted his cross.

True, there are limits to this law of love. But the sacrifice in question comes within those limits. So Paul thought. Though an inhabitant of Palestine, the land of vines and vineyards, he deemed it not only admissible, but also "*good neither to drink wine, nor anything whereby thy brother stumbleth, or is offended or is made weak.*"

Do you inquire, Who is my brother? So inquired a lawyer, "Who is my neighbor?" You remember that beautiful and touching narrative in which the answer was conveyed; you remember the hapless

Jew who fell among thieves; you remember the unfeeling priest and Levite who having stood and looked upon the sufferer, passed by on the other side, and left a countryman to perish; you remember the good Samaritan who flew to a stranger's and alien's rescue; and you remember too who it was that said, "Go thou and do likewise."

O! it is not to the narrow circle of kindred and of caste that the charities of man's common brotherhood are confined. The men around you are your brethren—bone of your bone and flesh of your flesh. God hath not only made of one blood all nations to dwell upon the earth, but he hath also bound together by ties of reciprocal dependence the different classes of the men which compose those nations.

It is for you, ye rich men who live in affluence and ease, it is for you that the husbandman toils and sweats by day, and the shepherd wakes and watches by night.

You owe the raiment you wear, the dwelling you inhabit, the furniture you use—you owe the sofa on which you recline, the carriages in which you ride—the steam car that conveys you by land, and the steamboat by sea, with so much dispatch and ease in your excursions of pleasure and business, to the skill and industry of the artificer; while that sailor boy that climbs the mast, that breasts the storm and perils his life upon the ocean, does this to furnish for your possession and enjoyment the comforts and the luxuries of other and distant countries.

But for these men, the men who conduct the agriculture, and the manufacture, and the commerce of the world; but for these men, you and yours must perish; or putting off your ornaments and relinquishing your life of ease, you must betake yourselves to the practice of those self-denials and the endurance of those hardships which these men in your behalf now practice and endure.

It is in behalf of these men, the sufferers of so many privations, and at the same time the producers of so many comforts; it is in behalf of these men, to whose wearisome days and sleepless nights you are so much indebted, it is in behalf of these men that we wish to apply the apostolic maxim: "It is good not to drink wine or any thing whereby thy brother stumbleth, or is offended or is made weak."

You have, as you affirm, the self-command to avoid excess. Be it so. Still they by whose industry you subsist, have not. You have the knowledge to distinguish the pure from the adulterated. They have not; and even if they had, they want the ability to profit by that knowledge. So long, therefore, as you continue the use of the former, they will remain the victims of the latter.

It is not in man to be insensible to the influence of fashion, or to set at naught the power of example. If you cannot forego the exhilaration of wine, you, living at ease and surrounded by comforts, how should it be expected that they should forego the exhilaration of whiskey, they, exhausted by fatigue and exasperated by privations?

Know you not that the poor drunken day laborer, standing with his tin cup and rum jug in his hand, finds an apology for his conduct in the demijohn and wine glass of his rich and moderate drinking employer; and that from those who lack fortitude and self-denial to abandon the one, exhortations come with an ill grace for the abandonment of the other?

And yet the other must be abandoned, or the mother continue to mourn, the wife and the widow to suffer, and the orphan to supplicate.

Nay, the poor-house, the prison-house, the house of silence, and even the hell that lies beyond it, must continue hereafter, as heretofore, to be supplied gratuitously, prematurely, and in numbers; numbers who might otherwise have lived for usefulness on the earth, and honor and immortality in heaven; Oh! for their sakes, if not for your own, we urge—we entreat you to lend to this enterprise the countenance of your example; especially for the sake of those who have already fallen, or who are about to fall.

Christians, patriots, men of humanity! will you not come along with us to their rescue, who, misguided by the example and emboldened by the counsel of others, have ventured onward in a course which threatens to prove fatal alike to their health, their happiness and their salvation?

Will you not, in place of casting additional impediments in the way of their return, contribute to remove those which already exist, and which, without such assistance, they will remain forever alike unable to surmount or remove?

On your part the sacrifice will be small, on theirs the benefit conferred immense; a sacrifice not indeed without requital; for you shall share the joy of their rejoicing friends on earth, and their rejoicing friends in Heaven, who, when celebrating their returns to God, shall say: "This, our son, our brother, our neighbor, was lost and is found, was dead and is alive again."

You see, Christians, that although you lived in Canaan, and in the vicinity of the Cana of Galilee where water was changed into wine, you would not be authorized to use wine as we now use it, and that you would not be required even to use it at all; that they were not saints, but men who forgot God, concerning whom it is recorded "that the viol and the tabret, and the harp and wine is in their feasts," and that its use as a beverage is nowhere commanded; that large classes of men, and men approved of God, abstained wholly from its use; and that it is not only lawful, but befitting for Christians always so to abstain, when the circumstances of those around them call for such abstinence.

This you see, and seeing this, I ask what, under present circumstances, is your duty?

In view of the prevailing usages of society in which you live, and the obvious inroads drunkenness is making on that society; in view of that frightful number of ministers at the altar and advocates at the bar, whom drunkenesss, robbing the church and the world of their services, has demented and dishonored; in view of those master spirits in the field and the

Senate chamber, whom drunkenness has mastered; in view of those families made wretched, those youth corrupted, and those poor-houses and prison-houses and graveyards peopled—and peopled with beings made guilty and wretched by drunkenness; I put it to your conscience, Christians, whether at such a time and under such circumstances you would be at liberty, though supplied with wine made from the grapes of Eshcol, to use it as a beverage?

At such a time and under such circumstances would Paul so have used it?

Would Timothy, or any other of those suffering and self-denying men, sent forth to reform the manners of the age in which they lived, and teach mankind the way of salvation; would these men, or either of them, were an effort making—no matter by whom, or with what want of insinuation of address or sauvity of manner—to stem the torrent of licentiousness, to change the current of public opinion, and purify the church and the world from drunkenness, would these men, in such a state of things, array themselves on the side of the many who drank, and against the few who abstained from drinking? Would they hesitate, and waver, and finally draw back and refuse to coöperate? Above all, would they lend their influence to weaken the resolution of the wavering, to reassure the faltering courage of the drinker, and to relieve the conscience of the drunkard by drinking themselves—moderately, I admit, but still by drinking and by declaiming against the fanaticism of all who refuse to drink?

I know not how others might, but I do not believe that Apostles or Apostolic men would act thus; and I dare not, therefore, act thus myself.

If, between the ultraism of relinquishing the use of even wine, and the ultraism of continuing to use it under existing circumstances, I am called to choose, it behoves me to make the choice of safety, not of danger.

And it seems to me that if I knew the day of judgment were at hand, as the day of death is, and were that day to come suddenly, as the day of death may come, I should prefer that my judge should find me standing and acting with a few fanatics, among whom no drunkards, already declared to be excluded from the kingdom of God, could be found, than with that multitude among whom, though no fanatics, many drunkards might be numbered; and many others, who, though not now drunkards, were pursuing the way to become so thereafter.

It was not concerning him who drank with the drunken, but concerning him who watched, that it was said: "Blessed is the servant, who when his Lord cometh, he shall find so doing."

In conclusion, I do not ask, Christians, whether you are, or propose to become members of a temperance society; or whether you have taken, or propose to take, the old, or the new, or the still newer pledge; but I do ask, whether you are not bound, by the very circumstances in which God has placed you, to refrain from the use of intoxicating liquors, of every name and nature, as a beverage, and whether you can, without sin, refuse to give your influence, your whole influence, to the cause of total abstinence?

Be it so, that this cause has advocates who are neither courteous nor conciliating, that their measures are often ill-chosen, and their spirit fanatical; still it is to be remembered, that to adopt ill-advised measures, is not peculiar to the advocates of total abstinence, and that whatever of fanaticism there may be in its advocacy, it is all in a safe direction; and for a long time to come, the interests of virtue and religion will have much less to fear from restraint than from indulgence; and besides, if devils be cast out, even by some who follow not with us, it were wiser to encourage than forbid them.

Paul rejoiced when Christ was preached, though preached out of envy, and in the hope of adding affliction to his bonds. So we, without any sacrifice of principle, may rejoice when temperance is advocated, though advocated by disguised enemies or misguided friends; and though advocated in no better spirit, or for no higher end than was apparent in those invidious preachers of whom the Apostle spoke.

LECTURE No. VII.

ADULTERATIONS.

The adulteration of the wines of commerce — Drunkenness and gluttony compared — Analogy between bad oil, bad milk and bad wine — An appeal to Patriots and to Christians.

In the preceding lectures we have seen that distinct kinds of vinous beverages existed in the Holy Land; the one a good, nutritious, sober beverage — the other a bad, innutritious, intoxicating beverage; the one conducive to health and virtue — the other to disease and crime; the one suited in its nature to the temperate festivals of Christians — the other to the drunken revels of Pagans — and both usually called by the same name in our translation of the Bible, and often in the original itself — that if in consequence of this, the advocates of total abstinence cannot prove by verbal criticism, when wine is commended, that unintoxicating wine is meant; so neither, for the same reason, can their opponents prove the contrary — that uninspired men deemed sober, moral, unintoxicating wine the best, and that the presumption is, that inspired men were of the same opinion; a presumption strengthened by the fact that such wine is usually spoken of with commendation — that though it were otherwise, though the Bible sanctioned the intoxicating wines of Palestine, it would not follow that it sanctions our own still more intoxicating wines.

Or, though even this absurdity would follow, that still the argument in favor of wine drinking among ourselves would be inconclusive — that, be the kind of wine, the use of which the Bible sanctioned, what it may, and even though it were conceded, for argument sake, to be intoxicating — still that its use was not commanded, or commended as a common beverage; the multitudes who feared God and worked righteousness, never used it; and that circumstances were liable to occur, even in Palestine, that would render its use improper, and make total abstinence even there a duty; that here the use of such wine, supposing it to be intoxicating, would be less admissible and more perilous, because here its effects would be liable to be aggravated by the action of other and intenser stimulants; which stimulants are everywhere accessible, and for which a national taste has been already formed — so that, were the wines in use among us as pure as the wines of Spain, France, Italy, or even the Holy Land, under existing circumstances, total abstinence would be an imperious duty, as it would have been in Palestine, if then and there, as now and here, it had caused a brother to stumble, to offend, or to become weak.

How much more imperious must that duty be felt to be, when it is considered that generally and truly speaking, we have no such article as even intoxicating wine, in the Bible sense of wine, in use among us.

Wine indeed, falsely so called, we have, and in abundance; but names, as we have elsewhere said, do not alter the nature of things.

The extract of logwood is not the less the extract of logwood, nor is the sugar of lead the less the sugar of lead, because combined with New England rum, western whiskey, sour beer, or even Newark cider, put up in wine casks, stamped Port, Champaigne, or Maderia, and sold under the imposing sanction of the collector's purchased certificate, passed from hand to hand, and perhaps transmitted from father to son, to give the color of honesty to cool, calculating, heartless imposition.

O! it was not from the vineyards of any distant grape-bearing country, that those disguised poisons, sent abroad to corrupt and curse the country, were derived. On the contrary, the ingredients of which they are composed were collected and mingled, and their color and flavor imparted, in some of those garrets above, or caverns beneath, the observation of men; caverns fitly called hells, where, in our larger cities, fraud undisguised finds protection, and wholesale deeds of darkness are securely and systematically performed.

I do not say this on my own mere authority. I had a friend who had been himself a wine dealer; and having read the startling statements, sometime since made public in relation to the brewing of wines, and the adulteration of other liquors generally, I inquired of that friend as to the verity of those statements. His reply was: "GOD FORGIVE *what has passed in* MY OWN *cellar, but the statements* MADE, ARE TRUE, ALL TRUE, I assure you."

That friend has since gone to his last account, as have doubtless many of those whose days on earth were shortened by the poisons he dispensed. But I still remember, and shall long remember, both the terms and tone of that laconic answer, "THE STATEMENTS *made are true, all* TRUE, *I assure you.*"

But not on the testimony of that friend does the evidence of these frauds depend. Another friend informed me that the executor of a wine dealer, in a city which he named, assured him that in the inventory of articles for the manufacture of wine, found in the cellar of that dealer, and which amounted to many thousand dollars, there was not one dollar for the juice of the grape. And still another friend informed me, that in examining, as an assignee, the papers of a house in that city which dealt in wines, and which had stopped payment, he found evidence of the purchase during the preceding year, of hundreds of casks of cider, but none of wine. And yet it was not cider, but wine, which had been supposed to have been dealt out by that house to its confiding customers.

I might proceed, but it is unnecessary. These are not, and are known not to be, solitary cases, but samples merely, of what is taking place in almost, if not quite, all our larger cities, and in many even of our towns and villages.

But to this it is replied, that although spurious wines may be fabricated at home, pure wine, and in quantity, is imported from abroad. Is it so? Where and by whom, I ask, is pure wine imported? No-where, and by no one; nor in the ordinary course of importation can it be. The ocean barrier lies between us and the vineyards of the east. The God of nature has placed it there, and it cannot be removed. To cross the sea, wine must be "brandied," and is "brandied," as analysis has shown.

And yet the Christian fathers refused the use of wine, even in the sacrament, unless mixed and diluted with water; whereas the purest wines we use are not only fermented, but also mixed with brandy, or otherwise rendered pungent and corrosive, by the introduction of some other ingredient, or of alcohol in some other if not intenser form.

Such is the boasted article, falsely called wine, with which our market is supplied. Would that it was the only article; but it is not, nor is it the worst. Spurious wines—wines of the vilest character, and in the greatest quantities, are imported from abroad, as well as manufactured at home. This the nation does not know, but they who supply the nation know this. In London alone, more port wine is drank than is furnished by the entire vintage at Oporto; and yet London supplies the whole civilized world with port. Whence is this excess derived? Not surely from the vineyards along the banks of the Douro, but from the caverns aside the bed of the Thames. Nor from these alone. At Oporto itself, at Madeira, and elsewhere, throughout the grape bearing region, similar, if not even greater frauds, are committed.

"It is not, perhaps, generally known," I quote from the London Times, "it is not, perhaps, generally known that very large establishments exist at Celte and Marseilles, in the south of France, for the manufacture of every description of wines, the natural products, not only of France, but of all other wine growing and wine exporting countries; some of these establishments are on so large a scale as to give employment to an equal, if not a greater number of persons than our large breweries.

"It is no uncommon occurrence with speculators engaged in this sort of illicit traffic, to purchase and ship imitation wines, fabricated in the places named, to Madeira, where by collusion with persons in the custom-house department in the island, the wines are landed in the entrepot, and thence, after being branded with the usual marks of the genuine Madeira vintage, reshipped, principally, it is believed, to the United States. The scale of gratuity for this sort of work to the officials interested, may be estimated by the fact that, on one occasion, seventy pipes were thus surreptitiously passed at a charge of $1000. It is a circumstance no less singular, that the same manufacture is said to be commonly carried on with counterfeit wine made up in Celte and Marseilles, and thence dispatched to Oporto, where the same process of landing, branding and reshipment as genuine Port, is gone through; the destination of this spurious article being most generally to the

United States. Such is the extent of this nefarious commerce, that one individual alone has been pointed out in the French ports, who has been in the habit of dispatching, four times in the year, twenty-five thousand bottles of champagne each shipment, of wines not the produce of the Champagne districts, but fabricated in these wine factories." A scientific gentleman purchased from the importer a bottle of champagne in New-York, and had the same analyzed. It was found to contain a quarter of an ounce of sugar of lead.

Correspondent to this, was that letter from Madeira by an officer of our navy, stating that but thirty thousand barrels of wine was produced on the island, and fifty thousand claimed to be from thence, drank in America alone.

In confirmation of this statement, a friend of mine, and a citizen of ours, James C. Duane, Esq., informed me that having been induced to purchase a cask of port wine, by the fact that it had just been received direct from Oporto, by a house in New-York, in the honor and integrity of which entire confidence could be placed, he drew off and bottled and secured with his own hands, its precious contents, to be reserved for the especial use of friends; and that having done so, and having thereafter occasion to cause that cask to be sawed in two, he found to his astonishment that its lees consisted of a large quantity of the shavings of logwood, a residuum of alum and other ingredients, the name and nature of which were to him unknown.

What secrets other wine casks would reveal, were their contents examined, is not difficult to conjecture, or if knowledge be preferred to conjecture, even that would not be of difficult attainment.*

---

* Would you wish to be informed what the ingredients are that enter into the composition of those fabrications called wines, so obligingly prepared in caverns or garrets at home, or no less obligingly supplied from the brew-houses of the grape bearing countries abroad? That wish may be gratified by consulting M. P. Orfila on poisons, (first American ed., 1819), from which author the following extracts have been made:

Page 198: "Wines adulterated by various substances. The object is to mask defects, or give color, odor, or strength."—*Jour. T. U.*, *p.* 43, *year* 1838.

Page 199: "Wines adulterated by lead. Sugar of lead, ceruse, and still more frequently, litharge, are mixed with acid or sharp tasted wines, in order to render them less so, and these substances do in fact give them a sweet taste."

Page 74, 5: Speaking of sugar of lead he says: "It gives a sweet, astringent, metallic taste, constriction of the throat, pain in the stomach, desire to vomit, or vomiting (47), fœtid eructations, hiccough, difficulty of respiration, thirst, cramps, coldness of limbs, convulsions, change of features, delirium, &c."

Page 202: "White wines adulterated with lead."

Page 208: "Red wines adulterated with lead. Wines adulterated with alum. The object of this adulteration is ——— and to give them an astringent taste; effects—digestion painful, vomiting from time to time, obstructions of bowels, and piles, are the results of drinking wine thus adulterated."

Page 306: "Wines adulterated with chalk. Design—to saturate acetic or tartaric acid, and destroy the sharpness."

Page 307: "Wines adulterated by brandy. It occurs sometimes that brandy is added to weak wines; in other circumstances, wine with a mixture of cider or other spiritous liquor, and brandy, logwood, sandal wood, or some other coloring matter being added."

Indeed chemistry has supplied such facilities, and avarice such motives for the adulteration of intoxicating liquors of every kind, that though fermented

---

Page 208: "Means employed to give color to wine—old wines being in general, of a deeper color than new wines. This is done by exposing to the air, by sugar, by the acid of sulphurous acid gas; and by vaccinum, myrtillus, logwood chips and other substances which also render them astringent."

Page 210: "Wines adulterated by sweet or astringent substances, sugar, raisins, extract of oak or willow bark."

Page 34, 35: "Sulphuric and nitric acid, and the alkalies, &c., inflame the parts with which they are placed in contact, but in different degrees. There are some which produce so great an inflammation that they may be regarded as caustics almost as powerful as the actual cautery. They are called corrosive or escharotics; they evidently cause a death in the same manner as burns. Such are the concentrated acids, alkalies, &c. There are others whose caustic effects are less intense, but which produce death in a more rapid manner, because they are absorbed, mixed with the blood, carried into the circulation, destroy the vital properties of the heart, lungs, brain, and nervous system."

Page 44: "The effect of the alkalies is nearly similar to that of the acids, &c."

Page 75: "If in place of taking a large dose of lead, water or wine, containing but a small portion, is taken, no immediate inconvenience will be felt; but if the practice be long continued, a disease similar to that of the cholic of painters will arise, which, in certain cases, is true palsy."

Page 100: "Nux vomica, cocculus indicus, introduced into the stomach, or applied to wounds, are repeatedly absorbed, and affect the brain or spinal marrow near the neck. They occasion a general rigidity and convulsions. The head is thrown back, the chest is dilated with difficulty, respiration is greatly impeded, and death is the consequence, and that in a very few moments, if the dose has been great. The effects on some are not continual, but give rise to fits from time to time, in the intervals of which the individual appears little affected Opium and poppy heads are more or less poisonous."

liquors were harmless, safety can only be found in TOTAL ABSTINENCE.

From Accum on Culinary Poisons, the following extracts are made:

Page 74: "It is sufficiently evident that few of these commodities, which are the objects of commerce, are adulterated to a greater extent than wine. Alum, Brazil wood, gypsum, oak saw dust and husks of filberts, are used to brighten, color, clear and make astringent, wines. A mixture of spoiled foreign and home made wines is converted into the wretched compound frequently sold under the name of genuine old Port."

Page 75: "Various expedients are resorted to for the purpose of communicating particular flavors to insipid wines. Bitter almonds, cherry, laurel water, &c., are used."

Page 76: "The sophistication of wines is carried on to an enormous extent. Many thousands of pipes of spoiled cider are annually brought hither from the country for the purpose of being converted into factitious wine."

Page 78, 80: "Artisans are regularly employed in staining casks and crusting casks and bottles, and making an astringent extract for old port. There are many other sophistications which are deceptive, and which are connected with another branch of an absolutely criminal nature."

Page 81: "Several well authenticated facts prove these adulterations of wine with substances deleterious to health to be practiced oftener than is perhaps expected."

Page 82: "The most dangerous adulteration of wine is by some preparations of lead. Lead is certainly employed for this purpose. Merchants persuade themselves that the minute quantity employed for that purpose is perfectly harmless. But chemical analysis proves the contrary, and it must be pronounced highly deleterious. Lead, in whatever state it is taken into the stomach, occasions terrible diseases. And wine adulterated with the minutest quantity of it becomes a slow poison.

"The merchant or dealer who practices this dangerous sophistication, adds the crime of murder to that of fraud; and deliberately scatters the seeds of disease and death among those who contribute to his emolument."

And yet when we mention total abstinence from even the adulterated liquors here in use, we are met as before, and sometimes even, alas! that it should be so, by good men too, with the authority of the Bible; as if the Bible had ever had anything to say in favor of this modern drunkard's drink, in any of its forms in use, in these ends of the earth.

Be it so, that the Bible sanctioned the fruit of the vine in Palestine, does it follow from this that it sanctions also the juice of the grapes of Sodom and the apples of Gomorrah? And yet it as truly sanctions these as it sanctions "that wine of dragons and poison of asps," in use as a beverage in America.

Can it be needful to repeat, in the conclusion of this article, what we said at its commencement, that it is only against bad wine, wine that Solomon reprobated, wine that causes woe and sorrow and wounds without cause, that we array ourselves?

The wine that David commended was good wine; the wine that Jesus Christ miraculously supplied was good wine—wine worthy of its Author, of the guests and the occasion; and when He shall again honor the bridal chamber by His presence and supply

---

These words of Accum are in perfect keeping with the recent confession of a wine dealer, who on his death-bed, acknowledged in the bitterness of penitential sorrow, "that he had often seen his customers wasting away around him, poisoned by that he had meted out to them, and that same wine which was the cause of their decline, was often prescribed by their physicians as a means for their recovery."

the guests by His agency, or when another in His name and by His authority shall do this, and we refuse that cup of blessings, it will be time enough to confront us with Christ's example, and accuse us of impugning His authority.

What influence there is in a name! Because Christ changed water into wine in Cana of Galilee, Christians may not abjure the use, not of the fruit of the vineyards of Palestine, not of the fruit of the vine at all, but the product of the still and the brewhouse in America! as if an inference, assented to by the intellect and binding the conscience, could be drawn from the one to the other.

Be it then distinctly understood, that it is not the mere fruit of the vine, the pure wine of Palestine, nay, nor pure wine at all, about the virtues of which we hear so much, that this dispute is concerned with; but it is about a brandied or brewed article, falsely called wine, in the sense the Bible speaks of wine with approbation, or even speaks of it at all, a factititious or spurious article, always supplied in fraud, and usually drank in ignorance; an article which is corrupting the morals of youth, paralyzing the energies of manhood, polluting even female virtue, and bringing the grey hairs of age down with dishonor to the grave. It is, I repeat it, so far as respects wine, such an article, with which this dispute is concerned. This is the true issue.

If there be a fruit of the vine in Palestine, or elsewhere, healthful, or even harmless, let the dwellers in those favored lands enjoy the full benefit thereof; but in the name of humanity and religion, I protest against their palming on us, under the guise of such an article, the vile compounds now in market. And in the same name, I protest against our consenting any longer to receive those compounds.

But, after all, it is asked, why this ultraism? No one thinks of abstaining, on account of gluttony, from eating; why then from drinking, on account of drunkenness? Especially why, since gluttony is quite as prevalent and injurious as drunkenness? Is it so, indeed? Where, then, I ask, is the evidence of the alarming fact? Where are the families that gluttony has beggared, the individuals it has brutalized?

Where is that utter degradation, in form, and feeling, and intellect, produced by gluttony, which is every day exhibited in those ragged wretches with which intoxication strews the very gutters of the streets along which we pass? Where are the poor-houses, and prison-houses and the lunatic asylums, that gluttony has peopled with its miserable victims?

That evils are occasionally produced by gluttony, I doubt not; but that those evils are either so frequent, or so frightful as the evils of drunkenness I have yet to learn; and the world has yet to learn this; or even, if it were so, be it remembered, these are evils allied to drinking, not to abstinence. Show me a glutton, and you will show me a drinker, if not a drunkard. And however numerous such pitiable objects may be in the ranks of moderate drinkers, in the ranks of "teetotalers" there are none of them. And you may go through the length and breadth of the land, and marshal the whole army of cold water drinkers, without finding one bloated, over eating gourmand among them all. So that drinking is chargeable with the double condemnation of both gluttony and drunkenness.

But were gluttony as prevalent, which it is not, as drunkenness, where would be the pertinence of the argument attempted by the comparison? Man cannot live without eating. Eating, then, be its incidental evils what they may, cannot be dispensed with. Not so with drinking; as far as the drunkard's drink is concerned, man cannot only live without it, but he can also live longer and better without than with it; all the tremendous evils, therefore, resulting from its use, are wanton and gratuitous.

Gluttony results from excess in the use of aliments of every kind. Not so with drunkenness—it is produced by distilled and fermented liquors only.

But were it otherwise; were gluttony confined, like drunkenness, to the use of a single article, and that the vilest and least nutritious article existing; and an article rendered vile and innutritious by voluntary debasement, in the manner of preparing it from other articles, which, in the state God created them, were both nutritive and healthful; were such the case with gluttony, who would not cry shame to the man who would still persist in selecting that article, to the neglect of other and unobjectionable articles, for the daily use of his family, cause it to be spread out before the eye of his children, and recommended to the taste of his guests?

Be it so, that drunkenness, unlike gluttony, springs only from the use of a single kind of beverage; still, to pretend that that beverage should be altogether abandoned on that account, is said to be not reason, but fanaticism. It is said that, up to that limit where sobriety ceases, and intemperance begins, men may indulge in the use of intoxicating liquors with safety, and ought not, therefore, to be deprived of the privilege of doing so.

Hearer! Christian! does wisdom counsel thus? To me, it seems her voice counsels the inquirer after safety to keep away from even the vicinity of that slippery, treacherous cliff, down which the feet of the presumptious sinner slide to ruin.

Is it forgotten who it was that taught his disciples, day by day, to offer up that petition: "Lead us not into temptation?" And shall God hold that man guiltless, who, having offered it, shall go away, and day by day spread temptation before his children, his family, his friends, and the stranger that comes within his influence?

"Up to the limit where sobriety ceases and intemperance begins, men may indulge in safety." Fatal maxim! And the man who, now acting on it, dares to approach that limit, will, hereafter, given up of God, transgress it, and become, what so many temperate drinkers have become already, an habitual drunkard.

But be the dangers of indulging what they may, in abstaining there are no dangers. I have heard of multitudes ruined in health, and fortune, and fame, by the use of intoxicating liquors; never of one, in either of these respects, by abstaining from their use.

It is safe, then, and therefore wise, for parents, for Christians, and especially for Christian ministers, to take the side of abstinence in its totality; and, standing between the living and the dead and the dying, to say, both by precept and example, "touch not, taste not."

Be not deceived by names. When you hear men quote the Bible in favor of a beverage that is filling the world with crime, disease and death, you may be assured that the quotation is made in error; that the article, here so fatal, is not the article which the Bible recommends, or that our manner of using it is not the manner which it sanctions. God wills the virtue and the happiness of his creatures, and cannot therefore will the use, I mean such use of anything as tends to the subversion of both.

Oil is as distinctly recommended in the Bible as wine; and yet who ever thought of insisting on the use of train oil, the oil of ambergris, or even of tobacco, on that account? And since there are more kinds of wine than of oil, it were at least as reasonable to defend the use of bad oil as of bad wine elsewhere, because good oil as well as good wine were once used in Palestine. The defence of the use of those kinds of oil, known to be offensive to the taste, or injurious to the health, and especially to the life of man, would be deemed an absurdity not to be entertained. Why then entertain a similar absurdity in the defence of the use of similar kinds of wine? Why should the term wine, any more than the term oil, consecrate the use of the poisons designated by it?

What would be thought of the apothecary who should insist that wine to which antimony had been added was Scriptural, and ought to be used as a common beverage, because wine to which no antimony had been added was allowed to be used in the Holy Land; especially, what would be thought of the apothecary who should insist on this in the face of the qualms, and retching, and faintness, and prostration apparent on every side, in consequence of the use of such poisonous wine? And yet, it is not perceived why this reasoning of the apothecary would not be as legitimate as that of the moralist who insists that wine to which alcohol has been added is Scriptural, and ought to be used as a common beverage in America, because wine to which no alcohol had been added was so used in the Holy Land; especially of the moralist who should insist on this, in the face of the withered intellect, the paralyzed energy, and the ultimate death which brandied wines were known to have occasioned?

Take another and a parallel case. Milk and honey were among the promised blessings of the land of promise, and they are employed in Scripture as emblems of the richest mercies; and yet who does not know that honey is often deleterious, and that there are times and places in which to taste of milk is death?

"At Logansport," I quote here from a letter in the Danbury Herald, dated July 11, 1833: "At Logansport, on the banks of the Wabash, I was cautioned by an elderly lady against using either milk, butter or beef, on my way to Vincennes; as a reason for her caution, she informed me that the milk sickness was common in the state. I had heard of it before, but knew little of it; she informed me that very many deaths occurred annually by this dreadful malady. There is a difference of opinion as to the cause that produces it, but the general opinion is, that it is occasioned by the yellow oxide of arsenic, in the low ground and woodland, and particularly near the Wabash river; and that some weed, yet unknown, imbibes the poison, and when eaten by the cattle, causes them to quiver, stagger, and die within a few hours. If cows eat it, the milk is poisoned, or butter that is made from the milk, and it is sure death to these who eat of either, as it is to the animal that eats the weed. Great care is taken to bury such cattle as die with it; for if dogs eat their flesh, they share the same fate, and it operates upon them as violently as upon the creature that was affected with it. The butcher, uniformly in this state, runs the victim of the knife a mile to heat the blood, and, if it has eaten the weed, it will at once, on stopping, quiver and shake; if it does not, it is considered safe to butcher; and this is the uniform test, even when the beef cattle show no signs of having ate the weed.

"Indiana is not alone in this misfortune; there have been many cases in some parts of Ohio, and south of St. Louis, and other southwestern states. I have seen many farms, with comfortable buildings and improvements, entirely abandoned, and their owners fled to avoid this dreadful curse."

Now what, I ask, would be thought of the sanity of a man who, with his Bible in his hand, and his finger pointing to the text that speaks of the milk and honey of the Holy Land, should undertake to rebuke that mother in Israel for presuming to recommend to that stranger traveler, not the moderate use, but total abstinence from an article, in Indiana, which God himself had authorized to be used in Palestine? What would be thought of the sanity of the man who, standing in the great valley of the west, amid the dying and the dead — and after having surveyed the sick rooms where the victims of milk were agonizing, or the fresh graves where their corses had been buried, should gravely talk, not of abstinence, but of moderation in the use of this fatal aliment — should provide it for his family, place it on his table, proffer it to his friends, and even make a show of tasting it himself, out of reverence for the Bible, and through the dread of appearing to give countenance to ultraism? What would be thought of the sanity of such a man? And yet what are all the ills which milk has occasioned on the other side of the mountains, since the foot of the white man first trod the great valley of the west, compared with those which intoxicating liquor occasions annually, in any one of the cities of the east?

If these cases are not parallel, their want of parallelism only gives additional force to the argument drawn from their comparison. For, the milk in the valley of the west, deadly as it may be, is, notwithstanding, truly the milk of kine; whereas the drunkard's drink of the east is not even the fruit of the vine, but the product of the brew-house; or, if it indeed ever partake of the fruit of the vine, it is not of that fruit in its purity, but in admixture with articles that debase it, so that the mixture no longer comes within the limits of that license granted to the wine of Palestine, whatever that license may be; hence the whole question of the merit or demerit of the intoxicating liquors here in use, and of the innocence or guilt of using them, is to be decided, not by appealing to the Bible, but to observation and experience. To that tribunal we appeal, and are prepared to abide the issue—the only rightful issue; and in making this appeal, we take no vantage ground; we claim no right to bind the conscience of others, or to sit in judgment on our brother.

If patriots shall think—I speak as to wise men—if patriots shall think, having examined the facts of the case, and with all these evils before their eyes, that it is befitting in them to continue the use of brandied, or even brewed wines; if they shall think, on the whole, that the happiness these liquors confer exceeds in amount the miseries they inflict, let them drink on and abide the consequence.

If Christians think—I speak as to conscientious men—if Christians think, having examined the facts of the case, and with all these evils before their eyes, that the benefits resulting from this drink of drunkards are so numerous or so signal as to require the influence of their example in the furtherance of its use, especially on gala days and at weddings, let them give to the good cause the benefit of their influence; but let them do this understandingly, and on account of the benefits which the church and the world are likely to derive from continuing its use, and not because the Bible sanctions it. If this drunkard's drink is to be hereafter drunk by Christians, let it be done by the authority of reason, and in the name of Ceres or Vesta, and not of Religion and Jesus. And why not by the authority of Religion and in the name of Jesus? Neither the Bible or its Author, whatever may have been said of the mere fruit of the vine in Palestine, has said any thing in commendation of the products of the still and the brew-house in America.

These unbidden, exciting, maddening mixtures are in every sense profane, and befit the orgies of Bacchus rather than the festivities of Christians. They are, at best, mixed wines, mixed with brandy, or even worse materials, which mixture the Bible nowhere tolerates, and which cannot, therefore, under its sanction, be distributed even to bridal guests. If hereafter, therefore, any Christian shall claim the liberty of countenancing the use of wine, falsely so called, on gala days and at weddings, let him do so as a man, not as a Christian; nor let him lay to his soul the flattering unction, that in doing so he is borne out by the Bible, and sheltered behind the example of his Savior. If the use of these articles as a common beverage can be vindicated at all, it is because of their utility, and only because of their utility, and not because religion either requires or sanctions such use; for no such article as even the brandied wine of commerce existed in our Savior's time; for brandy itself did not then exist. This intenser poison is a product of human skill, and of later times.

Having disabused our minds of the bewildering influence of that miserable sophism—that because the Bible authorized the use of good wine in Palestine it had also authorized the use of bad wine in America; that because it spoke in terms of commendation of vineyards and wine-presses there, it had, by implication, spoken in like terms of brew-houses and distilleries here; having disabused our minds of the bewildering influence of this sophism, having learned what God has not said in the book of Revelation, concerning the intoxicating liquors here in use, we are prepared to turn and open the Book of Nature, and learn what he has said, and is still repeating there

LECTURE No. VIII.

MORAL AND NATURAL LAWS AS APPLIED TO STRONG DRINK.

Books of Revelation and Nature — Misery springs from violations of law — Nature interrogated — Her answer returned — In crime, disease and death — Spontaneous combustion — Distinction between stimulants and aliments — Example of moderate drinkers more injurious than of drunkards — Iniquities of fathers visited on children — Expostulation with moderate drinkers.

The books of Revelation and of Nature were both written by the same unerring wisdom, and written for our instruction and reproof, on whom the ends of the world are come.

The moral laws of God's kingdom are embodied in the former, the physical in the latter. The knowledge of the former is acquired by reading and meditation; of the latter, by observation and experiment. As the character of moral agents is made manifest by the works they perform, so the nature of material elements is made manifest by the effects which they produce.

The laws of God, whether physical or moral, tend to promote the virtue and secure the happiness of all who are subject to those laws; and were that subjection entire and universal, happiness would also be entire and universal.

Misery never springs from obeying, always from disobeying the laws of the Creator. When we obey, we are in harmony—when we disobey, at variance with his government. Wherever misery exists, it always exists, therefore, in evidence that God's will has been disregarded, and some law of his physical or moral kingdom violated.

On carefully examining those varied productions of nature with which we are surrounded, and which, like the forbidden fruit of Eden, may appear pleasant to the eyes, good for food, and to be desired to make one wise, it will be perceived that some were designed of God for sickness, some for health, some for habitual use, some for occasional use, and some to be wholly avoided. What his design was with respect to each several production, is revealed to the inquirer after truth, by the effects which they severally produce.

That the use of every good creature of God, that is, such use as will, on the whole, conduce to happiness and virtue, is conformable to his will—and that such use of any of them as is subversive of either happiness or virtue, is contrary to his will, are truths inscribed alike on the pages of the book of Revelation and of Nature.

Let us then, keeping in mind this obvious rule of interpreting the manifestations of Providence, consult this latter oracle, as to the will of God and the duty of man, in relation to intoxicating liquors. Yes, let us enter and interrogate Nature in her own sanctuary, and let us attend to the response returned. Returned from whence? From the bar-room—the banquet—the harvest-field—the deck of the merchantman and of the man-of-war—from the poor-house—the prison-house—the mad-house and the graveyard; in one word, from every place on every part of the footstool of God where the inebriating cup is raised to human lips, or where the victims of its contained poison are assembled; from a thousand places, and in a thousand forms is this response returned. It is returned in the sigh of the widow—the supplication of the orphan—the wail of the mourner—the howl of the maniac, and the death-groan of the expiring.

But do not these evils spring from the abuse, not the use of the articles in question? Doubtless from the abuse of them, for to use them in a manner in which they were not intended to be used, is to abuse them.

If the use of intoxicating liquors as a beverage in health, be such use of them as God ordained, and as God approves, how comes it that their use and their abuse are so identified, that the one seems to follow from the other consequentially, and as if by some necessity of nature? It is not thus with rest, or sleep, or food, or any other of those bland restoratives which nature furnishes, and our exhausted strength requires. These all, though used habitually, and though their use be repeated from night to day, and from day to night, still operate benignly on the system, and lose nothing of their revivifying and invigorating efficacy.

Not so with intoxicating liquors. Here` by the very ordination of God, habitual use defeats itself, for it impairs the sensibility on which it operates. Hence the quantity must be increased as the sensibility is diminished, in order to keep up that pleasurable excitement at first produced; and hence by merely keeping up that excitement during a sufficient length of time, the constitution becomes impaired and the process of inebriation commenced.

But why debate this question, surrounded as we are by such numbers of wretched beings, whose enfeebled intellects or shattered constitutions evince that either alcohol is poison, or some other drug that is so, is combined with it in those fatal preparations dispensed alike from the bar-room and the grocery to unsuspecting multitudes, under the imposing names of Rum, Gin, Brandy, Wine, Beer and even Cider.

Here, at least, there is no mistake and no exaggeration. Our fellow creatures are literally dying around us, dying in numbers, dying in the city, dying in the country, dying of an insidious and loathsome disease, a disease that regards neither rank, or age, or sex; a disease distinctly marked and known to be induced by liquors purposely manufactured and distributed far and wide, as the common beverage of which the nation drinks.

Do any of you who hear me, doubt the truth of this? Go then yourselves to the bar-room and the grocery, as I have done; go see with your own eyes the haggard countenance, the emaciated forms, the trembling nerves and the demented looks of those wretched beings, once human beings, who appear like spectres from another world, within those dens of disease and death. Go, hear with your own ears their lascivious and silly jests, their idiotic laugh, their sepulchral moan, and that unearthly curse stammered forth from their quivering and blistered lips. Does any one still doubt? let him then interrogate the poor-house, and the jail, and the prison-house, and let them answer whence their wretched inmates are supplied! Let him ask the sepulchre, and let it say what sends such numbers, prematurely, and uncalled for, to its dread abode!

O! if the dead could speak, the response returned from thence would move alike the surface of the earth and the bosom of the sea; for there is scarcely a spot of either that has not witnessed the drunkard's degradation, and become itself the covering of a drunkard's grave.

Now, this whole downward process is an evidence of God's displeasure on account of abused mercies; a displeasure written on many a page of Providence in frightful characters, sometimes even in characters of fire.

The end or Nadab and Abihu, whom fire from the Lord consumed, was scarcely more signal or more terrible than the end of those miserable beings who are, with increasing frequency, consumed by the slow and quenchless fires which the use of intoxicating liquors hath gradually kindled in the living fibres of their own bodies.

When, a few years since, a case of spontaneous combustion, occurring in the person of an habitual drunkard, was referred to in a temperance address by a distinguished layman, it was generally regretted. Few of the friends of temperance were prepared to endorse what then seemed to them so improbable a statement, while the manufacturers and vendors, and drinkers of this fiery element took occasion to proclaim more loudly than ever the folly and fanaticism of men who could be so weak themselves as to believe, and so impertinent as to attempt to impose on others the belief of such ridiculous occurrences.

But these cases of the death of drunkards by internal fires, kindled often spontaneously, as has been supposed, have become so numerous and so incontrovertible, that I presume no person of information will now be found who will venture to call the reality of their existence in question.

Says Professor Silliman, after having examined this subject: "In all such cases (of consuming alive in consequence of drunkenness), the entire body having become saturated with alcohol, absorbed into all its tissues, becomes highly inflammable, as is indicated by the vapor which reeks from the lungs in the breath of the drunkard; this vapor, doubtless highly alcoholic, may take fire, and the body gradually consume."*

---

* It has been suggested by a learned friend (Rev. J. N. Campbell), that recent experiments made in France had failed to confirm the opinion of Professor Silliman, and that it was supposed that the real cause was the presence of phosphorus. It seemed due to truth to

For the information of those who may not heretofore have had their attention called to this visitation of God on drunkards, and of all the dwellers on the earth, only on drunkards, it may, perhaps, not be amiss to give the melancholy details of a single case; which details will be given in the words of the physician (Dr. Peter Schofield, of Upper Canada), who reported the same.

The case in question was, says he: "that of a young man about twenty-five years of age. He had been an habitual drinker for many years. I saw him about nine o'clock in the evening on which it happened; he was then, as usual, not drunk, but full of liquor; about eleven o'clock the same evening, I was called to see him. I found him literally roasted from the crown of his head to the soles of his feet. He was found in a blacksmith's shop, just across from where he had been. The owner, all of a sudden, discovered an extensive light in his shop, as though the whole building was in one general flame. He ran with the greatest precipitancy, and on throwing open the door, discovered a man standing erect in the midst of a widely extended silver-colored flame, bearing, as he described it, exactly the appearance of the wick of a burning candle, in the midst of its

---

mention this; although, should this supposition be confirmed, it will not materially affect the argument. For whether in these cases alcohol be the actual combustible, or merely the exciting cause of the combustion, the fact still remains, that of all the dwellers on the earth, inebriates are the most exposed to this frightful visitation of Providence.

own flame. He seized him (the drunkard) by the shoulder and jerked him to the door, upon which the flame was instantly extinguished. There was no fire in the shop, neither was there any possibility of fire having been communicated to him from any external source. It was purely a case of spontaneous ignition. A general sloughing soon came on, and his flesh was consumed or removed in the dressing, leaving the bones and a few of the larger blood vessels; the blood nevertheless rallied round the heart, and maintained the vital spark until the thirteenth day, when he died, not only the most loathsome, ill-featured and dreadful picture that was ever presented to human view, but his shrieks, his cries and his lamentations also, were enough to rend a heart of adamant. He complained of no pain of body; his flesh was gone. He said he was suffering the torments of hell; that he was just upon the threshold, and should soon enter its dismal caverns, and in this frame of mind he gave up the ghost. O! the death of a drunkard! Well may it be said to beggar all description. I have seen other drunkards die, but never in a manner so awful and affecting."

The following schedule contains nineteen cases, which have been selected, not from temperance addresses, but from medical reports, and all but one (by Dr. Lindsley*) from the "Dictionaire Medicine," a French work of high authority.*

No.	Time.	Combustion Entire, Except.	Immediate Cause.	Drunkard on What.	Situation of Remains.	Age.
1	1692	Part of skull and fingers, ...	....	Spirits for three years,	Upon a chair, ...	
2	1763	Skull, part of face and fingers,.	A lamp, ...	Camphorated spirits,.	On the floor, ...	62
3	....	Thigh and one leg, ...	Light aside bed,.	Pint rum per day, ...	Near bed on floor, ...	50
4	....	A few bones,...............	....	Habitual,..........	....	50
5	....	Skull and fingers,............	....	Brandy her only drink		
6	1744	Part of head and limbs, ...	A pipe,.........	Habitual,...........	Near chimney, ...	60
7	1745	do do	A fire, ...	do	On hearth.	
8	1749	A black skeleton,............	Fire on hearth,..	Brandy for years,....	On a chair by the fire,	80
9	1779	Hand and foot and a few bones,	Foot stoves, ...	Habitually.		
10	1782	do do do	Fire on hearth,..	do.	On hearth,..........	62
11	1820	Skull and portion of skin,.....	A candle,.......	Wine and cologne, ...	In bed,.............	90
12	1830	Right leg, ...	do	do do ...	Same bed together, ..	66
13	very old	Few parts of body,..........	Pipe, ...	....	Floor,.............	very old
14	1786	Right arm and skin of thigh, ..	Lamp,.........	....	Floor, lived four days,	
15	1799	Complete, ...	....	Brandy,...........	On a bench.	
16	....	Hand and thigh only burnt,...	....	....	Cured.	
17	....	One finger only,............	Candle, ...	....	do	17
18	1829	Muscles of thighs,..........	Foot stove, ...	Spirits,............	Chair,..............	51
19	....	Complete, ...	Reported by Dr. Schofield, of Upper Canada,.................			25

Now, I ask, what mean these indications of Providence? or can any sane man doubt what they mean? Is there anything obscure or equivocal in them? Are the loss of reason, conscience, self-respect, the loss of health, the loss of life — the loss of life by delirium tremens, and especially by the slow fires of a self-inflicted vengeance — Are these the bland and balmly rewards of obedience? or are they judgments, the fruits of sin; judgments as intelligible as awful? Doubtless they are judgments, all, all, judgments — death by drunkenness, by delirium tremens, and especially death by spontaneous combustion, requires no comment.

Those living human volcanos, exhibited usually, if not always, in the persons of inebriates, furnish a spectacle unutterably appalling; in the view of which, as well as in the view of those other indices of wrath, it would seem as if habitual inebriety was a violation of the laws of life, visited in the providence of God, by signal tokens of his displeasure.

How else are these signs and signs like these to be interpreted? or why this distribution of the bounties of providence into aliments and stimulants? why the marked and mighty difference in the effects which they produce by the ordination of God upon the constitution of man, if it be not intended to secure on his part a corresponding difference in the manner of their use?

Does, then, the habitual use of stimulants uniformly impair, and that of aliments as uniformly restore the sensibility on which they operate — and is this an ascertained, settled law of nature? then is it a law that cannot with impunity be transgressed, and they who do transgress it, array themselves against the established order of God's eternal providence, and they do this at their peril, no matter though done in ignorance—done, even on principle, done without the previous intention of offending God, or the knowledge thereafter of having offended Him—no matter though done by God's own children, still, true to his own unchanging nature of the government He ordained, He maintains inviolate his laws, even though that maintenance should embitter the joys and shorten the days of those who both love and fear his name.

Hence, on even the moderate use of intoxicating liquors, the frown of the Almighty is seen to rest; I say on the moderate use, for no one ever became at once a drunkard—the process is progressive; each successive victim is led down to ruin, by slow and almost imperceptible degrees; gradually his reason is impaired, his moral sense is impaired, his constitution is impaired; at length, brutalized in feeling, in character, in appearance, he is disowned by the human family, and stands forth apart, an outcast, a loathing and a by-word, till finally his abused constitution gives way, and the death scene prematurely follows; which death scene, together with the whole train of antecedent evils, are but the pre-ordained penalties of God's violated law; a law distinctly announced to transgressors, in every infliction of its penalty, that meets his eye, through the whole line of his forbidden and disastrous way.

If these things are so, then the manner of life persisted in by the wine drinker, beer drinker, and even cider drinker, as well as the rum and brandy and whiskey drinker, is at variance with the established order of nature, and the will of God as therein revealed. You, therefore, who persist in such a manner of life, cannot expect to attain that age to which you might otherwise attain, or to enjoy, even while life lasts, that blessedness which you might otherwise enjoy, or that your children, or your children's children will attain the one or enjoy the other.

Here, as elsewhere, the law of God will find the transgressor out. Yes, drinker, moderate drinker, know that ere long you will pay in your own person, or in the person of a son or daughter, or brother or sister, or other kinsman or friend, the mighty forfeit you have dared to stake on the issue of transgressing, with impunity, the established order of God's unchanging providence. Nor are the evils which you are about to bring upon yourselves, or on your family, the only evils. Your position is one which more than any other obstructs the onward movement of the temperance cause, and may be compared to that of those men of old, who, planting themselves before the gate of heaven, neither entered in themselves, nor suffered those who were entering, to go in.

Talk not of the innocence of such a course—I address myself to those on whose minds the full force of modern discovery has been brought to bear—talk not of the innocence of such a course; there was a time when it might have been admissible so to talk; but those days of ignorance, with regard to many, are past. New truths have been developed, additional light has been shed upon the world; the specific and deadly poison contained in intoxicating liquors has, in the providence of God, been fully revealed, and through that revelation he now calls on inebriates and the abettors of inebriation everywhere to repent. Yes, moderate drinker, he calls on you; you whose manner of life is at variance with the settled order of his providence; he calls on you not only to save yourself from the doom of drunkenness, but to save also those other misguided beings, whom you are urging forward by the force of your example to a like destruction.

The ragged, squalid, brutal rum-drunkard, who raves in the bar-room, consorts with swine in the gutter, or fills with clamor and dismay the cold and comfortless abode, to which, in the spirit of a demon, he returns at night, much as he injures himself, deeply wretched as he renders his family, exerts but little influence in beguiling others into an imitation of his revolting conduct. On the contrary, as far as his example goes, it tends to deter from, rather than allure to, criminal indulgence. From his degradation and his woes, the note of warning is sounded both loud and long, that whoever will may hear it, and hearing understand.

But reputable, moderate, Christian wine drinkers, that is, the drinkers of brandy or whiskey, in admixture with wine or other preparations falsely called wine, the product, not of the vineyard, but of the still or the brew-house; these are the men who send forth from the high places of society, and sometimes even from the hill of Zion and the portals of the sanctuary, an unsuspected, unrebuked, but powerful influence, which is secretly and silently doing on every side, among the young, among the aged, among even females, its work of death. It is this reputable, authorized, moderate drinking of these disguised poisons, under the cover of an orthodox Christian name, falsely assumed, which encourages youth in their occasional excesses, reconciles the public mind to holiday revelries, shelters from deserved reproach the bar-room tippler, and furnishes a salvo even for the occasional inquietude of the brutal drunkard's conscience.

Regard this conduct as we may, there can be no question how God regards it. He has not left himself without a witness of his displeasure, in any city, or town, or village, or hamlet throughout the land. His judgments are, and are seen to be abroad among us.

Which, even of our own families, or the families with which we have become connected, have not been visited in the person of some of the members thereof with the curse of drunkenness, that appointed retribution for the sin of drinking? Which? It is not, hearer, yours, or yours, or mine: certainly there are not many, perhaps not even one within my hearing, who has not seen some friend or relative in ruin, unutterable ruin, produced by this useless, injurious, and yet reputable habit of moderate drinking; a habit to which men cling, against their reason, against their conscience, often even against their inclination, and this because they shrink from acting on their own responsibility, and lack the courage to obey God speaking in his providence, rather than man.

If there were but one such pitiable object as a drunkard—a poor diseased, demented drunkard, within the whole circle of our acquaintance, on whose intellect, on whose moral sense, on whose whole organism was inflicted the vengeance which alcohol inflicts, it might well fill us with dismay; what ought our emotions then to be, when there is not perhaps a single family throughout that circle which does not, in its relations, contain more than one such object?

Is not God evidently visiting the iniquities of fathers upon children in this respect? The fathers, enterprising and industrious, accumulated wealth, acquired honors, but they conformed to the usages which fashion sanctioned, and presented the inebriating cup to their families, their friends, and even pressed it, early pressed it, to their children's lips. And where are those children now, and what is their condition? Ah, me! their condition is that of hopeless poverty, and they may be found, if not in prisons or hospitals, in the veriest rendezvous of vice, and among the most degraded and abandoned of the species. Or if not yet thus totally reduced and publicly disgraced, they may be found in concealment, disgraced in their own estimation, disgraced in the estimation of friends, humbled, agonized friends, who are struggling to keep up appearances, and conceal from the public eye those blasted hopes, those unnatural crimes, and that unutterable misery that exists, in all the aggravation that despair can impart to misery, within their once peaceful and perhaps envied and joyous place of habitation.

Why then in sober reason (for I may say as Paul said, "I am not mad, but speak the words of truth and soberness") why then, though no fanatic, and having no sympathy with fanatics—I repeat the interrogation, why should we, since neither revelation nor nature enjoins or even sanctions the procedure—why should we in the face of all the warnings of the present, of the past, of the word and the providence of God, persist in the use of intoxicating liquors as a beverage; especially in the use of such liquors as are bought and sold and drank among us?

Is there any absolute necessity, or even any plausible, I had almost said imaginable reason for it—I mean a reason which an intellectual, and moral, and immortal being would not blush to name?

Have those who use these liquors as a beverage any advantage over those who do not? If so, what is it? To say nothing of the guilt or innocence of their use, do those who use them live longer, or do they enjoy life better while they do live? Is their muscle firmer, their complexion more healthy, or their breath less offensive? Can they endure the summer's heat or the winter's cold longer? Are they more exempt from sickness, or when sickness comes, less liable to death? Have they a clearer intellect, a serener frame of mind, a less irritable temper or a more approving conscience?

With all this array of bottles, and decanters, and demijohns, and beer barrels, and rum jugs, is there one attribute of body or of mind, one joy of earth or hope of Heaven, in reference to which he who drinks has any advantage over him who does not drink of this profane, bewildering, intoxicating beverage?

Let us not lose our reason with our temper. Now that the times of that ignorance which God winked at are past; now that chemistry, which reveals to the brewer the methods of adulteration, reveals also to mankind the methods of detection; now that it is known not only that alcohol is poison, but also that other and intenser poisons are mingled with it in the distilled liquors, in the fermented liquors, nay, even in the very wines, falsely so called, which we drink; now that religion and philosophy are both arrayed against it; what is there to induce a Christian, a patriot, or even a political economist, to desire to perpetuate among his countrymen and kindred the use of liquors—liquors never necessary, often hurtful, and sometimes even deadly?

Whence this inconsistency? How comes it that individuals otherwise intelligent and sagacious, quick to perceive and prompt to pursue their true interest, should in this particular commit an error as flagrant as fatal, and already sad with disappointment and bleeding with wounds,—

"Still press against that spear,
On whose sharp point peace bleeds and hope expires?"

After all our experience, our bitter experience, of the fruits of intoxicating liquors, they must not be relinquished; must not, unless in very measured terms, be spoken against.

And yet it is not blessings, but judgments, numerous and grievous to be borne, that the use of these liquors has brought upon us; nor on us alone—pauperism and crime, disease and death, have marked their introduction, and their progress, as a beverage, on every continent and island, and among every kindred, and tongue, and people, on the planet we inhabit.

Drunkenness is terrible, and is admitted to be terrible. Half the miseries of the human family spring from drunkenness, and are known to spring from it; and yet we are unwilling to relinquish the use of the very articles that produce it, the only articles that produce it, and which, unless we change our habits, or the course of nature changes, will continue to produce it among our posterity, through all future generations!

Talk not of ultraism! than this, can there be greater ultraism? For Christians, for Christian parents, following the biers of neighbors, and friends, and kindred, and standing amid grave-yards filled with the victims of intoxicating liquors; for Christians and Christian parents thus situated to cling to their cups, and array themselves against the temperance reformation; or for them to lack the moral courage to remove at once and forever, from their tables and their sideboards, and from before the eyes of their children, those elements of temptation, which are the admitted cause of all this guilt and misery; if this be not fanaticism, and fanaticism the most adverse to the hopes of the country and of the world, then I know not whether anything exists upon this planet that deserves the name.

In the guilt of this infliction of misery and waste of life which intoxicating liquors occasion, we who practice total abstinence are not partakers. Whatever other sins may be laid to our charge, we are free from this one sin; we do not taste this treacherous cup ourselves nor put it to our neighbor's lips.

Since we became "teetotalers," we have not coöperated with the distiller, the beer brewer, or the wine brewer, or rum selling grocer, in training up victims for the dyspepsia, or dropsy, or consumption, or cholera, to operate upon.

Nay, we have done nothing to furnish, even indirectly, by inebriation, new recruits of paupers for the poor-house, criminals for the prison-house, maniacs for the asylum, or sots for the gutter or the graveyard. Of the thousands of the debased beings now begging in rags, toiling among convicts, or raving with delirium tremens, none owe their debasement or their misery to the influence of our counsel or example.

But so far as we are concerned, we have taken from the inebriate the shelter of both; we have put it out of his power, while haranguing to his companions in public, or communing with himself in private, to lay that flattering unction to his soul, that sober, reflecting, moral men, nay, that even professors of religion, nay, even teachers of religion, are on his side, and that in their conduct he can find a vindication of his own.

Especially have we put it beyond the power of those interesting youth, removed from their friends and their home, and entrusted to our care; youth surrounded by so many snares, exposed to so many temptations; especially have we put it beyond their power to find, in our precepts or example, either pretext or apology for tasting even of that fatal chalice which, by bewildering the reason and inflaming the passions, prepares the way for taking the inceptive step in that downward course that leads through the dram shop, the oyster cellar, the play-house, the gaming room and those other nameless places of juvenile resort, aye! places which I may not name, down to the abodes of death.

In this thought there is a consolation, as well as in that other thought, that whatever may be our future lot on earth, whatever unknown and unexpected ills may be held in reservation for us and ours, one thing is certain, come what will, if true to our principles, we are at least secure from that whole class of curses comprehended in the single curse of drunkenness.

Drinkers, I mean moderate drinkers, of all intoxicating liquors, whether students or citizens, professors of religion or not, be assured that neither revelation or nature are on your side, and that whether you hear or forbear, the uniformity of Providence will be maintained and the purposes and government of God will stand, and in the onward progress of time, what has been will be hereafter.

Pause, then, I beseech you; look back on the past, and see within the circle of your acquaintance how many families you can number up who have not furnished to this dread destroyer at least one victim. Here I might —— But I forbear. * * * * *

It were not befitting publicly to lift that veil that covers the painful reminiscences that occur. Let it rest; or rather lift it mentally, and in the retirement of that secret chamber of your hearts, lift it; yes, ye parents who have children now moderate drinkers—husbands that have wives now moderate drinkers—wives that have husbands now moderate drinkers—lift that veil, and, in the light the past sheds upon the future, consider what they will hereafter be, and prepare betimes for your coming destiny.

O! Great God! if the past be an index to the future!—and why should it not be?—if the past be an index to the future, who can, where intoxicating liquors, as a beverage, are in use, look around upon a family, however lovely, however innocent, however full of promise, without shuddering?

And why should not the past be an index to the future? Admit this,—and is there anything unreasonable in its admission?—admit this and I ask no more.

This admitted, and what discreet parent is there, what ingenuous child is there, who would not practice the self-denial and make the sacrifice, if there be either self-denial or sacrifice, that would be availing to change the course of destiny, and ward off from those we love the impending danger?

There is, hearer, as has been shown, such a self-denial and such a sacrifice.

Time will tell who of you have the magnanimity to act accordingly, and eternity reveal the mighty consequences of that action.

LECTURE No. IX.

MORAL AND NATURAL LAWS AS APPLIED TO STRONG DRINK.

Nature still farther interrogated — Another page turned — The response in the structure of creation and the orderings of Providence — Man made for temperance and chastity — Excess fatal — The intrepid engineer — The voice of Nature, the voice of God — His disapprobation of intoxicating liquors stamped on the whole human organism — Especially the human stomach — Explanation of the drawings of Doct. Sewal — The maniac.

In the preceding lecture we proposed to enter, and interrogate nature in her own temple, concerning the will of God, and the duty of man in relation to the use of intoxicating liquors. We have done so, and have heard the response that was returned.

Let us again enter the same temple — repeat the same interrogation — and turning another leaf in the book of nature, attend to the response returned — a response returned in the visible structure of creation and the daily orderings of Providence.

Throughout the entire empire of Jehovah design is apparent, and in all the provinces of that empire means are adapted to ends.

The oak, exposed to the onset of the tempest and liable to be riven by the lightnings of thunder, while it raises upwards its massive trunk, and spreads out its giant branches, sends downwards its roots of strength amid the crevices of the everlasting rocks, and thus stays itself on its broad, deep, strong foundations. Whereas the ivy that entwines that trunk, and the osier that grows beneath the shadow of those branches, are frail, delicate, and proclaimed by their very structure to be designed, not to furnish, but to receive protection.

The eye and the wing of the eagle "that dwelleth upon the crag of the rock and seeketh her prey afar off," are suited to her daring flight and extensive field of vision.

Strength is given to the war horse; his neck is clothed with thunder—the sinews of Behemoth are like brass, his bones like bars of iron. The album of the forest tree is protected by its rind; the organism of fish by their scales; of brutes by their fur; of birds by their plumage; but the human organism is furnished with no adequate corresponding protection, against either the summer's heat or the winter's cold, and yet that organism is frail, delicate and complicated, beyond all imagining.

What means this difference of structure and of defence, if it do not indicate a corresponding difference of design? In this, O man, "fearfully and wonderfully made," thou hearest the voice of thy Creator saying, "thou wast made for temperance and chastity—for the government of reason, for the restraints of conscience and of religion—destined to partake of purer joys and presently to enter on a higher and holier state of being, for which thou canst only be prepared by a practiced self-government, and a voluntary self-denial; thy frail mechanism cannot endure the unrestrained cravings of excited appetite or the rude impulses of inflamed passion.

In health, aliments alone supply all the energy that such a structure as thine can endure; and it is on rare and great occasions, only in sickness or other marked crises of thy being, that additional and auxiliary stimulants are admissible; and the man who indulges in the habitual use of such stimulants, does this in defiance of law, a law written by the finger of God, in living characters, on the delicate organism of his own body;* an organism against

---

* Aliments are necessary as well to provide for the growth of the body in early life, as to repair the waste which, in old and young alike, is ever taking place.

Lavoisier, a celebrated French chemist, states "that the skin alone, during every twenty-four hours, parts with twenty ounces of useless matter. To this important source of waste may be added that of the alimentary canal and various organs of excretion, not omitting also the impure air which is continually being emitted from the lungs. This large separation of useless matter indicates the necessity of a continual supply of fresh nourishment. The system otherwise would be liable to premature dissolution or decay. To effect this restoration the *reparative* organs must be in a healthy condition. Derangement of the digestive functions, in particular, is inimical to healthy restoration. The lungs, the heart, the liver, &c., have each their separate functions, and contribute their appropriate share towards restoring the waste of the system. Derangement, then, of any or all of these functions is more or less injurious to health by preventing those processes which are essential to its continuance."

To supply this waste which is perpetually taking place (Anti-Bacchus, p. 178), "our food is digested, converted into blood, and circulated to every point, both external and internal, of our frame, and by this

which, by such indulgence, he is performing a suicidal act, the effect of which act soon becomes apparent,

---

means we are nourished and our strength is renewed. Animal food, wholesome bread, nutritious vegetables and fruits, when properly digested, amply and suitably supply the waste and absorption of the body. The gastric juice is produced in exact proportion to the wants of the system. In a laboring man the expenditure and exhaustion is much greater than in one who is inactive, and it is a well known fact that in the stomach of the former there is a larger quantity of gastric juice ready to digest or chyme a greater quantity of food, and for this reason, the recluse, if he eat as much as the plowman, must suffer from indigestion, because his stomach finds it difficult to digest more than his absorption actually requires. It must also be observed that nothing but 'solid substances' can be digested. The stomach cannot digest water or any other liquor, and therefore cannot turn it into blood. Dr. Beaumont found, in the case of St. Martin, that liquids, as soon as they entered the stomach, were absorbed by the venous capillary tubes which are spread over that organ, and consequently carried out of the body by the kidneys. Milk was immediately coagulated, the whey absorbed and the curd digested; soups, by these little tubes were filtered, the solid parts retained for digestion and the liquid or water taken into the veins. The same is the case with beer, cider and wine. The water which they contain, and the spirit, or strength, which is lighter than water, are taken up by the absorbents, and the very, very small portion of solid matter which is left, is, if not too hard for such a process, subjected to digestion.

"Aliments are indispensable to health and vigor, and even to life itself. It is otherwise with stimulants. Stimulants, whether local or diffusible, that is, whether acting merely on a single organ or on several, neither repair the wastes of the organism, or add to the energy of the vital principle. They accelerate, merely for the time being, the action of the system, and by accelerating exhaust the *vis vitæ*, as well as blunt the sensibility of the whole nervous structure on which they operate.

Local or simple stimulants (Bacchus, p. 323), irritate the parts with which they come in contact, and affect the other parts of the

in the deranged movement of that organism; in the suspended performance of its several functions; and

---

system only by reason of the vital connection which exists between the parts injured, and the other portions of the system. A strong stimulant, for instance, applied to the stomach, injures its functions, and consequently more or less interferes with its capability to carry on perfect digestion. Hence other organic functions suffer *indirectly*, in part, by reason of their being deprived of proper nourishment, and partly because of the morbid sympathies which are excited in that important organ.

2d. *Diffusive stimulants* also act injuriously on the parts with which they come in contact, but differ from the former class in their influence, being extended over the whole of the system. If an individual swallow a small proportion of pure spirit on an empty stomach, a sensation of burning or irritation ensues. Other and more distant organs, however, shortly afterwards participate. The brain in particular exhibits marks of disorder, and a species of temporary delirium, or mental excitement follows, in addition to general physical disturbance. All of these symptoms indicate some peculiar influence by which diffusive stimulants expand and operate over the whole of the animal functions. The organic medium by which this is effected will subsequently be referred to.

For these reasons it will easily be perceived how incomparably more dangerous are the class of diffusive stimulants than those designated as "simple stimulants." The latter exercise their injurious powers on a limited scale only; while the former possess the property of injuring one or more of the vital functions at the same time. The brain, for example, may be silently undergoing destructive changes, while at the same period the stomach and its functions may be so disordered as to hinder digestion and nutrition; and thus the two grand sources of life and energy suffer either simultaneously or successively from the same pernicious cause.

The brain in this case, of course, is affected through the medium of the nervous system, which is essential to life, and supplies all the functions through their respective organs with their vital energy; consequently an injury done to the nervous, necessarily extends its deleterious effects to all the operations of the system, and this in the speedy and inevitable dissolution of all its parts —I say suicidal, because this premature dissolution

---

proportion to the susceptibility and energy of the different parts, as regulated by their organic constitution.

The peculiar powers of the nervous system bear an important relation in regard to the present inquiry. In relation to diet, one of nature's sentinels consists in the *distinct sensation* which is experienced when the stomach is loaded with food, either improper in its quantity or injurious in its quality. The class of diffusive stimulants, however, when taken in moderate quantities, produce more or less injury without exciting *conscious sensation* in the stomach. General exhilration usually follows moderate vinous indulgence, but the stomach itself, when in a state of health, may or may not display conscious gratification or dislike.

In this consists the great danger of moderate drinking. Individuals commonly do not *feel* any uneasy sensations consequent on moderate indulgence in wine. They cannot, therefore, for a moment suspect the slightest possibility of injurious consequences arising from a cause apparently so innocent and devoid of danger. Experience and extended observation, however, lead us to a contrary conclusion. The healthy relations of the system may for some time be almost imperceptibly undermined, and its harmonious operations disturbed, and not the slightest suspicion be entertained that these changes have originated in some injurious though silent action on the digestive organs. "This circumstance," remarks Dr. Johnson, "leads us to divide into two great classes those symptomatic or sympathetic affections of various organs in the body, dependent on a morbid condition of the stomach and bowels, viz: into that which is accompanied by *conscious sensation*, irritation, pain, or obviously disordered functions of the organs of digestion — and into that which is *not* accompanied by *sensible* disorder of the said organs or their functions. Contrary to the general opinion, I venture to maintain, from very long and attentive observation of phenomena in others, as well as in my own person, that this *latter* class of human afflictions is infinitely more prevalent, more distressing and more obstinate than the *former*. It is a class of disorders, the source, seat and nature of which are, in nine cases out of ten, overlooked, and for

of a structure, formed originally for greater endurance, is not owing, either in its inception, its progress

---

very obvious reasons, because the morbid phenomena present themselves anywhere and everywhere except in the spot where they have their origin."—*Essay on Indigestion*, *page* 8.

Thousands and tens of thousands of individuals are in the present day martyrs to indigestion, and more or less suffer from organic disorders of various kinds, altogether attributable to the moderate and habitual use of intoxicating liquors.

Stimulants not only diminish the excitability of the system, they also diminish the vital power, "*that property possessed by the human frame which may be denominated the self preserving power of nature.*" The vital power is that mysterious influence which pervades all living matter, imparting life, vigor and animation, in addition to the power of sustaining existence for a limited period. It sustains man through extraordinary physical exertion, and endows his constitution with the power to resist, to a certain extent, the effects of excessive heat or cold, labor and fatigue. Man is peculiarly subject to the vicissitudes of climate and of seasons. Business or pleasure may direct him to countries, the climates of which are either in the extremes of heat or cold. In his own or foreign lands, he may be exposed to sudden impressions, arising from the changes of the seasons. All of these vicissitudes the vital power enables him to sustain with comparative impunity, *provided he has not exhausted its influence by intemperate habits.* The same power, in a healthy condition, preserves him from the injurious influence of *marsh miasma*, poisonous vegetable exhalations, and other noxious effluvia, to the dangers of which most persons, more or less subject.

The vital power is the same in all human beings; modified, it is true, by peculiar circumstances. It is possessed by the native of the torrid, as well as the frigid and temperate zones, and sustains him in all the physical exertions to which he is liable. The *tenacity* of this principle of nature displays itself in the wonderful exertions of travelers.

The Arab, with a very small proportion of sustenance, traverses scorching deserts for hundreds and even thousands of miles; the soldier, in the midst of the most trying physical circumstances,

or its consummation, to any unavoidable accident—to any necessity of nature, but to the violence of a

---

endures long and enervating marches. A light proportion of food, a few hours' rest, and the body is invigorated, and again capable of encountering labors of an astonishing character. Such is the sustaining and life preserving influence of the .vital power. How important, then, that mankind should minutely ascertain those circumstances which contribute to enervate and destroy this active principle.

It may be observed, that this power can only be secured in a healthy state by the regular and harmonious action of all the functions of the system. It is subject to, and a consequence of a due performance of the organic laws. Proper food, air, exercise and rest are essential to its continuance. Every circumstance, therefore, which tends to derange or enfeeble the animal functions, diminishes in a greater or lesser degree the force of the vital power. Many circumstances contribute to this result, but among other causes none have so great a tendency to decrease the vitality of the system as that of intemperance. Intoxicating liquors for a time increase the excitability of the vital power. This effect, however, is quickly succeeded by languor and exhaustion. Intemperance thus shortens the duration of human life. Each act of indulgence decreases the energy and strength of the vital power, until at last the unhappy victim of strong drink falls an unavoidable and premature victim to his unnatural career.

To obtain a more familiar notion of the nature of the vital power, it may be interesting, by way of illustration, to compare the human frame to a machine of limited powers, in other words, one which, by previous experiment, is calculated to undergo for a limited period a certain degree of labor. Produce more labor from this machine than it is calculated to perform, and in the same proportion will be the limit of its duration. There is an exact analogy in this case with respect to the human frame. The Creator has given to our physical constitution a power sufficient for all natural purposes. If by intemperance, of whatever character, or arising from whatever source, we excite irregular action in the system, the human machine becomes proportionably debilitated in its power and limited in its duration.

pressure to which it had been subjected through the rashness of the agent to whose supervision it had by its Maker been subjected.

These general remarks will enable the reader to understand why it has been asserted that the length of a man's life may be estimated by the pulsations he has strength to perform. An ingenious author, from this circumstance, makes the following calculations: If we allow seventy years for the usual age of man, and sixty pulsations in a minute for the common measure of pulses of a temperate person, the number of pulsations in his whole life would amount to 2,207,520,000. If by intemperance he force his blood into a more rapid motion, so as to give seventy-five pulses in a minute, the same number of pulses would be completed in fifty-six years. His life by this means would be reduced fourteen years. The celebrated physician, Dr. Hufeland, appears to lay much stress on the circulation with respect to longevity. He remarks that "*a slow uniform pulse* is a strong sign of long life and a great means to promote it." And again, "a principal cause of our internal consumption or spontaneous wasting, lies in the continual circulation of the blood. He who has a hundred pulsations in a minute may be wasted far more quickly than he who has only fifty. Those therefore whose pulse is always quick, and in whom every trifling agitation of mind or every additional drop of wine increases the motion of the heart, are unfortunate candidates for longevity, since their whole life is a continual fever." Dr. Dod informs us that under the increased excitement of alcohol "the circulation is quickened and the diameter of the vessels through which the blood has to flow is diminished." More work is demanded at the very time that the capacity of these wonderful tubes for their labor is decreased. In the wise economy of nature, "a given amount of blood, with a given force in a given time," and through pipes of a given and proper "diameter," is to be circulated; by drinking intoxicating drinks, we increase the quantity of fluid which we have changed into fiery, contaminated blood, we increase the force that propels it, we shorten the time in which it is to be done, and at the same moment decrease the diameter of the tubes through which it is to pass — and is it any wonder that blood vessels burst, sometimes on the brain and cause instant death? sometimes in the lungs, and

When during the late storm on the great western lakes, that intrepid engineer, of whom we have heard so much, planted his foot upon the lever of the safety valve, and caused his fires to be plied with that inflammable combustible, which suddenly supplied in such

---

afflict for life that mysterious purifier of the blood? Is it wonderful that by the bursting of overworked, overheated and poisoned vessless, "diseased deposits" should be formed which may ulcerate the lungs, ossify the heart, produce cancers and calculi of various descriptions and kinds?

Bleeding at the nose, hæmorrhiodal and other diseased fluxes and swellings occur from the same cause. As alcohol especially, seeks the heart, the seat of life, and propels it with a deadly velocity, and seeks the brain, the seat of thought, intelligence and moral judgment, and, by loading the blood vessels of that delicate organ, encumbers the head, is it to be wondered at that palpitation of the heart ensues, or that the mind is too confused to think, or that the eye becomes dim, the ears deaf, and the tongue clammy? Persons that drink stimulating liquors have a swimming in their heads, a dimness before their vision, a ringing in their ears, a nervous sense of obstruction in the organs of speech, a supposed ball rising up in their throats, and a palsied shake of the hand and tottering of the limbs. And nothing could be more natural than that it should be so.

Dr. Gordon, of the London hospital, states that from actual observations on his own patients, he knew that seventy-five cases of disease out of every hundred could be traced to drinking. He also declared that most of the bodies of moderate drinkers, which, when at Edinburgh, he had opened, were found diseased in the liver; and that these symptoms appeared also in the bodies of temperate people which he had examined in the West Indies. He more than once says "that the bodies whose livers he had found diseased were those of moral and religious people." The same witness observed that "the mortality among the coal whippers who are brought to the London hospital is frightful." He also adds that "the moment these beer drinkers are attacked with any acute disease, they are unable to bear depletion, and die directly."

quantities the mighty agent by which that noble steamer, in despite of the billows and the tempest, forced her way off from that rock-bound shore on which she had been driven, and which threatened all on board with instant and inevitable death—when during that storm that intrepid engineer planted his foot on the lever of his safety valve and caused his fires to be plied with such inflammable combustible, would he have done this, think you, in the same assurance of hope, had his manner been, reckless of consequence, to subject his boilers and machinery, on every trivial occasion, to the like extreme and frightful pressure; or had these been so subjected and weakened and rent thereby, would they have responded to the demand made upon them in this hour of danger? Ah no! it was because that engineer, prudent as well as intrepid, had hitherto spared his machinery and husbanded his resources, that when the crisis came, awful as it was, he was prepared to meet it.

There are crises in other voyages to which the crisis just alluded to is quite analogous, when unwonted energy of action is demanded, an energy which stimulants are availing to call forth. But even stimulants avail not where the organism itself, or the sensibility of the organism on which stimulants operate, has been impaired by stimulants. And hence the victim of disease often becomes prematurely the victim of death, because he has familiarized in health, and by familiarizing in health rendered impotent in sickness, those remedial agencies which God in mercy has provided for those seasons of affliction.

Know you not, drinker, that by the use in health of that which was provided for sickness, you are reversing the order of nature, and rendering health more precarious, sickness more speedy and more violent, and recovery therefrom more doubtful and more difficult?

Ask your physician, and he will tell you that even the moderate use of intoxicating liquors in health shortens its duration, and increases in sickness the chances of death.* And how should it be otherwise?

---

* Those who have been accustomed to live freely, invariably fall an easy prey to the attacks of disease. With such persons the slightest injury is frequently attended with the most serious results. The vital functions are unable to perform their accustomed labors, and consequently the *vis naturæ* is incapable of resisting the effects either of internal or external injuries. Thus the slightest cold or comparatively trifling physical injury, is in general attended with danger and often with loss of life. In some inebriate cases the principle of vitality is so small that it is suddenly extinguished by little more than ordinary exertion or exposure to unusual heat or cold; and even, as has not unfrequently happened, *by simple indulgence in a glass of cold water.* The substance of the following remarks not very long ago went the round of the public papers: Medical men of experience in the metropolis are familiar with the fact that confirmed beer drinkers in London can scarcely scratch their fingers without risk of their lives. A copious London beer drinker is all one vital part; he wears his heart upon his sleeve, bare to a death wound even from a rusty nail or the claw of a cat. The worst patients brought into the metropolitan hospitals are those apparently fine models of health, strength and soundness, the London draymen. It appears that when one of these receives a serious injury it is always necessary to amputate in order to give the patient the most distant chance of life. The draymen have the unlimited privilege of the brewer's cellar. Sir Astley Cooper on one occasion was called to a drayman, a powerful, fresh colored, healthy looking man, who had suffered an

What are intoxicating liquors? They are liquors, containing poison not merely, but containing it in quantity and intensity sufficient to disturb the healthy action of the system when used as a beverage, and were they not so, they would not be intoxicating. And are such liquors fit for use?

The Providence of God has answered this interrogation, which answer is conveyed in ruins, stamped by his appointment, from its first inception to its final consummation, on the whole living human organism. I say human organism, for of all God's creatures having organs, man alone is chargeable with the folly, I had almost said the madness, of making use of poison as a beverage. On man's whole organism, therefore, is the influence of that poison stamped—on the brain, the heart, the lungs, the stomach, the viscera, nay not on these only, but also on the intellect, the passions, the moral sense, on the whole man in both natures, corrupting the body in anticipation of the sepulchre, and effacing the image of God from the soul.

And can liquors which produce such ruins be a beverage fit for man? fit to be placed on the side-

---

injury in his finger from a small splinter of a stave. Suppuration had taken place in the wound, which appeared but of a trifling description. This distinguished surgeon as usual opened the small abscess with his lancet. Upon retiring, however, he ascertained that he had forgotten his lancet case. Returning to recover it, he found his patient in a dying state. In a few minutes, or at most a few hours, the unfortunate man was a corpse. Every medical man in London, concludes the writer of this statement, above all things dreads a beer drinker for his patient in a surgical case.

board, and on the table in private families, to be provided for guests in the retirements of friendship, and spread out before the eye and proffered to the taste of youth, at New Year's salutations, on public occasions, and in promiscuous assemblies?

O that I could present before you the outer man, scathed and blasted, as it stands forth in real life, bearing on every fibre, and on every feature, that loathsome, leprous, vinous impress, of which those dark, dismal lines traced on canvass, about to be exhibited to-night, are merely symbols.

O that I could present before you the inner man, still more scathed and blasted, bearing on every attribute and element of its immortal nature that same loathsome, leprous, vinous impress, but in coloring so horrible, that no lines ever drawn on canvass, however dark, can become an appropriate symbol thereof.

Could I do this, I would not ask, nor attempt to return an answer to the question, whether such liquors—liquors which enervate and disease the body, degrade and defile the soul, were a beverage fit for immortal, heaven-descended, heaven-aspiring man to drink of.

Nor would it be needful that I should do so. In that array of guilt and misery, with which these poisons have filled our world, there is a tongue that speaks, and speaks for God, and its language is (as I have before said) to you, to me, to all, touch not, taste not, handle not.

That voice not only speaks for God, but it is God's voice that speaks. Yes, throughout the whole of nature, God's voice is heard. It is heard in the ocean's roar, the tempest's howl, and in the mutterings of thunder. Aye, it is heard, too, in the murmer of the rill, the rustle of the leaf, the whisper of the breeze, and in that deeper stillness in which no breeze whispers, nor leaf rustles; the temple of nature is God's temple, and throughout all its chambers he is present, is heard, is seen, is felt. He it is that "warms in the sun, refreshes in the breeze."

Think not that God is heard only in the book of revelation. The book of nature, as well as the book of revelation, is a book of God. Both were written by him, and hence David bound them up together, and in the 19th Psalm you will find a summary of both.

"The heavens," saith he, "the heavens declare the glory of God," and having said this, he adds in unbroken continuity, "the law of the Lord is perfect, converting the soul."

These two books, which David more than thirty centuries since bound up together, have not yet been separated, and are both, with reverence, now, as formerly, to be consulted; and both, consulted on the question now at issue, return the same answer. It is the book of nature, however, with which chiefly we are now concerned. Let us examine its contents. Let us obey its teachings.

Whatever obscurity there may be elsewhere, here there is no obscurity; here there are no opposing phenomena to explain — no contradictory testimony to reconcile. After a lapse of six thousand years, the original law of God, concerning intoxicating poisons, with its awful and unchanged penalty, stands out to view, written, on the living organism of those who drink it, in characters so broad and bold, and plain, that he who runs may read.

In view of this recorded prohibition of those poisons, talk not of temperate use; such use belongs to authorized healthful beverage — to water, milk and wine; I mean good, refreshing wine, such as might have been drank in Palestine, such as was drank at Cana; even such wines, when used, are to be used temperately; and there may be times, and I think the present is such a time, when from motives of humanity as well as religion their use should be dispensed with.

But poisonous beverage, even poisonous wine, wine that intoxicates, wine the mocker; that serpent's tooth, that adder's sting, against which the book of revelation warns, and to which warning the book of nature in accents long and loud responds; of such wine there is no temperate use. Such wine is poisonous, and is therefore to be everywhere and at all times utterly rejected. The chalice that contains it, contains an element of death. It is not even to be received, or, having been received, is to be rejected; and happy the youth — the man — who dashes it untasted from his hand.

This is not declamation — it is not the speaker, but thy Maker, hearer, that counsels thus. That counsel, as we have said, is made apparent in ruins stamped by the ordination of Jehovah in every age, in every clime, and on every organ of every human being who transgresses his published law in regard to poisons. Yes, in ruins, stamped from their first inception in the moderate drinker, to their final consummation in the death of the drunkard by delirium tremens.

The shadowing forth of these ruins, as seen in a single organ, transferred by the pencil from the dissecting-room of the surgeon* to the canvass of the painter, I shall now proceed to exhibit and very briefly to illustrate.

The organ in question is the human stomach, with its triple coatings, with its inlet for food, its outlet for chyme, its mysterious solvent for converting the former into the latter, and its contractile power for transmitting the same (when so converted) through other viscera, to be absorbed in the repairing of the wastes of an ever-perishing and renovated organism.

Fig. I represents the inner surface of this organ, exposed to view in its natural and healthy state — the state in which it was created, and in which it would ordinarily continue through life, but for those elements of ruin with which, by the indiscretion of man, it is so early and often brought in contact.†

---

* Dr. Thomas Sewal.

† When this lecture was delivered, Dr. Sewal's drawings of the human stomach were exhibited, and the text is the explanation of them severally, as then given.

Fig. II represents the changed aspect of this same organ, as it appears in the person of the temperate drinker. You perceive how that delicate and beautiful net-work of blood-vessels, almost invisible in the healthy stomach, begins to be enlarged—how the whole interior surface, irritated and inflamed, exhibits the inception of that progressive work of death about to be accomplished.

This change is effected by a well known law of nature, to wit, the rushing of the blood to any part of a sensitive texture to which any irritant is applied. You know what is the effect produced by even diluted alcohol when applied to the eye; you know what the effect is, of holding even undiluted brandy in the mouth; what, then, must be the effect of pouring such an exciting and corrosive poison into that delicate and vital organ, the human stomach?

Fig. III represents the stomach of the habitual drunkard, with its thickened walls, its distended blood-vessels, and its livid blotches, visible at irregular intervals to the eye, like the unsightly rum blossoms that overspread the countenance, in token of the havoc which disease, unseen, is making with the viscera within.

Fig. IV exhibits the ulcerated stomach of the habitual drunkard—with its loathsome, corroding sores, eating their way through its triple lining, and gradually extending over the intervening spaces: all bespeaking the extent of the hidden desolation which has already been effected.

Fig. V represents the frightful stomach of the habitual drunkard, rendered still more frightful by the aggravation of a recent debauch. Its previously inflamed surface has become still more inflamed, and its livid blotches still more livid. Grumous blood is issuing from its pores, and its whole putrid aspect indicates that the work of death is nearly consummated.

Fig. VI represents the cancerous stomach of the drunkard, or rather a cancerous ulcer in such a stomach, the coats of which stomach, as the surgeon who performed the dissection affirms, were thickened, and schirrous, and its passages so obstructed as to prevent for some time previous to death the transmission of any nutriment to the system.

Fig. VII represents a stomach in which this progressive desolation is completed—it is the stomach of the maniac, the drunken maniac—as seen after death by delirium tremens, than which there is no death more dreadful,—signalized as it ever is by unearthly spectres, hydras and demons dire.

It may have been the lot of some of you to have witnessed such a death scene; if it has, you will bear me out in saying that no language can express its horrors.

The following lines convey but a faint idea of the frightful ravings of a poor inebriate who died of delirium tremens in an asylum to which he had been removed, and who, amazed at the situation in which he found himself placed, conceived the idea that, though sane himself, the friends who had placed him there were deranged. Excited to phrenzy and haunted by this illusion—

Why am I thus, the maniac cried,
  Confined, 'mid crazy people? Why?
I am not mad—knave, stand aside!
  I'll have my freedom, or I'll die.
It's not for cure that here I've come—
I tell thee, all I want is rum—
  I must have rum.

Sane? yes, and have been all the while;
  Why, then, tormented thus? 'Tis sad!
Why chained, and held in duress vile?
  The men who brought me here were mad.
I will not stay where spectres come—
Let me go hence; I must have rum,
  I must have rum.

'Tis he! 'tis he! my aged sire!
  What has disturbed thee in thy grave?
Why bend on me that eye of fire?
  Why torment, since thou canst not save?
Back to the churchyard whence you've come!
Return, return! but send me rum,
  O! send me rum.

Why is my mother musing there,
  On that same consecrated spot
Where once she taught me words of prayer?
  But now she hears—she heeds me not.
Mute in her winding sheet she stands—
Cold, cold, I feel her icy hands—
  Her icy hands!

She's vanished; but a dearer friend—
  I know her by her angel smile—
Has come her partner to attend,
  His hours of misery to beguile;
Haste! haste! loved one, and set me free;
'Twere heaven to 'scape from hence to thee,
  From hence to thee.

She does not hear — away she flies,
  Regardless of the chain I wear,
Back to her mansion in the skies,
  To dwell with kindred spirits there.
Why has she gone? Why did she come?
O God, I'm ruined! Give me rum,
      O! give me rum.

Hark! hark! for bread my children cry —
  A cry that drinks my spirits up;
But 'tis in vain, in vain to try —
  O give me back the drunkard's cup:
My lips are parched, my heart is sad —
This cursed chain! 'twill make me mad!
      'Twill make me mad!

It wont wash out, that crimson stain!
  I've scoured those spots, and made them white —
Blood reappears again,
  Soon as morning brings the light!
When from my sleepless couch I come,
To see — to feel —— O! give me rum,
      I must have rum.

'Twas there I heard his piteous cry,
  And saw his last imploring look,
But steeled my heart, and bade him die —
  Then from him golden treasures took:
Accursed treasure — stinted sum —
Reward of guilt! Give — give me rum,
      O! give me rum.

Hark! still I hear that piteous wail —
  Before my eyes his spectre stands,
And when it frowns on me, I quail;
  O! I would fly to other lands!
But, that pursuing, there 'twould come —
  There's no escape! O! give me rum,
      O! give me rum.

Guard! guard those windows — bar that door —
  Yonder I armed bandits see;
They've robbed my house of all its store,
  And now return to murder me;
They're breaking in, don't let them come;
Drive — drive them hence — but give me rum,
    O! give me rum.

I stake again? not I! — no more,
  Heartless, accursed gamester! No!
I staked with thee my all, before,
  And from thy den a beggar go.
Go where? A suicide to hell!
  And leave my orphan children here,
In rags and wretchedness to dwell —
  A doom their father cannot bear.

Will no one pity? no one come? —
  Not thou! O come not, man of prayer!
Shut that dread volume in thy hand —
  For me damnation's written there —
No drunkard can in judgment stand!

Talk not of pardon there revealed —
  No, not to me — it is too late —
My sentence is already sealed;
  Tears never blot the book of fate.
Too late! too late these tidings come;
There is no hope! O give me rum,
    I must have rum.

Thou painted harlot, come not here!
  I know thee by that lecherous look —
I know that silvery voice I hear —
  Go home, and read God's holy book.
For thee there's mercy — not for me;
  I'm damned already — words can't tell
What sounds I hear, what sights I see!
  I'm sure it can't be worse in hell!

See how that rug those reptiles soil!
  They're crawling o'er me in my bed!
I feel their clammy, snaky coil
  On every limb — around my head —
With forked tongue I see them play;
I hear them hiss — tear them away!
    Tear them away!

A fiend! a fiend! with many a dart,
  Glares on me with his bloodshot eye,
And aims his missiles at my heart —
  O! whither, whither shall I fly?
Fly? no! it is no time for flight!
  I know thy hellish purpose well —
Avaunt, avaunt, thou hated sprite,
  And hie thee to thy native hell!

He's gone! he's gone! and I am free;
  He's gone, the faithless braggart liar —
He said he'd come to summon me —
  See there again — my bed's on fire!
Fire! water! help! O haste! I die!
  The flames are kindling round my head!
This smoke! I'm strangling! cannot fly —
  O! snatch me from this burning bed!

There! there again — that demon's there,
  Crouching to make a fresh attack!
See how his flaming eye-balls glare —
  Thou fiend of fiends, what's brought thee back?
Back in thy car? For whom? For where?
  He smiles — he beckons me to come —
What are those words thou'st written there?
"IN HELL THEY NEVER WANT FOR RUM!"*
    In hell they never want for rum.
Not want for rum! Read that again —
  I feel the spell! haste, drive me down
Where rum is free! where revelers reign,
  And I can wear the drunkard's crown.

---

* The rum maniac varied.

Accept thy proffer, fiend? I will,
  And to thy drunken banquet come;
Fill the great cauldron from thy still
  With boiling, burning, fiery rum —
There will I quench this horrid thirst!
  With boon companions drink and dwell,
Nor plead for rum, as here I must —
  There's liberty to drink in hell.

Thus raved that maniac rum had made —
  Then starting from his haunted bed —
On, on, ye demons, on! he said,
  Then silent sunk — his soul had fled.

Scoffer beware! he in that shroud
  Was once a temperate drinker too,
And felt as safe — declaimed as loud
  Against extravagance, as you.

And yet ere long I saw him stand
  Refusing, on the brink of hell,
A pardon from his Savior's hand,
  Then plunging down with fiends to dwell.

From thence, methinks, I hear him say,
  Dash, dash the chalice, break the spell,
Stop while you can, and where you may —
  There's no escape when once in hell.

O God, thy gracious spirit send,
  That we, the mocker's snare may fly,
And thus escape that dreadful end,
  That death eternal, drunkards die.

LECTURE No. X.

THE TRAFFIC—APPEAL TO DEALERS.

The injurious effect of abandoning the liquor trade considered — The expedient of total abstinence — The manner in which it should be enforced — an appeal to dealers.

BUT *would not the abandonment of intoxicating liquors, could the community be induced to abandon them, throw many an industrious individual out of employment, and deprive many a needy family of bread?* I admit for a short time, and to a considerable extent, this would be the case: and I also admit that this is a circumstance that deserves to be considered, and that, where kindness dwells, cannot fail to be regretted.

Some indeed there are who seem to think and speak of those engaged in the manufacture and sale of intoxicating liquors as mere wretches, infamous alike in person and in occupation, whose feelings and whose wants were not deserving of regard but I do not so estimate character, nor have I thus learned Christ.

It is not ours to sit in judgment on our brethren. We see the outward appearance, God alone seeth the heart. I have known and still know men of talents and integrity, and so far as man can judge, of religion too, who have long been engaged, and who are still engaged in these (to me) abhorred occupations : but I know also and rejoice to know that as information reaches and light breaks in upon their minds, one after another of their number is led first to doubt, then to disbelieve the innocence of his occupation, and then forever to abjure it.

This change of opinion and of practice in relation to the manufacture and sale as well as use of intoxicating liquors, is still progressive, and it will continue to progress; others, and yet others, and yet others, instructed by the counsel and moved by the example of their brethren, will be induced to practice the same self-denials, and make the same sacrifices, until neither drunkard, nor vender of the drunkard's drink, shall remain within the limits of a purified and reclaimed city. Nor within its limits only ; for the entire race are destined to experience a moral renovation, and the earth which man inhabits, to become covered with works of righteousness, as well as filled with the knowledge of God.

The doom of drunkenness, as well as of oppression and every other vice, is settled—settled in the councils of that Godhead who has declared, from his throne of mercy, that virtue shall prevail, and crime of every name and nature cease from off a ransomed, disinthralled planet. Already from that throne of mercy a redeeming spirit has been sent abroad among the nations, which begins to be apparent in their quickened moral feeling and onward moral movement. The conscience of the world begins to be enlightened and turned towards the prevailing sin of drunkenness—the source and centre from which so many other sins are sent abroad over the face of the whole earth. If there be encouragement in the indications of Providence, or hope in the predictions of prophecy, this frightful abuse of the products of the harvest field and the vineyard, so wantonly manifested in the manufacture and sale and use of intoxicating liquors, must be corrected, and it will be corrected, or the glory of this republic will depart not only—but the progress of civilization be arrested also, and even the chariot wheels of the Son of God be rolled back.

Let us then, cheered by the successes of the past, and encouraged by the promise of the future, urge forward, with renewed energy, our work of mercy.

There was a time when the whole Christian church could be congregated in an inner chamber at Jerusalem. Now its numbers, reckoned by millions, are spread abroad over continents and islands. Within even our own recollection, the same inner chamber would have contained all the advocates of total abstinence in Christendom. Now their number too is reckoned by millions, and their influence is felt by the inhabitants of many a kingdom, and the seamen that navigate the waters of many a sea.

During the ages gone by, the ruinous, loathsome and brutalizing effects of intemperance were extensively experienced and deplored and counteracted. Governments legislated, moralists reasoned, Christians remonstrated, but to no purpose. In the face of all this array of influence, intemperance not only maintained its ground, but constantly advanced; and advanced with constantly increasing rapidity. Death indeed came in aid of the cause of temperance, and swept away, especially during the prevalence of the cholera, crowds of inebriates, with a distinctive and exemplary vengeance. Suddenly the vacancies thus occasioned were filled up; and, as if the course of life whence these supplies were furnished was exhaustless, all the avenues of death were not only reoccupied but crowded with augmented numbers of fresh recruits. The hope even of reclaiming the world by any instrumentalities then in being, departed, and fear lest Christendom should be utterly despoiled by so detestable a practice, took possession of many a reflecting mind.

In that dark hour, the great discovery, THAT DRUNKENNESS IS CAUSED BY DRINKING; moderate, temperate, continuous drinking; and that entire sobriety can be restored and maintained by ABSTINENCE: in that dark hour, this GREAT DISCOVERY was made and promulgated to the world. A discovery which, simple and obvious as it seems to be, had remained hid for ages—during which no one dreamed that mere drinking, regular, reputable, temperate drinking, injured any one; much less that it produced, and by a necessity of nature produced, that utter shameless drunkenness which debased so many individuals, beggared so many families, and brought such indelible disgrace on community itself. This discovery, though not even yet generally known throughout community, has relieved more misery, conduced to more happiness, prompted to more virtue, and reclaimed from more guilt; in one word, it has already shed more blessings on the past, and lit up more hope for the future, than any other discovery, whether physical, political or moral, with which the land and the age in which we live have been signalized.

By this great discovery it has been made apparent that it is not drunkards, but moderate drinkers with whom the temperance reformation is chiefly concerned; for it is not on a change of habits in the former, but the latter, on which the destiny of the state and the nation hangs suspended.

Drinking, and the manufacture and sale of that which makes drunkards, operates reciprocally as cause and effect on all the parties concerned.

The manufacturer and vender furnish the temptation to the drinker, and the drinker in return gives countenance and support both to the manufacturer and the vender.

All these classes must be reformed before the triumph of the temperance cause will be complete; and the reformation of either contributes to the reformation of all. Every dram shop that is closed narrows the sphere of temptation, and every teetotaler that is gained contributes to the shutting up of a dram shop. And they must all be shut up, the rum and the wine and the beer selling grocery, and temperate drinking relinquished, or drunkenness can never be prevented, society purified from crime, relieved from pauperism, freed from disease, and human life extended to its allowed limits.

But how can this be effected, how can the prejudices of whole classes of community be overcome, and the very habits of masses of men changed? How have those mighty changes, even national changes, elsewhere and in former ages, been brought about?* How? sometimes by *appealing to physical force; sometimes to wrong, and sometimes to right principles of voluntary action.*

To *physical force*, in the present instance, it were vain for us to appeal. There are those, indeed, who have it in their power to answer by force, arguments even that are unanswerable by argument, and who, though unable to gain the mind by persuasion, can crush the body by violence. But thus it is not with the friends of total abstinence. We have not, and it is well we have not, at our disposal, either pains or penalties. We cannot even abridge the perfect freedom of the moral agents that surround us, perverse and erring as in our opinion their conduct may be. We cannot inhibit access either to the side-board or the rum jug, and thus render inebriation either to the man of fortune, or even the day laborer, physically impossible; for we can neither point the bayonet to the breast or apply the lash to the back of the refractory inebriate. Ours is a free country, and this an

---

* Changes from barbarism to civilization—from bondage to liberty—and in the Emerald Isle, of late, from riot to order—from inebriety to temperance—how have these changes been brought about?

enlightened age. Here men will think and speak and act according to their own convictions of duty; and they ought to do so. Unconvinced, I would not relinquish the manufacture, or sale, or use of intoxicating liquor at the bidding of another; and I have no right to require that another should do this at my own bidding, and though I had, I could not by any pains or penalties at my command enforce that right. Compulsion then is out of the question.*

---

* The author of course means "compulsion" by individuals, or temperance societies, and not compulsion by the law-making power of the state. No part of this lecture can justly be quoted against prohibitory legislation. It was written before that great device, "The Maine Law," was advocated, or thought necessary to the success of temperance. When the author says he would not relinquish the manufacture or sale of liquor "at the bidding of another," he certainly does not mean that he would not do so, if he was so bidden by the officers of the law.

To the above we add: The liquor traffic is not, and its public repute is not, what it was when this lecture was written. The liquor has grown worse, and the character of the vendors has grown worse. As the pernicious effects of the traffic have been made apparent, one after another of the better class of persons who used to sell liquor (the most virtuous of men once engaged in it without scruple) have abandoned it, until it is now in the hands of persons, but a small proportion of whom were born in the midst of the temperance agitation. Of seven hundred and seventy-five liquor sellers in Albany (see the *Prohibitionist* for March, 1856), it was found that less than one hundred were born in America; all the rest being foreign emigrants. Of all who were convicted of selling liquor contrary to the prohibitory law, in the city of Portland, Maine, not one, it is said, was born in the United States. And so it will be found that the grog-shop system, as it now exists in the United States; from dram-selling up to the state prison and the gallows; including all its monstrous brood of evils, in the shape of Intemperance, Pauperism and

To WRONG PRINCIPLES OF VOLUNTARY ACTION we may, and alas! too often do appeal. But such appeal,

---

Crime, — fully three-fourths of this whole grog-shop system, constituting the load, the oppression, the giant curse of the country, will be found to be a foreign importation. The quality of these wares, always bad and demoralizing, has deteriorated with the character of the vendors. Adulterations are not only not disguised, but they are publicly advertised in the newspapers. This new rascality in science is reduced to a trade, even in the case of what are called the best of liquors; while the frauds in the more common liquors are so flagrant and fatal, that nothing but intense vulgar avarice is visible in the motive, and hardly anything short of downright murder in the result. The following epithets, not invented by "Temperance fanatics," but by drinkers themselves, are now part of the stock phrases of all the bar-rooms in the country: "Fighting brandy;" "Jersey lightning;" "Sword-fish;" "Red-eye;" "Rot-gut;" "Blue ruin;" "Liquor that will kill at forty paces;" and such like. These, be it noted, are a sample of the dismal epithets, which are now used in grim earnest, by habitual drinkers, — a sort of ground swell of detestation, from even the best friends of intoxicating liquors. And public sentiment, in regard to the traffic, has kept pace. From being thought to be an indispensable good, it has come to be regarded as at best but a necessary evil. In several states of the American Union, also in the British Province of New Brunswick, laws have been enacted prohibiting the sale of liquor (for a beverage) entirely. In some of these states, these laws have been embarrassed or overthrown, on technical grounds, by the courts; in others, mostly from political and party motives, they have been repealed. In these states, in several cases, some flagrant outrage has turned the point of public endurance. The arm of the municipal law withdrawn, the great law of self-preservation has been applied, to stay the desolations of the liquor traffic; and it has been forcibly abated, as a public nuisance, by the direct hand of the people.

In the *Prohibitionist* for the month of June, 1857, will be found recorded no less than nineteen such cases, which have been reported by exchanges, in less than as many months. In Huron, in the State of Ohio, the sudden death, by means of the grog-shops, of an old

by whomsoever made, is not in keeping with the benevolence of an enterprise, which has as its object the

---

woman, aroused public resentment to a degree which was no longer to be restrained. Some fifty women immediately armed themselves with hatchets and axes, proceeded to the places of sale, and demolished jugs, casks and demijohns, and spilt every drop of whiskey, brandy, wine and beer they could find. The same thing, pretty much, transpired at Wakeman, in the same state. Also in Lima, Salem, Albany, Moscow, Bellville and Kirkland — all in the State of Ohio. And so at Ellsworth, in the State of Maine; at Rockport, in Massachusetts; at Jamestown, in New-York; at Plattsville, in Wisconsin; at Chesterfield, in South Carolina; and California, in Kentucky. And so, with circumstances slightly different, at two places in Illinois — Earlville and Hanover. And in Indiana, three places — at Vienna, Princeton and Moorsville. In all these cases, the execution of the "search, seizure and destruction clause" was done by *women*. In one case, by the sister of a woman who was made drunk; and in the other cases, by companies of women, numbering from a dozen to fifty. At Bellville, the women were tried for riot; they were acquitted by the jury. At Wakeman they were also tried; these were discharged by the court. At Logansport, in Indiana, Mr. Wright (himself a judge), whose little boy had been made drunk by a liquor seller, armed himself with an axe, stove in the door of the groggery, broke all the bottles and spilt all the liquor he could find; then put on his Sunday clothes, and went to church.

Such is a specimen (for details, see page 41 of vol. 4 of the *Prohibitionist*) of the most noticeable and significant signs of the times. For it is not merely that such things are done, but that they are publicly applauded, and approved of probably in every case, by nine persons out of every ten. They show that the liquor traffic has lost its hold on public favor, and point unmistakably where the sympathy of the people runs; that it is coming to be very generally regarded as a NUISANCE — which in truth it is, and the greatest of nuisances: nor would it be an extravagance to say, that it is fruitful of more mischief than all other nuisances united.

Prohibitionists are charged with being revolutionary. But it is their opponents who are revolutionary. The advocates of prohibi-

amelioration of the condition, and the elevation of the character of the beings on whose destiny it is intended to bear.

---

tory liquor laws, seek to rid the community of a vast and intolerable evil, by peaceable and lawful means, and which are as old as the Common Law. This is reform; not revolution. But they who seek to protect and perpetuate the traffic in Intoxicating Liquors — to keep so vast a wrong, and so complicated a system of wrongs, in a community of men and women who abhor it, and rise to cast it off, as an infamy and a scourge — the attempt to keep society where it is, when its first and strongest instincts compel it to a point beyond — this is revolution, and the most unnatural and violent kind of revolution.

Eleven years ago, we knew a student, at Union College, who sent a copy of these Lectures to his father, who was then engaged in liquor selling. He soon sent back word that he had read them, and was about to employ his capital in other business. Doubtless there are some such persons still remaining in the trade, whose hearts and consciences, if this volume were sent to them, would be similarly touched. We should be glad to have the experiment tried in the case of all the two hundred or two hundred and fifty thousand liquor sellers in the United States.

If anything in the way of "moral suasion" can affect the hearts of the men who still deal in intoxicating liquors, it will be these powerful and searching appeals by Dr. Nott. For he seems to exhaust all the arts, not only of the orator, but the Christian orator. But it must not escape our notice, that all these same appliances, uniting the skill of the rhetorician and the zeal of the missionary, are equally proper to be used, and ought to be used, with the counterfeiter and the forger, the keeper of gambling-houses, and the horse thief. But while these pious efforts on the part of individuals cannot be too much applauded, society at large does not wait, and cannot wait, until these wrong-doers are personally reclaimed. The pains and the penalties of the prohibitory laws are resorted to in the case of lesser evils than liquor-selling; and government cannot refuse to employ them in the case of the greater, without abandoning its pri-

Before the eye of the philanthropist there is spread out one vast field of crime and misery, the admitted consequence of inebriation; deliberate, customary, I had almost said fashionable inebriation. Evils so appalling require the immediate universal application of that only remedy.

TOTAL ABSTINENCE.

But be it remembered that they alone who can apply this remedy are free, untrammeled, intelligent, moral agents; as such agents they must be addressed;

---

mary functions, and resigning all pretensions to maintain social security.

To prove conclusively, that the author would not have any part of these Lectures quoted against the agitation for legislative prohibition, we close this note by quoting the following passage from an address delivered by the author, at the Annual Meeting of the New-York State Temperance Society in Albany, on the 18th of January, 1856: "It is in these public and long-established rendezvous of vice that the occasion is furnished and the temptation presented; here the elements of death are collected, here are mingled, and here the fatal chalice that contains them is presented to unsuspecting and confiding guests, as containing an innocent, cheering and even healthful beverage; and, by being so presented in the midst of boon companions, an appeal is made, guilefully made, to the kindly instincts and generous impulses of man's social nature, — an appeal which few long subject to its seductive influences are able to withstand. Merely to shut up these moral Golgothas, these shambles of the soul, would be a noble triumph. But how are these progressive triumphs to be accomplished, this final victory achieved? How? By the force of public opinion — settled, decided public opinion — and *such public opinion embodied, and expressed in the form of authoritative public* LAW, — and thus embodied and expressed as fast and as far as it is formed." — [EDITOR.]

addressed as agents who, in view of evidence and motives, are to form their own opinions and decide for themselves their own characters and course of conduct; and hence, agents who can only be gained to abstinence by forming each for himself the high resolve and carrying out the same in action. The change in contemplation is a change on principle — a moral change, a voluntary change, a change to be effected by each individual on himself and by himself; a rightful change — a change in which appetite is denied, reason enthroned, and homage paid to the behests of duty and the authority of truth, so that in the advocacy of this cause its friends are estopped from appealing to physical force, not only, but also from appealing to all wrong principles of even voluntary action.

It is easy to rail at the rum and even the wine seller, as well as the rum and the wine drinker; to injure his business, to asperse his character, and to make him odious in community, and thus compel him, especially where our influence is controlling, to dissemble, while paying to our abhorred principles an external but reluctant homage.

It is easy, perhaps natural, convinced as we are of the goodness of our cause, to do this. But is it kind, is it fraternal? especially, is it Christian? Have we then forgotten how much and how long God has borne with us? See we not how long He bears with others? How His sun shines and His showers fall even yet upon the wicked? O! it was the disciples and not their Master who, when treated less urbanely than was befitting, by a village of Samaritans, it was the disciples who proposed to call down fire from Heaven and consume that village: to whom, rebuking their rashness, He said, "Ye know not what manner of spirit ye are of, for the Son of man is not come to destroy men's lives, but to save them."

But though estopped from appealing to physical force, estopped from appealing to wrong principles, we are not estopped from appealing

TO RIGHT PRINCIPLES AND VOLUNTARY ACTION.

"*I*," said the Savior of the world, "I, if I be lifted up, will draw all men unto me."

The event has verified the prediction. It is not the terrors of Sinai that have driven, but the attractives of Calvary which have drawn so many souls to Jesus. Now, as formerly, there is a charm in kindness, and to the powerless reformer, persuasion is still an arm of power. Let us then, in place of offending by our rudeness and repelling by our censure, endeavor to convince by our arguments, and conciliate by our entreaties, both the manufacturer and the vender as well as the consumer of intoxicating liquors.

Abhorrent as the manufacture and sale, as a beverage, of intoxicating liquors may be, to the fully instructed and confirmed advocates of total abstinence, it is still to be considered that these are occupations which, at no distant period, the prevalent, I had almost said the universal, usages of society called for; which law sanctioned and even religion itself was believed and is still believed by many to sanction;

occupations which even temperance men patronized and engaged in without compunction. Under these alleviating circumstances the capital of the manufacturer and vender has to a considerable extent been invested and his habits formed, and he cannot now transfer the one or change the other without inconvenience; perhaps not without sacrifice, perhaps not even without suffering. It is no easy thing for a man whose little all is thus invested, and who thereby obtains his daily bread, and who knows not how otherwise to obtain it; it is no easy thing for such a man to gird himself up to the performance of the painful duty to which our doctrines summon him. On the contrary, it requires great magnanimity, great decision of character, and great self-sacrifice to do this.

Think not, therefore, that those whose hard lot it is to breathe the air of the brewer's vats, or to barrel the liquid that flows from the distiller's still; or that those whose still harder lot it is, standing at the counter or the bar, to measure out by the gill to drinkers the drunkard's drink; think not that these men are from the very nature of their profession greater sinners than other men. On the contrary, *they* are now *what many of us*, and without any change of moral character, once were. And *many of them* may, and doubtless will, without any change of moral character, become what *we* now are. Even now they have the same hopes and fears and sympathies, the same love of life and liberty and country and kindred and of man, as other men have.

Among them may be found those who would shrink from crime with as instinctive a shuddering, look on misery with as tender an eye, and stretch forth for its relief as willing an arm, as any among ourselves; in one word, there may be found among them, as among us, men who fear God and in other respects work righteousness: but owing to their education or occupation, to their misapplied experience, to their ignorance of facts, to the influence of habit, to the force of prejudice, or perhaps to our own unchristian advocacy of the cause itself; our unwarranted assumptions, our insidious slanders, our want of charity, our want of candor or fidelity; owing to these or other similar causes, they have not yet learned what we, though placed in more favorable circumstances, and enjoying greater light, were slow to learn (not that drunkenness is at once a crime, a curse and a dishonor, but)

That drunkenness, by a necessity of nature, is produced by drinking; MODERATE, CUSTOMARY, REPUTABLE DRINKING; and that such is the settled, unchanging order of Providence: and hence the frequent, frightful, loathsome manifestation of this abhorred malady, among, and only among temperate drinkers, so called; that is, among those who have the rashness, the temerity, I had almost said the impiety, in the face of this settled order of God's unchanging providence, to subject the living fibre of their own organism to the corrosive action of intoxicating poisons; poisons furnished by the Author of all good for medicine, not for aliment—and not intended, and declared by the effects they produce not intended, for habitual use.

This discovery is not fancy but fact; an ascertained, palpable, indubitable fact, at the knowledge of which we have arrived by collating the data furnished during other ages and in other countries, and comparing the same with the state of things existing in our own; in the prosecution of which inquiry we have visited the localities where intoxicating liquors are manufactured, and sold, and drank. We have marked their effect in the hut of ignorance, and the parlor of fashion; we have actually taken the dimensions of the miseries they have occasioned, and summed up the number of the dead which they have slain; and while doing this, we have been surprised to learn, that drunkenness was not, as we had once supposed, a calamity resulting from some single, sudden, overwhelming indiscretion, or at most from some few flagrant, wanton cases of criminal indulgence, into which men of every class were liable to be surprised; but that it was a calamity confined to a single class, the moderate drinking class; that the victims were never "teetotalers," but always moderate drinkers, and the process always moderate drinking—a process not sudden, but gradual, beginning when drinking began: continuing with its continuance: and making its silent, undiscovered, unsuspected advance, covertly and without sign of progress or note of warning; till suddenly friends and kindred are awakened to the knowledge of the alarming truth, that, seduced by moderate drinking into drunkenness, a father, a son or a brother lies in ruins.

And having discovered this truth, to wit, that drinking, I mean temperate drinking, is what makes drunkards; a truth momentous indeed, and big with everlasting consequence—but a truth hid for ages—and still hid from numbers; having discovered this truth, we hasten to announce it both to the vender and the drinker; to announce it, not in the language of rebuke and crimination, but in that of Heaven's own mercy—saying, as an Apostle said, "Brethren, I wot that through ignorance ye have done this, as did also your rulers," who have licensed and by licensing sanctioned the doing. And full well we know that even God winketh at those bygone days of ignorance, though now, and far as the light shineth, *commandeth all men everywhere to repent.*

That self-denials and sacrifices will be required, in effecting that change in our social habits which is called for by this discovery of the deleterious effects of even the moderate use of intoxicating liquors on the human constitution, must be admitted. And it must also be admitted that, so far as sacrifices are concerned, manufacturers and venders will be the chief, I had almost said, the only sufferers. Still it must be recollected that these are sacrifices that patriotism as well as religion sanctions; and such too as are elsewhere called for, whenever in this onward movement of society any new and valuable improvement is introduced. Not a canal can be excavated, a railroad constructed, a steamboat started, or even a spinning jenny or a power loom put in motion, without impair ing the fortune of some and taking away the means of procuring bread from others.

And yet these partial temporary evils are submitted to, and often without a murmur, even by the sufferers, cheered as they are by the prospect of public, enduring, superabounding good.

But never was the endurance of private temporary evils encouraged by the promise of requital in the bestowment of such public enduring and superabounding good as in the case before us.

O! could the employment of capital, and the consumption of provisions, and the waste of labor, in the manufacture of intoxicating liquors, be prevented; and could the moral and physical energy, now paralyzed by their use, be directed to the production of comforts, how different would be the condition of all classes—especially of the laboring poor, who now, small as their earnings are, eagerly purchase, and unheedingly press to their lips, that cup which is ever, to those who taste of it, the cup of affliction—often even the cup of death!

Brethren, inn-keepers, grocers, whose business it has been to sell to drinkers the drunkard's drink, has it never occurred to your minds that the liquors dispensed were destined, though unseen by you, to blanch some glow of health, to wither some blossom of hope, to disturb some asylum of peace, to pollute some sanctuary of innocence, or plant gratuitous, perhaps enduring misery, in some bosom of joy? Have you never in imagination followed the wretched inebriate whose glass you have poured out, or whose jug or bottle you have filled; have you never in imagination followed him to his unblessed and comfortless abode? Have you never mentally witnessed the faded cheek and tearful eye of his broken-hearted wife; never witnessed the wistful look and stifled cry of his terror-stricken children, waiting at night-fall his dreaded return; and marked the thrill of horror which the approaching sound of his footsteps sent across their bosoms? Have you never in thought marked his rude entrance, his ferocious look, his savage yell, and that demoniac phrenzy, under the influence of which, father, husband as he was, he drove both wife and children forth, exposed to the wintry blast and the peltings of the pitiless storm; or, denying them even this refuge, how he has smitten them both to the earth beneath his murderous arm?

If you have never heretofore considered these things, will you not now consider them, and give up an occupation so subversive of virtue, so conducive to crime, so productive of misery? You would not willingly, even though it were desired, you would not directly furnish your customers with pauperism, insanity, crime, disease and death; why then supply them with what produces these, and more than these; more of misery than eye hath seen, or ear heard, or than it hath entered into the heart of man to conceive?

But the sale of liquors is your employment, and it furnishes you and yours subsistence. Be it so; still, is it a desirable employment? Are you willing to live, and that your family should live, on the miseries endured, and the crimes committed by others, in consequence of poisons by you dispensed? Are you willing to receive and treasure up the profits, which arise from the widow's tears, the orphan's cries, the maniac's loss of reason, the convict's loss of liberty, and the suicide's loss of life? Are you willing that death should find you still corrupting youth, dishonoring age, and sending waste and want and battle into the families of the poor; and disgrace, disease and death into those of the rich; and subverting, in both, the course of nature, so that in the habitations of maternal kindness, and under the tutelage of paternal virtue, in place of wise and good and useful men, debauchees and paupers and criminals are reared up? Are you willing death should find you still preparing victims for the poor-house and prison-house and grave-yard?

And ye, men of fortune, manufacturers, importers, wholesale dealers, will you not for the sake of the young, the old, the rich, the poor, the happy, the miserable, in one word, for the sake of our common humanity, in all the states and forms in which it is presented, will you not shut up your distilleries, countermand your orders, and announce the heaven-approved resolution, never hereafter to do aught to swell the issue of these waters of woe and death, with which this young republic is already flooded?

Have you never thought, as you rolled out and delivered to the purchaser his cask, have you never thought how many mothers must mourn, how many wives suffer, how many children must supplicate; how many men of virtue must be corrupted, men of honor debased, and of intelligence demented, by partaking of that fatal poison, dispensed from you, seller, and to be paid for as per invoice?

Have you never thought what a moral blight there was to be set abroad over that hamlet or village, where the vile disease and crime-producing contents of that cask, drained to its dregs, was to be palmed, under the guise of a healthful beverage, on the orderly, uninformed and unsuspecting inhabitants thereof? In your own poor-houses and prison-houses and grave-yards, in the beggars that frequent the city, in the loafers that infest the suburbs, and in the shop-lifters and incendiaries so common in both, you see something, indeed, but not a tithe of the whole evils which the traffic in these accursed liquors produce, sent forth, in quantities, as they are, along those extended channels that connect the far-off lakes with the ocean—along the no less extended seaboard, and up the great valley of the west, to every islet and glen, over every railroad or other avenue, to every inland village or shanty or cabin, inflicting everywhere the same miseries inflicted in the city from whence this element of evil was sent abroad—impairing the health, diminishing the vigor, and sowing the seeds of death in the constitution of the hardy laborer in the field, the ruddy housewife in the family, and the pale infant in the cradle—sharpening the avarice of the trader, inflaming the vengeance of the natives, raising the war cry amid the hunting grounds of the wilderness, and rendering savage life itself less secure and more comfortless, to the foot of the Rocky Mountains, and even the regions that lie beyond them.

But it were vain to attempt to portray the severity or take the dimensions of the evils produced by a single cask of intoxicating liquors, inconsiderately sent forth from the warehouse of the sober, moral, and often religious dealer, to the far-off west, or perhaps to some other continent, or to the islands of some distant sea, there to execute unseen, and on beings unknown, its work of death—there to sadden the missionary, to "demonize" the savage, and cause the hopeful convert to apostatize from the faith he had professed. These are evils, however, which God registers in the book of his remembrance, and which the day of judgment will bring to light; as well as those other evils nearer home of which we have already spoken, and, would time permit, might still farther speak; for at home and abroad, in the city and country, in the solitude and by the way side, it is not blessings, but curses, that the venders of intoxicating liquors dispense to their customers.

Said a venerable grocer, looking along a street in which in early life he had planted himself—"That street has twice changed most of its inhabitants since I commenced business in it; and the present occupants, untaught by the fate of their predecessors, are drinking themselves to death as speedily as practicable." "I admit," said another grocer, "that what you say is true; we know we sell POISON; all the world know this; mankind have acquired a taste for poison, and will have it; we merely administer to that taste, and if people will kill themselves, it is their own, and not our fault."

A wine dealer's wife, in the commercial capital of the state, whose conscience was ill at ease in relation to the traffic in intoxicating liquors, availing herself of an auspicious moment, said to her husband, "I do not like your selling liquor; it seems to me to be a bad business; you do not, I suppose, make more than one or two hundred dollars a year by it, and I should be very much rejoiced if you would give it up." "I know," answered her husband, "as well as you do, that it is a bad business; I should be as glad to give it up as you would be to have me, and if I did not make more than one, or two, or even five hundred dollars a year by it, I would give it up." "How much, then," inquired his wife, "do you make?" "Why," replied her husband, "I make from two to three thousand dollars a year, an amount quite too large to be relinquished." "What you say," she rejoined, "brings to my mind the remarks of a lecturer I once heard, who having repeated what Walpole said in relation to every man having his price in politics, added that it was much the same in religion. Satan, continued he, is a broker—not a wheat, or cotton, or money broker, but a soul broker: some can be procured to labor in his service for a hundred, some for a thousand, and some for ten thousand dollars a year. The price at which you estimate your soul, I see, is three thousand dollars a year. My dear husband, look you well to it—to me it seems that even three thousand dollars a year is a paltry price for that which is truly priceless."

On the mind of that husband sudden conviction flashed; and liberal as was his portion in those rewards of unrighteousness which Satan proffered, he resolved, and avowed the resolution, to receive it no longer.

Dealer in these disguised poisons, how stands this profit and loss account with you? Have you summed up the items and ascertained the total to be by you received in exchange for that which "angels dare not bid for, and worlds want wealth to bny?"

Not without reason did the poet say, in reference to the debasing influence of sinful mercenary pursuits—

> "How low the wretches stoop! how deep they plunge
> In mire and dirt: they drudge and sweat and creep
> Through every fen, for vile contaminating trash.
> Since prone in thought their nature is their shame;
> And they should blush, their forehead meets the skies."

In an address at a late temperance anniversary, said a speaker: "During the cholera season there came into my office in New-York, one forenoon, a grocer with whom I had been acquainted, and said with much agitation, I am going to give up selling spiritous liquors. Why? said I. Because, rejoined he, there came into my store this morning, at a very early hour, a young man, who, looking up to the brandy bottle which stood upon the shelf, exclaimed, with a fearful oath, Come down! come down! You killed my grandfather—you killed my father;

come down now, and kill me. What that young man said, continued the grocer, was but too true. His grandfather died a drunkard, and with liquor obtained at my store. His father died a drunkard, and with liquor obtained at my store. Both drank from the same bottle and both were dead; both the grandfather and father; and now the son had come to claim the sad privilege of drinking from the same bottle, and dying as his grandfather and father had died. I looked at that young man—I thought of the past, and it seemed as if the way to hell from my store was very short—that I could, from behind the counter where I stood, look quite into it; I felt that the business of selling liquor was a bad business, and I made up my mind to quit it."

And, true to his purpose, he did so — and before the sun went down every keg and decanter was removed from his premises to return to it no more. A blessing followed that decisive act; and having refused any longer to receive the wages of unrighteousness, he has enjoyed the visitation of the Spirit, and been made, and his family have been made, partakers in the purer, higher, holier pleasures of religion. Inn-keepers, grocers, dispensers, from the counter or the bar room, of the same disguised poison, you have heard this brief but affecting narrative; and having heard it, I ask, how does your experience tally with the proclaimed experience of your fellow-laborer in that common occupation in which you have been engaged? Have your brandy bottles, or beer casks, or rum jugs, been more or less effective than his in this work of death?

Can you recall the names, or sum up the number, of those customers of yours, who, reeling one by one, in succession, from your dispensaries of sin and suffering, have disappeared and sunk down to the abodes of death? Is the way longer from your counter or your bar room to the grave yard, or even to that hell beyond it, than it was from his? Could you, in fact, look into the latter as he did in fancy — what think you would be the discoveries such a vision would unfold? Could you see the horror-stricken countenances, could you hear the unceasing wail of those to whom, standing at your counter or your bar, you have meted out by measure, and for pay, this well known element of death — even of the second death — could you do this, what would your emotions be as your eye met theirs who are now suffering in hell,- the torments brought upon them by indulging in those appetites to which on earth it was your unworthy and cruel office to have ministered?

And are you willing that death should find you to the last thus occupied? Are you willing to go direct from the rum or beer selling bar to the bar of God's righteous retribution? Having posted your books and made out your bills for all the poisons you have ever dispensed — the families you have made wretched — the individuals you have brutalized, and the criminals you have sent prematurely and uncalled for to meet their eternal doom; having posted your books and made out your bills for all these services, which in your day and generation you have rendered mankind, are you willing to present this summary to your final Judge and abide the issue? Think you that He who bestowed your talents and fixed the bounds of your habitation, saying, "Creature of my beneficence and my power, occupy till I come;" think you that He, having examined these doings of yours, the motives from which they sprung, and the results to which they led, will add, "Well done, good and faithful servant, thou hast been faithful over a few things, I will make thee ruler over many things, enter thou into the joy of thy Lord?"

If not, then change your position while you may, and like that repentant grocer of whom you have heard, form the high resolve to quit at once, and at whatever sacrifice, a servitude so debasing, and to spend the remainder of your stay on earth in some blameless, if not higher and holier occupation.

LECTURE No. XI.

RECAPITULATION — GENERAL APPEAL IN BEHALF OF TEMPERANCE.

Appeal to Parents — To Youth — To Women — Conclusion.

In the preceding lectures, we have shown that a kind of wine has existed from great antiquity, which was injurious to health and subversive of morals; that these evils, since the introduction of distillation, have been greatly increased; that half the lunacy, three-fourths of the pauperism, and five-sixths of the crime with which the nation is visited, is owing to intemperance; that there are believed to be five hundred thousand drunkards in the republic, and that thousands die of drunkenness annually. We have also shown that drunkenness results from moderate drinking, and that drunkenness must continue, by a necessity of nature, as long as habitual temperate drinking is continued; that it is not the drinking of water or milk, or any other necessary or nutritive beverage, but of intoxicating liquors only, that produces drunkenness; that as the existing system of moderate drinking occasions all the drunkenness that exists, so that system must be abandoned, or its expense in muscle and sinew and mind, provided for by this, and all future generations; that even moderate drinking is now more dangerous than formerly, because intoxicating drinks are more deadly—to the poison of alcohol, generated by fermentation, other poison having been added by drugging, and *that* alike to intoxicating liquors, whether fermented or distilled. We have enumerated the kinds of poison made use of in the products of the still and of the brew-house, and met the objection that the use of wine was sanctioned by the Bible, by showing that there were different kinds of wine, some of which were good and some bad, and that the former only were commended in the Bible; that though it were allowable to use pure wines in Palestine, it would not follow that it was allowable to use mixed wines here, where intenser poisons exist, and where the use of wine leads to the use of brandy, and the use of brandy to drunkenness: We have shown that even in Palestine it was good not to drink wine, when it caused a brother to offend, and therefore not good elsewhere, and especially here, and at the present time, when the tremendous evils of intemperance in some classes of community render total abstinence befitting in all classes, in conformity to that great law of love which Jesus Christ promulgated, and in conformity to which the apostles of Jesus Christ acted, and the disciples of Jesus Christ are bound to act.

We have shown that the books of Nature and Revelation both proceeded from God, and both contain, though with unequal degrees of clearness, an expression of his will: that the import of the one is discovered by reading and meditation, of the other by observation and experiment; that in this latter oracle mankind are distinctly taught, that aliments restore the waste of the human organism, but that stimulants impair the sensibility on which they operate, and hence that the latter are not intended for habitual use, that they who so use intoxicating liquors violate an established law of nature, and that the drunkenness, disease and death, which result from such use, are the penalty which follows, by the appointment of God, the violation of that law; that God wills the happiness of his creatures, and when the authority of the Bible is plead in behalf of any usage that leads to misery, it may be known that the Bible is plead in error in behalf of such usage; that in the present instance, and so far as the wines of commerce are concerned, to appeal to the Bible as authority, is absurd; that the Bible knows nothing and teaches nothing directly, in relation to these wines of commerce — the same being either a brandied or drugged article, never in use in Palestine; that in relation to these spurious articles the book of nature must alone be consulted, and that being consulted, their condemnation will be found on many a page, inscribed in characters of wrath.

In the view of these and other truths, we have addressed ourselves to the manufacturer and vender of these legalized poisons; and there are yet others to whom, in the view of the same truths, we would, in conclusion, address ourselves.

Fathers, mothers, heads of families, if not prepared at this late hour to change your mode of life, are you not prepared to encourage the young, particularly your children, to change theirs? Act as you may, yourselves, do you not desire that they should act the part of safety? Can you not tell them, and truly tell them, that our manner of life is attended with less peril than your own? Can you not tell them, and truly tell them, that however innocent the use even of pure wine may be, in the estimation of those who use it, that its use in health is never necessary; that excess is always injurious, and that in the habitual use of even such wine there is always danger of excess; that of the brandied and otherwise adulterated wines in use, it cannot be said, in whatever quantity, that they are innocent; that the temptation to adulterate is very great, detection very difficult, and that entire safety is to be found only in total abstinence? Can you not truly tell them this? Will you not tell them this? And having told them, should they, in obedience to your counsel, relinquish at once the use of all intoxicating liquors, would their present condition, you yourselves being judges, would their present condition be less secure, or their future prospects less full of promise, on that account? Or would the remembrance, that the stand they took was taken at your bidding, either awaken in your bosoms misgivings now, or regrets hereafter? Especially, would it do this as life declines, and you approach your final dissolution and last account? Then, when standing on the verge of that narrow isthmus, which separates the future from the past, and connects eternity with time; then, when casting the last lingering look back upon that world to which you are about to bid adieu forever, will the thought that you are to leave behind you a family trained to temperance not only, but pledged also to total abstinence, will that thought, then, think you, plant one thorn in the pillow of sickness, or add one pang to the agonies of death? O! no, it is not this thought, but the thought of dying and leaving behind a family of profligate children, to nurture other children no less profligate, in their turn to nurture others,—thus transmitting guilt and misery to a remote posterity; it is this thought, and thoughts like this, in connection with another thought, suggested by those awful words, "For I, the Lord thy God, am a jealous God, visiting the iniquities of the fathers upon the children, to the third and fourth generation, of them that hate me;"—it is thoughts like these, and not the thought of leaving behind a family pledged to total abstinence, that will give to life's last act a sadder coloring, and man's last hour a denser darkness. Between these two conditions of the dying, if held within our offer, who of us would hesitate?

Ye children of moderate drinking parents; children of so many hopes, and solicitudes and prayers; the sin of drunkenness apart, the innocence of abstinence apart, here are two classes of men, and two plans of life, each proffered to your approbation, and submitted for your choice: The one class use intoxicating liquor, moderately indeed, still they use intoxicating liquor in some or many of its forms; the other class use it in none of them: The one class, in consequence of such use of intoxicating liquor, furnish all the drunkenness, three-fourths of all the pauperism and five-sixths of all the crime, under the accumulating and accumulated weight of which our country already groans. Yes, in consequence of such restricted use of intoxicating liquors, the one class pays an annual tribute in muscle and sinew, in intellect and virtue, aye, in the souls of men; a mighty tribute, embodied in the persons of inebriates, taken from the ranks of temperate drinkers and delivered over to the jail, the mad-house, the house of correction, and even the house of silence!

The other class pays no such tribute; no, nor even a portion of it. The other burthens of community they share indeed, in common with their brethren; a portion of their earnings goes even to provide and furnish those abodes of woe and death, which intoxicating liquors crowd with inmates; but the inmates themselves are all, all trained in the society, instructed in the maxims, moulded by the customs, and finally delivered up from the ranks of the opposite party—the moderate drinking party.

Now, beloved youth, which of these two modes of life will you adopt? To which of these two classes will you attach yourselves? Which think you is the safest, which most noble, patriotic, Christian? In one word, which will insure the purest bliss on earth, and afford the fairest prospect of admission into heaven?

For the mere privilege of using intoxicating liquors moderately, are you willing to contribute your proportion annually to people the poor-house, the prison-house and the grave-yard? For such a privilege, are you willing to give up to death, or even to delirium tremens, a parent this year, a wife, a child or brother or sister the next, and the year thereafter a friend or neighbor? Are you willing to do this, and having done it, are you further willing, as a consequence, to hear the mothers', the wives', the widows', and the orphans' wailings, on account of miseries inflicted by a system deliberately adopted by your choice, sustained by your example, and perpetuated by your influence? Nor to hear alone; are you willing to see also the beggar's rags, the convict's fetters, and those other and more hideous forms of guilt and misery, the product of intemperance, which liken men to demons and earth to hell?

That frightful outward desolation, apparent in the person and the home of the inebriate, is but an emblem of a still more frightful inward desolation. The comfortless abode, the sorrow-stricken family, the tattered garments, the palsied tread, the ghastly countenance, and loathsome aspect, of the habitual brutal drunkard, fill us with abhorrence. We shun his presence, and shrink instinctively from his polluting touch. But what are all these sad items, which affect the outer man only, in comparison with the blighted hopes, the withered intellect, the debased propensities, the brutal appetites, the demoniac passions, the defiled conscience; in one word, in comparison with the sadder moral items which complete the frightful spectacle of a soul iu ruins; a soul deserted of God, possessed by demons, and from which the last lineaments of its Maker's image have been utterly effaced; a soul scathed and riven, and standing forth already, as it will hereafter stand forth, frightful amid its ruins, a monument of wrath, and a warning to the universe.

Be not deceived, nor fear to take the dimensions of the evils that threaten, or to look that destroyer in the face, which you are about to arm against yourselves. Not the solid rock withstands forever the touch of water even, much less the living fibre that of alcohol, or those other and intenser poisons mingled with it, in those inebriating liquors of which a moiety of the nation drinks. The habitual use of such liquors in small quantities prepares the way for their use in larger quantities, and yet larger quantities progressively, till inebriation is produced. Such is the constitution of nature; it is preposterous, therefore, to calculate upon exemption. Exceptions indeed there may be; but they are exceptions merely. The rule is otherwise. If you live an habitual drinker of such liquors, you ought to calculate to die a confirmed drunkard: and that your children, and your children's children, should they follow your example, will die confirmed drunkards also. And if life shall be prolonged to them, and they so live, they will so die, unless the course of nature shall be changed.

In the view of these facts and arguments which the subject before you presents, make up your minds, make up your minds deliberately, and having done so, say whether you are willing to take along with the habitual moderate use of intoxicating liquors, as bought and sold, and drank among us, the appalling consequences that must result therefrom. Are you willing to do this? and if you are not, stop,—stop while you may, and where you can. In this descent to Hades there is no half-way house, no central resting place. The movement once commenced, is ever onward and downward. The thirst created is quenchless, the appetite induced insatiable. You may not live to complete the process—but this know, that it is naturally progressive, and that with every successive sip from the fatal chalice, it advances, imperceptibly indeed, still it advances towards completion. Yon demented sot, once a moderate drinker, occupied the ground you now occupy, and looked down on former sots, as you, a moderate drinker, now look down on him, and as future moderate drinkers may yet look down on you, and wonder;

"Facilis decensus averni."

Let it never be forgotten that we are social beings. No man liveth to himself; on the contrary, grouped together in various ways, each acts, and is acted on by others. Though living at a distance of so many generations, we feel even yet, and in its strength, the effect of the first transgression. Now, as formerly, it is the nature of vice, as well as virtue, to extend and perpetuate itself. Now, as formerly, the existing generation is giving the impress of its character to the generation which is to follow it—and now, as formerly, parents are by their conduct and their counsel, either weaving crowns to signalize their offspring in the Heavens, or forging chains to be worn by them in hell.

Hearer, time is on the wing; death is at hand; act now, therefore, the part that you will in that hour approve, and reprobate the conduct you will then condemn.

It has not been usual for the speaker, as it has for some others, to bespeak the influence of those who constitute the most numerous, as well as most efficient part of almost every assembly, where self-denials are called for, or questions of practical duty discussed. And yet, no one is more indebted than myself to the kind of influence in question.

Under God, I owe my early education, nay, all that I have been, or am, to the counsel and tutelage of a pious mother. It was, peace to her sainted spirit, it was her monitory voice that first taught my young heart to feel that there was danger in the intoxicating cup, and that safety lay in abstinence.

And as no one is more indebted than myself to the kind of influence in question, so no one more fully realizes how decisively it bears upon the destinies of others.

Full well I know, that by woman came the apostacy of Adam, and by woman the recovery through Jesus. It was a woman that imbued the mind and formed the character of Moses, Israel's deliverer—it was a woman that led the choir, and gave back the response of that triumphal procession, which went forth to celebrate with timbrels, on the banks of the Red Sea, the overthrow of Pharoah—it was a woman that put Sisera to flight, that com-composed the song of Deborah and Barak, the son of Abinoam, and judged in righteousness, for years, the tribes of Israel—it was a woman that defeated the wicked counsels of Haman, delivered righteous Mordecai, and saved a whole people from utter desolation.

And not now to speak of Semiramis at Babylon, of Catharine of Russia, or of those Queens of England, whose joyous reign constitute the brightest periods of British history, or of her, the young and lovely, the patron of learning and morals, who now adorns the throne of the sea-girt Isles; not now to speak of these, there are others of more sacred character, of whom it were admissable even now to speak.

The sceptre of empire is not the sceptre that best befits the hand of woman; nor is the field of carnage her field of glory. Home, sweet home, is her theatre of action, her pedestal of beauty, and throne of power. Or if seen abroad, she is seen to the best advantage, when on errands of love, and wearing her robe of mercy.

It was not woman who slept during the agonies of Gethsemane; it was not woman who denied her Lord at the palace of Caiaphas; it was not woman who deserted his cross on the hill of Calvary. But it was woman that dared to testify her respect for his corpse, that procured spices for embalming it, and that was found last at night, and first in the morning, at his sepulchre. Time has neither impaired her kindness, shaken her constancy, or changed her character.

Now, as formerly, she is most ready to enter, and most reluctant to leave, the abode of misery. Now, as formerly, it is her office, and well it has been sustained, to stay the fainting head, wipe from the dim eye the tear of anguish, and from the cold forehead the dew of death.

This is not unmerited praise. I have too much respect for the character of woman, to use, even elsewhere, the language of adulation, and too much self-respect to use such language here. I would not, if I could, persuade those of the sex who hear me, to become the public, clamorous advocates of even temperance. It is the influence of their declared approbation; of their open, willing, visible example, enforced by that soft, persuasive, colloquial eloquence, which, in some hallowed retirement and chosen moments, exerts such controlling influence over the hard, cold heart of man, especially over a husband's, a son's, or a brother's heart; it is this influence which we need;—an influence chiefly known by the gradual, kindly transformation of character it produces, and which, in its benign effects, may be compared to the noiseless, balmy influence of Spring, shedding, as it silently advances, renovation over every hill, and dale, and glen, and islet, and changing, throughout the whole region of animated nature, Winter's rugged and unsightly forms, into the forms of vernal lovliness and beauty.

No, I repeat it, I would not, if I could, persuade those of the sex who hear me, to become the public, clamorous advocates of temperance. It is not yours to wield the club of Hercules or bend Achilles' bow. But, though it is not, still you have a heaven-appointed armour, as well as a heaven-approved theatre of action. The look of tenderness, the eye of compassion, the lip of entreaty, are yours; and yours, too, are the decisions of taste, and yours the omnipotence of fashion. You can therefore,—I speak of those who have been the favorites of fortune, and who occupy the high places of society,—you can change the terms of social intercourse and alter the current opinions of community. You can remove, at once and forever, temptation from the saloon, the drawing-room and the dining-table. This is your empire, the empire over which God and the usages of mankind have given you dominion. Here, within these limits, and without transgressing that modesty which is heaven's own gift and woman's brightest ornament, you may exert a benign and kindly but mighty influence. Here you have but to speak the word, and one chief source of the mother's, the wives', and the widow's sorrows, will, throughout the circle in which you move, be dried up forever. Nor, throughout that circle only. The families around you and beneath you will feel the influence of your example, descending on them in blessings like the dews of Heaven that descend on the mountains of Zion; and drunkenness, loathsome, brutal drunkenness, driven by the moral power of your decision, from all the abodes of reputable society, will be compelled to exist, if it exist at all, only among those vulgar and ragged wretches, who, shunning the society of woman, herd together in the bar-room, the oyster cellar and the groggery.

This, indeed, were a mighty triumph, and this, at least, you can achieve. Why, then, should less than this be achieved? To purify the conscience, to bind up the broken-hearted, to remove temptation from the young, to minister consolation to the aged, and kindle joy in every bosom throughout her appointed theatre of action, befits alike a woman's and a mother's agency,—and since God has put it in your power to do so much, are you willing to be responsible for the consequences of leaving it undone?

Are you willing to see this tide of woe and death, whose flow you might arrest, roll onward by you to posterity, increasing as it rolls forever?

O! no, you are not, I am sure you are not; and if not, then, ere you leave these altars, lift up your heart to God, and, in his strength, form the high resolve to purify from drunkenness this city. And, however elsewhere others may hesitate, and waver, and defer, and temporize, take you the open, noble stand of ABSTINENCE; and, having taken it, cause it by your words, and by your deeds, to be known on earth and told in Heaven, that mothers here have dared to do their duty, their whole duty, and that, within the precincts of that consecrated spot over which their balmy, hallowed influence extends, the doom of drunkenness is sealed.

Nor mothers only; in this benign and holy enterprise, the daughter and the mother alike are interested.

Ye young, might the speaker be permitted to address you, as well as your honored parents, and those teachers, their assistants, whose delightful task it is to bring forward the unfolding germs of thought, and teach the young idea how to shoot—might the speaker, whose chief concernment hitherto has been the education of the young, be permitted to address you, he would bespeak your influence, your urgent, persevering influence, in behalf of a cause so pure, so full of mercy, and so every way befitting your age, your sex, your character.

O! could the speaker make a lodgment, an effectual lodgment, in behalf of temperance, within those young, warm, generous, active hearts within his hearing, or rather within the city where it is his privilege to speak, who this side Heaven could calculate the blessed, mighty, enduring consequence? Could this be done, then might the eye of angels rest with increased complacency on this commercial metropolis,* already signalized by Christian charity, as well as radiant with intellectual glory;—but then lit up anew with fire from off virtue's own altar, and thus caused to become, amid the surrounding desolation

* Philadelphia.

which intemperance has occasioned, more conspicuously than ever, an asylum of mercy to the wretched and a beacon light of promise to the wanderer.

Then from this favored spot, as from some great central source of power, encouragement might be given and confidence imparted to the whole sisterhood of virtue, and a redeeming influence sent forth, through many a distant town and hamlet, to mingle with other and kindred influences in effecting throughout the land, among the youth of both sexes, that moral renovation called for, and which, when realized, will be at once the earnest and the anticipation of millennial glory.

O! could we gain the young,—the young who have no inveterate prejudices to combat, no established habits to overcome; could we gain the young, we might, after a single generation had passed away, shut up the dram-shop, the bar-room and the rum selling grocery, and, by shutting these up, shut up also the poor-house, the prison-house, and one of the broadest and most frequented avenues to the charnel house.

More than this, could we shut up these licensed dispensaries of crime, disease and death, we might abate the severity of maternal anguish, restore departed joys to conjugal affection, silence the cry of deserted orphanage, and procure for the poor demented suicide a respite for self-inflicted vengeance.

This, the gaining of the young to abstinence, would constitute the mighty fulcrum on which to plant that moral lever of power, to raise a world from degradation.

O! how the clouds would scatter, the prospect brighten, and the firmament of hope clear up, could the young be gained, intoxicating liquors be banished, and abstinence with its train of blessings introduced throughout the earth.

Appendix of texts in which the fruit of the vine is spoken of with approbation; usually, if not always, when so spoken of, in its natural and unintoxicating state, i.e., the state in which it exists in the cluster, the press and the vat; the state being either self-evident from the text or inferable from the other articles in connection, or from the design in view, or the effect ultimately produced.

TIROSH—[WITH APPROBATION.]

TERMS USED WITH APPROBATION.	Book.	Chapter.	Verse.	Rendered in English.	Rendered in Septuagint.	Rendered in Vulgate.	With what connected.
TIROSH is used thirty-six times with APPROBATION, for the fruit of the vine in its NATURAL and UNINTOXICATING STATE.	Genesis, ...	27	28	wine,	οἴνου,	vini,	With dew and rain — causing the growth of corn and other products, as a blessing.
	"	27	37	"	οἴνῳ,	vino,	
	Deut., ...	11	14	"	οἶνον,	vinum,	
	"	33	28	"	οἴνου,	vini,	
	"	28	51	"	οἶνον,	vinum,	
	Isaiah, ...	24	7	new wine,	οἶνος,	vindemia,	
	Hosea, ...	2	9	wine,	οἶνον,	vinum,	With corn failing through drought or otherwise, as a judgmen'
	"	9	2	new wine,	οἶνος,	"	
	Joel, ...	1	10	"	"	"	
	Haggai, ...	1	11	"	οἶνον,	"	
	Nehemiah, ..	5	11	"	"	vini,	
	Psalms, ...	4	7(8)	"	οἴνου,	"	With the restoration or increase.
	Hosea, ...	2	22	"	οἶνον,	vinum,	

TIROSH—AUSIS—HHAMER—HHEMER—HHAMRA—ESHISHA—[WITH APPROBATION.]

Terms used with approbation.	Book.	Chapter.	Verse.	Rendered in English.	Rendered in Septuagint.	Rendered in Vulgate.	With what connected.
TIROSH continued, with approbation, for the fruit of the vine in its natural and unintoxicating state.	Joel, ...	2	19	wine,	οἶνον,	vinum,	With corn and plenty and rejoicing, as blessings.
	2 Kings, ...	18	32	"	οἴνου,	vini,	
	2 Chronicles,	32	28	"	"	"	
	Isaiah, ...	36	17	"	"	"	
	"	62	8	"	οἶνον,	vinum,	
	Jeremiah, ...	31	12	"	"	vino,	
	Deut., ...	7	13	"	"	vindemiæ,	
	Zechariah, ..	9	17	new wine,	οἶνος,	vinum,	
	Judges, ...	9	13	wine,	οἶνον,	vinum,	With vines, grapes and vats, gushing out as blessings.
	Proverbs, ...	3	10	new wine,	οἴνῳ,	vino,	
	Isaiah, ...	65	8	"	ῥὼξ,	granum,	
	Joel, ...	2	24	wine,	οἶνον,	vino,	
	Micah, ...	6	15	sweet wine,	"	vinum,	
	Numbers, ...	18	12	wine,	οἶνον,	vini,	With first fruits, and as tithes and offerings.
	Deut., ...	12	17	"	"	"	
	"	14	23	"	"	"	
	"	18	4	"	"	"	
	2 Chronicles,	31	5	"	"	"	
	Nehemiah, ..	10	37	"	"	vindemia,	

	Nehemiah, ..	10	39	new wine,	οἶνον,	vini,	With first fruits, and as tithes and offerings.
	" ..	13	5	"	"	"	
	" ..	13	12	"	"	"	
	Hosea, ...	2	8(x)	wine,	οἶνον,	vinum,	With corn and oil.
AUSIS is used four times with APPROBATION, for the fruit of the vine in its natural and unintoxicating state.	Canticles, ...	8	2	juice,	νάματος,	mustum,	With other natural productions.
	Joel, ...	1	5	new wine,	εὐφροσύνη,	vinum in dulcedine,	
	"	3	18 (H. 4)	"	γλυκασμόν,	dulcedinem,	
	Amos, ...	9	13	sweet wine,	"	"	
HHAMER, one.	Deut., ...	32	14	pure blood of the grape,	αἷμα, σταφυλῆς,	sanguinem, uvæ,	With butter, milk, &c.
HHEMER, one.	Isaiah, ...	27	2	red wine,	ἀμπελών, καλός,	meri,	With the vineyard.
HHAMRA, two.	Ezra, ...	6	9	wine,	οἶνον,	vinum,	With sacrifice.
	"	7	22	"	οἴνου,	vini,	
ESHISHA, four.	2 Samuel, ...	6	19	flagon of wine,	λάγανον,	frixam,	Probably used for grape.
	1 Chronicles,	16	3	"	ἀμορίτην,	"	
	Canticles, ...	2	5	flagons,	μύροις,	floribus,	
	Hosea, ...	3	1	"	πέμματα,	vinacia, uvarium,	

YAYIN—[USED WITH APPROBATION.]

TERMS USED WITH APPROBATION.	Book.	Chapter.	Verse.	Rendered in			With what connected.
				English.	Septuagint.	Vulgate.	
YAYIN — used with APPROBATION for the fruit of the vine, evidently in its NATURAL and UNINTOXICATING STATE, i. e., as it exists in the *cluster*, the *press* and the *vat*.	Genesis, ...	49	11	wine,	οἴνῳ,	vino,	In connection, for the most part, with grapes, wines, vineyards, ingatherings and wine presses, &c.; which show that it is used in these instances for the wine of the CLUSTER, the PRESS and the VAT.
	1 Chronicles,	27	27	"	οἴνου,	vinariis,	
	Nehemiah, ..	5	18	"	οἶνος,	vina,	
	" ..	13	15	"	οἶνον,	vinum,	
	Job, ...	32	19	"	γλεύκους,	mustum,	
	Psalms, ...	104	15	"	οἶνος,	vinum,	
	Canticles, ...	5	1	"	οἶνον,	"	
	" ...	7	9 (10)	"	οἶνος,	"	
	" ...	8	2	"	οἴνου,	vino,	
	Isaiah, ...	16	10	"	οἶνον,	vinum,	
	Deut., ...	28	39	"	"	"	
	Jeremiah, ...	40	10	"	"	vindemiam,	
	" ...	40	12	"	"	vinum,	
	" ...	48	33	"	οἶνος,	"	
	Lamentation,	2	12	"	"	"	
	Hosea, ...	14	7 (8)	"	"	"	
	Amos, ...	5	11	"	οἶνον,	"	
	"	9	14	"	"	"	
	Micah, ...	6	15	"	"	"	

YAYIN with approbation for the wine of the cluster, press or vat.	Zephaniah,	1	13	wine,	οἶνον,	vinum,	Continued for wine of cluster and vat.
	Joel,	1	5	"	"	"	
	Genesis,	14	18	"	"	"	In connection with corn, oil, raisins, fruit, and other natural productions.
	Deut.,	29	6 (5)	"	"	"	
YAYIN, with APPROBATION, for the fruit of the vine continued. Probably in its natural and unintoxicating state.	Judges,	19	19	"	οἶνος,	"	
	1 Samuel,	25	18	"	οἴνου,	vini,	
	2 Samuel,	16	1	"	"	"	
	"	16	2	"	οἶνος,	vinum,	
	1 Chronicles,	12	40	"	οἶνον,	"	
	2 Chronicles,	2	10 (9)	"	οἴνου,	vini,	
	"	2	15 (14)	"	οἶνον,	vinum,	
	"	11	11	"	"	vini,	
	Nehemiah,	5	15	"	οἴνῳ,	vino,	
	Ezekiel,	27	18	"	οἶνον,	"	
	Ecclesiastes,	9	7	"	"	vinum,	
	Exodus,	29	40	"	οἴνου,	"	In connection with oil, &c.; and in offerings.
	Leviticus,	23	13	"	"	vini,	
	Numbers,	15	5	"	οἶνον,	vinum,	
	"	15	7	"	"	"	
	"	15	10	"	"	"	
	"	28	14	"	οἴνου,	vini,	
	1 Samuel,	1	24	"	"	"	
	"	10	3	"	"	"	
	"	16	20	"	"	"	
	1 Chronicles,	9	29	"	"	vino,	

YAYIN—[USED WITH APPROBATION.]

TERMS USED WITH APPROBATION.	Book.	Chapter.	Verse.	Rendered in			With what connected.
				English.	Septuagint.	Vulgate.	
YAYIN continued, with approbation.	Hosea, ...	9	4	wine,	οἶνον,	vinum,	With oil, &c., and in offerings.
	Deut., ...	14	26	"	οἴνῳ,	"	
	Proverbs, ...	9	2	"	οἶνον,	"	Mixed by wisdom.
	" ...	9	5	"	"	"	
	Zachariah, ..	9	15	"	"	vino,	With different things, by way of comparison, in a good sense
	" ..	10	7	"	οἴνῳ,	"	
	Canticles, ...	1	2	"	οἶνον,	"	
	" ...	1	4	"	"	vinum,	
	" ...	4	10	"	οἴνου,	vino,	
	Genesis, ...	49	11	"	οἴνῳ,	"	
	Psalms, ...	78	65	"	οἴνου,	"	
	Isaiah, ...	29	9	"	"	"	
	"	51	21	"	"	"	

Appendix of texts in which the fruit of the vine is spoken of with disapprobation ; usually, if not always, when so spoken of, in its artificial state, i.e., the state in which it exists in the bottle and cask ; the state being self-evident from the text, or inferable from the other articles in connection, or from the design in view, or the effect ultimately produced.

TIROSH AND YAYIN—[WITH DISAPPROBATION.]

TERMS USED WITH DISAPPROBATION.	Book.	Chapter.	Verse.	Rendered in			With what connected.
				English.	Septuagint.	Vulgate.	
TIROSH, once.	Hosea, ...	4	11	wine,	οἶνον,	vinum,	With whoredom.
YAYIN, many times with DISAPPROBATION—for the fruit of the vine fermented, as it exists in the *bottle* and the *cask*.	Genesis, ...	9	21	"	οἴνου,	"	Drunkenness—of Noah—Nabal—Ephraim—prophets—priests—drunken men—nations—Hannah supposed—denied.
	"	9	24	"	"	vino,	
	1 Samuel,...	25	37	"	"	vinum,	
	Proverbs, ...	23	31	"	οἶνος,	"	
	Isaiah, ...	28	1	"	οἴνου,	vino,	
	"	28	7	"	οἶνον,	"	
	"	28	7	"	οἴνῳ,	"	
	Jeremiah,...	23	9	"	οἴνου,	"	
	" ...	13	12	"	"	ebrietate,	
	" ...	51	7	"	"	vino,	
	1 Samuel,...	1	14	"	οἶνον,	vinum,	
	"	1	15	"	"	"	

YAYIN [WITH DISAPPROBATION.]

TERMS USED WITH DISAPPROBATION.	Book.	Chapter.	Verse.	Rendered in English.	Rendered in Septuagint.	Rendered in Vulgate.	With what connected.
YAYIN, with disapprobation, for fruit of the vine in its artificial and fermented state, as it exists in the bottle and the cask.	Genesis, ...	19	32	wine,	οἶνον,	vino,	Incest — Lot.
	"	19	33	"	"	vinum,	
	"	19	34	"	"	"	
	"	19	35	"	οἴνῳ,	"	
	2 Samuel,...	13	28	"	οἶνος,	vino,	Murder of Ammon.
	Deut.,.......	32	33	"	"	vinum,	Poison of dragons—the mocker—drinker—astonishment—dregs — violence—drunken men—whoredom.
	Proverbs, ...	20	1	"	"	"	
	" ...	23	30	"	οἶνον,	vino,	
	Psalms, ...	60	3(5)	"	οἴνου,	"	
	"	75	8(9)	"	οἴνῳ,	vini,	
	Proverbs, ...	4	17	"	οἴνου,	vinum,	
	Jeremiah,...	23	9	"	οἶνον,	vino,	
	Hosea, ...	4	11	"	"	vinum,	
	Genesis, ...	27	25	"	οἴνου,	"	Falsehood and deception.
	Joshua,......	9	4	"	"	"	
	"	9	13	"	οἶνον,	vinarios,	
	Micah, ...	2	11	"	"	vini,	
	Amos, ...	2	8	"	"	vinum,	Wine of the condemned.

YAYIN, with disapprobation — continued as above.	Deut., ...	32	38	wine,	οἶνον,	vinum,	With idolatry—transgression.
	Habakkuk, ..	2	5	"	"	"	
	Proverbs, ...	21	17	"	"	"	Festivity, licentiousness and feasting.
	Ecclesiastes, .	2	3	"	"	vino,	
	" .	9	7	"	"	vinum,	
	Isaiah, ...	5	11	"	οἶνος,	vino,	
	"	5	12	"	οἶνον,	vinum,	
	"	5	22	"	"	"	
	"	22	13	"	"	"	
	"	56	12(13)	"	"	"	
	Hosea, ...	7	5	"	οἴνου,	vino,	
	Amos, ...	6	6	"	οἶνον,	vinum,	
	Joel, ...	3(4)	3	"	οἴνου,	vino,	
	Esther, ...	1	7	"	οἶνος,	vinum,	
	"	1	10	"	"	mero,	
	"	5	6	"	πότῳ,	vinum,	
	"	7	2	"	"	vino,	
	"	7	7	"	συμποσίου,	convivi	
	"	7	8	"	"	"	
	Leviticus, ...	10	9	"	οἶνον,	vinum,	Prohibition for priests, nazarites and Manoah.
	Ezekiel, ...	44	21	"	"	"	
	Numbers, ...	6	3	"	οἴνου,	vino,	
	Judges, ...	13	4	"	οἶνον,	vinum,	
	"	13	7	"	"	"	

YAYIN—SHECAR—SOBHE, MESECH, [WITH DISAPPROBATION.]

Terms, how used —state of fruit.	Book.	Chapter.	Verse.	Rendered in English.	Rendered in Septuagint.	Rendered in Vulgate.	With what connected.
YAYIN, with disapprobation—continued as above.	Judges,.....	13	7	wine,	οἶνον,	vinum,	Prohibition.
	"	13	14	"	οἴνου,	vinea,	
	"	13	14	"	οἴνῳ,	vinum,	
	Proverbs,...	31	44	"	οἶνον,	"	
	Amos,.....	2	12	"	"	"	Temptation to priests, Nazarites and Daniel.
	Jeremiah,...	35	2	"	"	"	
	" ...	35	5	"	"	"	
	Daniel,.....	1	5	"	οἴνου,	vino,	
	"	1	8	"	οἴνοῳ,	"	
	Jeremiah,...	35	6	"	οἶνον,	vinum,	Refusal of Rechabites and Daniel.
	" ...	35	6	"	"	"	
	" ...	35	8	"	"	"	
	" ...	35	14	"	"	"	
	Daniel,.....	1	16	"	"	"	
	"	10	3	"	οἶνος,	"	
"SHECAR."	Leviticus,...	10	9	strong drink,	σίκερα,	omne quod inebriare potest,	Prohibition to priests and Nazarites.

"SHECAR," in connection with Yayin, is used eighteen times with disapprobation for intoxicat'g drinks.	Numbers, . . .	6	3	strong drink,	σίκερα,	omne quod inebriare potest,	Prohibition to priests and Nazarites.
	" . . .	6	3	"	"	ex qualibet alia potione,	
	Judges, ...	13	4	"	μέθυσμα,	liceram,	Prohibition to the mother of Sampson.
	"	13	7	"	"	"	
	"	13	14	"	"	"	
	1 Samuel, . . .	1	15	"	μέθυσμα,	omne quod inebriare potest,	Drunkenness denied.
	Psalms, ...	69	12	drunkards,	οἱ πίνοντες, τὸν οἶνον,	qui bibevat vinum,	Drunkards.
	Proverbs, . . .	20	1	strong drink,	μέθη,	ebrietas,	Drunkenness and woe
	" . . .	31	4	"	"	"	
	Isaiah, ...	5	11	"	σίκερα,	ebrietatem,	
	"	5	22	"	"	"	
	Micah, ...	2	11	"	μέθυσμα,	"	
	Isaiah, ...	28	7	"	σίκερα,	ebrietate,	
	"	28	7	"	"	"	
	"	28	7	"	μέθμ,	"	
	"	24	9	"	σίκερα,	amara potio,	
	"	29	9	"	"	ebrietate,	
"SOBHE."	Hosea, ...	4	18	drink,	"	convivium,	Whoredom.

SOBHE—MESECH [WITH DISAPPROBATION.]

Terms, how used — state of fruit.	Book.	Chapter.	Verse.	Rendered in			With what connected.
				English.	Septuagint.	Vulgate.	
"SOBHE," and its cognates, used six times with disapprobation.	Isaiah, ...	1	22	wine,	οἶνον,	vinum,	Dross.
	Nahum, ...	1	10	drunken,		convivium pariter potantium,	Stubble.
	Deut., ...	21	20	drunkard,	οἰνοφλυγεῖ,	convivium,	
	Proverbs, ...	23	20	"	μέθυσος,	vacantes potibus,	Drunkenness.
	Isaiah, ...	56	12	fill ourselves,		impleamur ebrietate,	
"MESECH" and its cognates, used four times with disapprobation, twice with approbation.	Proverbs, ...	23	30	mixed,	πότοι,	epotandis,	Inebriety.
	Psalms, ...	75	8	mixture,	κεράσματος,	misto,	Dregs.
	Isaiah, ...	65	11	drink offering,	κέρασμα,	libatis,	Forsaking God.
	"	5	22	mingle,	κεράννυντες,	miscendam,	Inebriety.
Indifferent.	Psalms, ...	102	9	mingled,	ἐκίρνων,	miscebam,	Ashes.

WITH DISAPPROBATION OR DOUBTFUL.

Terms, how used — state of fruit.	Book.	Chapter.	Verse.	Rendered in English.	Rendered in Septuagint.	Rendered in Vulgate.	With what connected.
SHEMARIM with disapprobation.	Psalms, ...	75	8	dregs,	τρύγιας,	faex,	Dregs.
TIROSH, doubtful.	Hosea, ...	7	14	wine,	οἴνῳ,	vinum,	Corn.
YAYIN, doubtful.	Nehemiah, ..	2	1	"	οἶνος,	"	King of Babylon.
	"	2	1	"	οἶνον,	"	
	Job, ...	1	13	"	"	"	Feasting.
	"	1	18	"	"	"	
	Isaiah, ...	24	9	"	"	"	A song.
SHECAR,	"	24	9	strong drink,	σίκερα,	amara potio,	Bitterness.
YAYIN,	Haggai, ...	2	12	wine,	οἴνου,	vinum,	Oil and meat.
SHACKER with YAYIN,	Deut., ...	29	6(5)	wine and strong drink,	οἶνον καὶ σίκερα,	vinum et siceram,	Wilderness.
HAMRA,	Daniel, ...	5	1	wine,	οἶνος,	vinum,	Festivity.
	"	5	2	"	οἴνου,	"	
	"	5	4	"	οἶνον,	"	
	"	5	23	"	"	"	
HHAMAR,	Psalms, ...	75	8(9)	red,	οἴνου, ἀκράτου,	vini meri,	Dregs.
SHECKAR, good.	Numbers, ...	28	7	wine,	σίκερα,	vini,	Sacrifice.
"	Isaiah, ...	56	12	strong drink,	"	ebrietate,	Drunkenness.

LETTER

FROM

MR. DELAVAN TO GOVERNOR KING.

OFFICE NEW-YORK STATE TEMPERANCE SOCIETY,
ALBANY, N. Y., JANUARY 21ST, 1857.

To His Excellency JOHN A. KING,

Governor of the State of New-York:

DEAR SIR—Your elevation to the high and responsible station of the Chief Magistrate of the Empire State, so greatly multiplies your influence over all classes and ages of your fellow-citizens, that I confess myself desirous that your sympathies and active coöperation should be enlisted on the side of the cause of Temperance. With this motive, I take the liberty to ask you to read this communication, which cites a part of the proofs that this movement has already achieved very considerable results for the public good. I lay these facts before you with more encouragement and hope, because I am of the impression that, to statements which are honestly submitted, you will listen with candor, even when you are not prepared to endorse the reasoning and inferences which accompany them. It is by calm and kind appeals to the judgments and consciences of men, that so many, both of the humble and the great, have been brought to advocate and support the cause of Abstinence and Prohibition. And it is on such means that the friends of the cause should rely to bring distinguished public men, like your Excellency, among the number.

EFFECTS OF PROHIBITION ON CRIME IN NEW-YORK.

When some of our opponents survey the field as it is now, they say that there never was more selling in the State than at present, and that therefore all the efforts of Temperance men have wrought no good, but have made even matters worse. But this is not fair. They should revert to the period when the Prohibitory Law was in force, by which the commitments for crime in this State were reduced two-fifths from the number under the License Law. The operations of the Prohibitory Law were such, that during the six months after it came in force, there were in nine counties but 2898 commitments for crime, compared with 4960 in the same counties during the same period under the License Law. The fearful and sudden increase in drunkenness since that law was laid prostrate, so far from proving that the efforts of Temperance men are of no avail, only demonstrates the deplorable effects of thwarting those efforts. For if that law had been sustained by the Court of Appeals, as it had already been by a majority of the Judges of the Supreme Court, what a vast abatement would it by this time have wrought in Intemperance, Pauperism and Crime! And perhaps the disastrous consequences which resulted from annulling that law were necessary to work a complete conviction of the wisdom and policy of Prohibition.

But the enactment, and the temporary enforcement of the Prohibitory Law in this State, and the enactment and permanent enforcement of such a law in Connecticut, Vermont,

New Hampshire, and other States, is only one of the fruits of the Temperance Reform.

It was stated by the Executive Committee of this Society, in their Report* to the Meeting on the 18th of December, that "during the twenty-nine years since your Society was organized, such a reformation has been wrought in the habits of the civilized world as has never before been witnessed in the same length of time." I think that facts will fully bear out this statement.

LIQUORS ON THE TABLE AND SIDE-BOARD.

1. When the Temperance Reform began, thirty years ago, every family who could afford it had intoxicating liquors on the table and side-board. These included not only wine, but brandy and rum. Every guest and every caller was invited to drink, and it was about as uncivil not to drink as not to invite to drink. In this respect the usages of society have undergone a striking change. The family tables which have liquors are now the exception. In many of these cases they are furnished only when guests are present, and the liquors are almost universally limited to wines.

DRINKING USAGES AMONG FARMERS.

2. Hardly a farm in the land was worked without spirits; and such a case was a matter of remark, and was pointed to as an evidence of niggardliness in the owner. It would now be a matter of unfavorable remark, if a farmer should furnish his workmen with intoxicating liquors. Not one in a thousand, if one in ten thousand does it.

---

* See *Prohibitionist* for December, 1856, p. 90, vol. iii.

3. Every farmer, having an orchard, had a cider mill, or used his neighbor's. Cider was as plenty in the farmer's cellar, as water in his well; and it was drank in place of water by men, women and children. The falling off in the use of cider is, of itself, a striking and conclusive proof of the revolution which the Temperance Reform has wrought in the drinking usages of society.

4. Intoxicating liquors were almost universally brought into our workshops. Now, almost never.

AMONG SAILORS AND TRAVELERS.

5. Time was when nearly every merchant vessel which sailed on the ocean, the rivers or lakes, furnished spirit rations to the men. I doubt if any do so now. This change is very marked as to fishery and whaling ships; a class of facts which, a mutual friend informs me, your Excellency is well acquainted with.

6. When the ocean steamships began to cross the Atlantic, their tables were supplied with spirits as free as water. This was the case in the Great Western, when I crossed in her, in one of her earliest voyages, in 1839. When off Great Britain, the passengers held a meeting (Lord Lenox in the chair), and, to the number of one hundred and twenty, signed a petition to the owners, at Bristol, requesting them to discontinue this custom. It happened, to the undersigned, to be appointed to present said petition. I did so; and the liquors disappeared thereafter from the table. I believe every steamship now adopts the same rule.

7. At the period referred to, there was not a hotel table or steamboat table at which ardent spirits were not furnished *free*. It would have been considered as unfurnished, as if it was without bread or salt. Now there is not a public table in the land where intoxicating liquor is furnished gratuitously.

And probably not one person out of twenty, at our public tables, calls for such liquors.

REFORMATION OF THE DRUNKARD.

8. When the reform began, it was thought that moderation would save the drunkard. Since that time, even temperance advocates have supposed that the avoidance of ardent spirits would save him. Now it is pretty generally admitted, on all hands, that the drunkard is safe only when he abstains entirely from all liquors, wines included. It being admitted that abstinence is of vital consequence to the drunkard, it follows that it is the duty of others to abstain, so as not only to remove every temptation, but to strengthen him by the force of example.

9. The testimony of convicts that their crime began with drink; and of drunkards generally, that they learned the habit from their parents, or from the example of professing Christians, have united with science to impress upon all parents, and all good men, the solemn conviction that as Abstinence is the only safe practice for themselves, so it is the only proper example for others.

PUBLIC SENTIMENT AS TO THEIR HEALTHFULNESS.

10. The belief that all use of intoxicating liquors as a beverage is injurious, and never beneficial, has pretty generally taken the place of the idea that the moderate use of it is safe, and almost entirely of the error that such liquors are essential to health as a beverage.

11. Since the Temperance agitation commenced, the most eminent physicians of this and other countries have declared by thousands that intoxicating liquors are not only unnecessary as a beverage, but positively injurious. That even in sickness it is rarely necessary; while in health it is

always injurious, impairing the functions of the brain, the stomach, and indeed the whole human organism.*

IN CONNECTION WITH RELIGIOUS SOLEMNITIES.

12. Thirty years ago, liquors were brought forward as a matter of course, at weddings, at christenings, and even at funerals. After burial, the friends returned to the house of the mourners to drink. Now intoxicating liquors are the exception at weddings, seldom furnished at christenings, and almost never at funerals.

13. It used to be thought that the Bible favored the use of intoxicating liquors as a beverage. Now the idea is extensively prevalent that where the Bible approves of wine as a beverage, it means the unintoxicating wine of the cluster, the press, and the vat, while intoxicating wine is condemned as "the mocker."

14. When fifteen years ago I instituted an inquiry as to the kind of wine, intoxicating or unintoxicating, which it was proper to be used at the Communion, great numbers of church members were sorely troubled for fear of harm to the solemn rites of Religion. Very many journals, both religious

---

* Since this letter was written, the following resolution, which goes beyond any expression which has heretofore emanated from any large body of the Faculty, was passed unanimously by the Medical Society of the State of New York, 4th February, 1857:

"*Resolved*—That in view of the ravages made upon the morals, health and property of the people of this State by the use of alcoholic drinks, it is the opinion of this Medical Society that the moral, sanitary and pecuniary condition of the State would be promoted by the passage of a Prohibitory Liquor Law."

For a detailed account of this important event in the Temperance world, and which, strange to say, was not even mentioned in any newspaper report of the society's proceedings, see the *Prohibitionist* for March, 1857, vol. iv., p. 20.

and political, denounced the movement. Within a few months I have caused, on my own responsibility, some 20,000 pamphlets to be issued on the same subject, and not one word of disapprobation has yet reached me.

HABITS AND SENTIMENTS OF THE CLERGY.

15. An aged Divine, now living, well acquainted with the clergy in Albany and vicinity, once drew my attention to the fact that, some thirty years ago, every clergyman when he made his pastoral visits was invited to drink. If he visited twenty of his parishioners, he was invited to drink, and sometimes did drink, twenty times. The same Divine found that fifty per cent of the clergy, within a circuit of fifty miles, died drunkards.* Now it is only a small proportion of the clergy

* A writer in the New-York *Observer* questions the correctness of the statement of an aged clergyman in Albany to Mr. Delavan, that a minister of former days was exposed in twenty visits in a day to twenty strong drinks, and that fifty per cent of the ministers in a circuit of fifty miles were drunkards. As to the first, every man living, who was in the ministry in 1820, knows it was true. Good Dr. Fisher said, in conversing on this subject a little before his death, that it was the greatest wonder he was not a drunkard; he was in his early ministry so forced to drink, lest he should, by refusal, offend his parishioners. The mug of cider or brandy sling were brought out at every house. As to the proportion of intemperate ministers, this is, no doubt, in general, incorrect; though it was not, as can be confirmed by men living as far back as 1810, in some of our cities. And there was no reason why it should not be so. Ministers have the same flesh and blood and nerves with other men; and if they will drink poison, why should they not suffer ? "Can a minister take fire in his bosom and not be burned ? Can he walk on hot coals and his feet not be burned ?" Thanks be to Him who takes care of his church, that the ministry have been pulled from the fire; though sad it is, that some are yet trifling with it, and are boasting how strong they are.—*Journal of the American Temperance Union.*

who drink a drop; and those who do drink show themselves extremely sensitive when the fact is alluded to in print, as if they regarded it as a reflection upon their standing as Ministers of the Gospel.

16. It is thirty years since, at a large assembly of the Ministers of the Gospel, in New England, one of their number, impressed with the evils of the Drink-System, urged them to adopt a resolution pledging themselves to abstain—not from wines—but from Ardent Spirits, while at the convention. It failed. These pious and devoted clergymen could not see why they should be called upon to give up a "good creature of God." Now there are vast religious bodies, who, were they to see one of their ministers drink intoxicating liquors, would be affected almost as much as if they were to hear him swear.

FASHION—THE PRESS.

17. Though few of the rich and fashionable have openly professed adherence to the Temperance cause, yet many now express their sympathy with it and are beginning to aid it pecuniarily, as a movement which inures to the public good. Many of our most distinguished citizens have lately given large social entertainments without wine; and this is not so significant, as that public opinion sustains and applauds it.

18. There was a time when the Temperance movement was the common theme of ridicule with the press. Now there are but few journals, even those which are opposed to Prohibition, which do not approve voluntary abstinence, and which do not compliment private citizens, or public bodies, who give entertainments without intoxicating liquors.

19. The spirit-ration has been abolished in the army. I am of the impression too that it has been diminished in the navy.

MANUFACTURING ESTABLISHMENTS.

20. Before the Temperance Reform began, and while we were ignorant of the nature and effects of strong drink, Nathaniel Prime, Lynde Catlin, and others, myself among the number, formed a chartered company, with a capital of $300,000, for the manufacture of steam engines and other heavy iron work. Thinking to do good to the workmen, and further the objects of the company, we directed that strong beer should be passed, gratis, to every man two or three times a day. We soon found that our work was badly done, almost every contract was in consequence litigated in the courts, and the company failed; by which failure the company not only sunk the whole capital of $300,000, but (to save their own credit) ten of the stockholders contributed ten thousand dollars each, to pay off further liabilities, of which eight thousand dollars of my contribution (including my whole stock) proved a dead loss. On a review of the whole subject, I firmly believe that this catastrophe is mainly ascribable to the unfortunate drinking habits which, from the best of motives, we ourselves encouraged.

21. Another company, formed to manufacture nearly the same kind of article, and who employed about 100 workmen, had their attention drawn to the evils of strong drink among operatives. One of the partners drew up a Total Abstinence Pledge, signed it, and induced nearly every workman to adopt the same principle. When the step was taken, hardly one of the workmen was beforehand in the world, and many were in debt. After four years upon the Temperance principle, none were in debt, and many had bought lots of land, and erected cottages for their families; and one of the partners told me that the aggregate amount saved by these 100 men during the four years since they abandoned strong

drink, would make capital enough to carry on the business operations of the company.

EFFECTS OF THE REFORM ON NATIONAL WEALTH.

22. A manufacturer who employed 300 hands, informed me that after they all, or nearly all, adopted the Total Abstinence principle, the prosperity of the establishment was vastly promoted, and that their improved steadiness, fidelity and style of workmanship were as good to him as a protective duty of twenty-five per cent. At this rate, what sums have accrued to the National wealth from the adoption of Temperance principles by the hundreds of thousands of abstainers!

23. The late Abbott Lawrence, that merchant prince and public benefactor, and late United States Minister to the Court of St. James, was asked, before he died, what had occasioned the great increase in wealth and prosperity in the United States? He instantly replied: "Our prosperity, in my opinion, is greatly owing to the Temperance Reformation. The influence of this movement is felt in the work-shop, on the farm, and in every branch of human industry. Before the Temperance Reform was started, a vast number of the farms in New England were mortgaged for rum bills,—now hardly one."

24. Until the subject of Temperance was agitated, the frauds of the liquor traffic were not suspected. All liquors were supposed to be what they pretended to be. Now the matter of adulteration, though but partially understood yet, is the theme of common conversation even among drinkers.

25. When the Temperance Reform commenced in this State there were about 1100 flour mills, and more than that number of distilleries. The population has about doubled since that time, and now there are 1464 flour mills and only 88 distilleries. It must be admitted, however, that the

distilleries now in operation are on a much larger scale than the average of those of the former period.

CLASSES OF DEALERS WHO HAVE LEFT THE TRAFFIC.

26. Of the great number of native citizens in the United States who used to sell intoxicating liquors, a vast number have left the business. The Temperance agitation has *educated* them to regard the traffic as immoral and degrading. It is found in the great cities that seven out of eight of all who sell liquor are foreign emigrants. The great majority of those who now sell liquor in America are a proof, not that the Temperance Reform does nothing, but of what the moral sense of our countrymen would have been on this subject, at this time, had this Reform never been agitated.

27. Formerly, church members and church officers of all our churches used to be engaged in the traffic; now, vast bodies of them denounce the traffic as an immorality; and the number of church members, American born citizens, who make or sell liquor, is probably not one to five hundred of the former proportion.

28. Witness, as a proof of the effects of the Temperance Reform, the growing idea that liquor when offered for sale, as a beverage, is a nuisance to be abated like any other nuisance.

29. What but the Temperance agitation has changed the policy of so many States; substituting laws aiming at Prohibition, in the place of laws which allowed rum to be sold by the authority of the State?

PROHIBITION APPLIED TO THE DRUNKARD.

30. Not only is the moderation theory now abandoned, and Total Abstinence held to be essential to the refor-

mation of the drunkard, but Physicians,* Clergymen and Judges agree that Asylums should be established by the State for the resort of inebriates, where no strong drinks can be procured—which, as far as the drunkard is concerned (of whom there are over 50,000 in the State of New-York), is an emphatic endorsement of the humanity and necessity of prohibition. The advocates of Temperance extend the same principle, and by a general enactment, prohibiting the sale of liquors throughout the State, aim to remove the temptation from all who have this habit partially formed, as well as those who have it fully formed, and so, by the united influence of moral and legal suasion, aim to create such *an asylum in every household in the land.*

These facts and illustrations might be greatly extended, but I forbear. Enough has been said to indicate a vast improvement in the drinking usages of society.

THE NEXT STEP IN THE REFORM.

But it will be said, if the Temperance agitation has done so much, why not go right on in the old way, without a resort to legislation. The same question might be asked of gambling, of lotteries and of duelling. A stage is at last reached, where legislative enactments are essential. Not that moral suasion is to be abandoned, but, in addition to this, the public sentiment regarding these evils must be embodied into statutory enactments. Of this, those who have used moral suasion most, and with the greatest success, are the most

---

* The following resolution was adopted by the Medical Society of the State of New-York, on the 4th of February, 1817:

"*Resolved*, That this Society commend the object sought to be attained by the project for an Asylum for Inebriates, to the favor and earnest support, not only of the Legislature of the State but to the public at large."

profoundly convinced. After obtaining millions of signatures to the Total Abstinence Pledge, Ireland was ripe for Prohibition. But it was not applied. The golden opportunity was lost; and the consequence is, that nearly as much liquor is drank in Ireland, now as before Father Mathew commenced his remarkable labors. The language of this beloved and renowned Apostle of Temperance, penned a year or two before his death, and published in the *Prohibitionist* for July, 1855, should teach a solemn lesson to the world on the subject of Temperance:

"The question of prohibiting the sale of ardent spirits, and the many other intoxicating drinks which are to be found in our country, is not new to me; the principle of Prohibition seems to me *to be the only safe and certain remedy for the evils of Intemperance. This opinion has been strengthened and confirmed by the hard labor of more than twenty years in the Temperance cause.* I rejoice in the welcome intelligence of the formation of a Maine Law Alliance, which I trust will be the means under God of destroying this fruitful source of Crime and Pauperism."

The friends of Prohibition in Great Britain are now making up for lost time; they are pressing on steadily, firmly and perseveringly, and the triumph of Prohibition is only a question of time.

OUGHT NOT EVERY GOOD MAN TO COÖPERATE?

When the Temperance Societies began, the general view of religious men was, that the work should be done through the churches. I submit that, in the main, what has been done, *has* been done by the churches. The Temperance Reform originated in the churches. If I may refer to myself in this connection, it was a devout and learned minister of the Gospel who converted me to the movement. If, since that time, I have been enabled to do more in my way than some of my fellow citizens, it is only because Providence has placed me in circumstances to do so. But it is the fervent, effectual prayer of the righteous, and the widow's mite, offered in faith, which points to the secret of the success of Temperance. Nor can I ever review the history of this benign and arduous enterprise without being deeply and profoundly penetrated with the conviction, that the great motive power, from the first and always, has been the Grace and Spirit of Almighty God, as shed abroad in the hearts of thousands of His pious servants, both men and women, and who are to be found in all religious denominations throughout the Christian world.

It is the religious sentiment of the country; it is the divine principle of self-denial, taught by our blessed Savior, which has wrought whatever has been done for this reform, and which I have ever regarded as the handmaid of Religion. There are good men who still think this work should be restricted to the churches, or perhaps to their own particular church. I put it to their hearts, would they go back to where we were thirty years ago? Would they have undone what has been done? And ought not every believer in Christianity, to whatever particular church he may belong, to unite as one man—in pressing forward with yet greater vigor, with the united energy of faith and prayer and works, by his example, his influence, and by contributions of his substance—the cause of personal Abstinence and legislative Prohibition? And if this is true of the Christian in private life, how important to the poor drunkard, to his wife, his children, and the whole community, do such duties become, when, as in the case of your Excellency, the private citizen is clothed by the people with great authority and official power! So sacred and important are the interests at stake, and so great is now your Excellency's influence for good, that I feel that I have not exceeded the privilege of your humblest fellow-citizen in attempting to enlist your personal and official coöperation on the side of a cause which has been so signally approved and blessed of God, and which redounds so palpably to the physical, the moral and the religious interests of the human family.

I remain, with great respect, your Excellency's friend and obedient servant,

EDWARD C. DELAVAN,
President New-York State Temperance Society.

ADULTERATION OF LIQUORS.

Since the foregoing Lectures were written, in one of which the adulteration of liquors was exposed, that nefarious practice has made prodigious strides, and it has been thought desirable that the later developments of this great fraud upon the American people and the world should find a place in this work, and President NOTT has suggested that we add some extracts, bearing upon this point, from the address of E. C. DELAVAN, made at the meeting of the New-York State Temperance Society, at the Capitol, Albany, 16th June, 1857.

"I have long known the fact that arsenic was employed in the manufacture of whiskey, and the reason why. Ever since the year 1833, I have been aware of the horrid adulterations that have been practiced in the manufacture of alcoholic drinks, rendering the same, by the addition of intense poisons, still more injurious to property, virtue, reason and life, of which I have never from that year ceased warning the public. My facts have been, in all cases, obtained from the manufacturers themselves, generally after they have abandoned the murderous business. The profit made has been enormous. In one case an individual engaged in the manufacture and sale, assured me that his sales in a single year amounted to 33,000 barrels, the average cost to him being about eighteen cents per gallon, while he sold it at a rate varying from fifty cents to five dollars the gallon.

"I have not known until recently of the use of that deadly poison, strychnine, in the manufacture of whiskey. This is described as endowed with a greater amount of destructive energy than any other poison except prussic acid. One-third of a grain killed a hog in ten minutes. It first produces agitation and trembling; these run into a general spasm, in which the head is bent back, the spine stiffened, the limbs extended and rigid, and the respiration interrupted by the fixing of the chest. So powerful are the spasms, that the body sometimes retains, for some hours after death, the attitude and expression impressed on it by their terrible action during life.

"This fearfully destructive agent is used for the same purpose as arsenic, and is, to a great extent, a substitute for it, the great object being the largest amount of whiskey out of the least quantity of grain; and whether it kills men, hogs or fishes, it makes but little difference with the distiller, so long as he can accumulate a fortune by its sale.

"I quote from an article recently published in the *Tribune:*

"'The use of strychnine in the manufacture of whiskey is henceforth to be punished as a felony in Ohio. By means of this drug, used in connection with tobacco, sharp distillers were making five gallons of whiskey from one bushel of grain, whereas the quantity obtained by the old process was but half so much. The topers never complained of the new liquid, but swallowed all they could get, and then smacked their lips for more; but the hogs, not being so case-hardened, could not stand it, and died off by hundreds of what is called "Hog Cholera." The fish, too, in the rivers into which the refuse of the distilleries was drained, began to die off in shoals; and a chemist reported that a barrel of this strychnine whiskey contained poison enough to kill twenty men. (So does a barrel of *any* whiskey, if administered to produce that result.) Ohio could not bear to have the quality of her poison distrusted, and so has made the use of strychnine, in whiskey, a state prison offence. Making the whiskey without strychnine is not even declared a misdemeanor as yet.'

"We all know that whiskey is the basis of the wine, brandy and gin now sold in the country, whether imported or domestic, the grape having in a great measure failed in wine producing countries. The demand for wines having increased, the resort has been to the distillery and poisonous preparations, to supply its place. And so the grains of the earth, which God designed for food, are laid under contribution for its production. Ohio, the great grain-producing state, answers the call, and her distillers worm it through their thousand distilleries. But they are not content to furnish the pure alcoholic poison. They call upon the druggist, and by means of strychnine and the decoction of tobacco, double the effect, by thus doubling the poison. This abominable compound is exported abroad, but is soon returned with such ingredients as foreign ingenuity can devise, and after paying duties abroad as whiskey, and at home under the names of wine and brandy, is sold at enormous profit, and drank by all classes. So extensively was adulteration practiced in France, that the Rev. Dr. Baird stated that certain persons appointed by government to test the purity of liquors by tasting, were compelled to resign, to escape from death by poisoning. And yet, these are the *pure* wines and brandies that circulate so freely through the higher circles, the only evidence of their purity consisting in the extravagant prices charged and paid for them.

"But the useless formality of sending across the ocean is often dispensed with. There exists ingenuity on this as well as on the other side of the water. This same Ohio whiskey is purchased in New-York and other large cities, where it is easily transformed into imported liquors, and sold as such often with the brands of the most celebrated dealers.

"So alarmingly extensive is the evil becoming, that the political press of all parties is sending out its voice of warning; and, in no measured terms, condemning and denouncing this wholesale poisoning of the people by the makers and vendors of these abominable compounds. We rejoice to see these evidences of moral life in the political press; we hail them as proofs that it is still mindful of its duty as a sentinel on the outposts of danger. We welcome it as a co-worker with us in this moral reform; for there clearly can be no perfect escape from these poisonous compounds, except in the adoption and enforcement of the prohibitory principle.

"I have called your attention to these enormous evils, now becoming so generally known and acknowledged, for the purpose of showing what kind of substances our legislature have legalized the sale of by the license law.

"It must be apparent to all that there is but one mode of escape, that of total abstinence, succeeded by prohibition. It is idle to waste time or thought upon any half and half measures.

"But while dwelling upon these adulterations and their enormity, we ought not to forget that alcohol itself, in these liquors, is an active poison, and that the other poisons added, only render the compound the more poisonous. Our warfare commenced against alcohol alone; we supposed all liquors pure, but that their very purity was poisonous as a beverage.

"All medical works pronounce alcohol itself a poison, and, like others, dangerous to health and life. The dark array of adulterations and poisonous compounds have come in since, but they have come only to stimulate us to stronger efforts and more determined perseverance to free the state and the nation from this monstrous iniquity; and in view of these horrid adulterations, and the miseries they are inflicting upon us—demoralizing the people, as well as rapidly deteriorating our race—should not all, of whatever denomination of Christians, or whatever party, having the love of God or man in their hearts, arouse themselves and unite with us in our efforts to arrest and finally eradicate this great and growing evil? The question of the rightfulness of using pure intoxicating liquors as a beverage should no longer be a barrier—for none such, with the least degree of certainty, can be had."

ADDRESS ON THE DRINKING USAGES OF SOCIETY.

BY A. POTTER, D. D., LL. D.,

Bishop of the Diocese of Pennsylvania.

WE have assembled, ladies and gentlemen, to contribute our aid in arresting a great and crying evil. We do not aim to promote directly that Temperance which forms one of the noblest and most comprehensive of the Christian virtues. Our simple object is to prevent drunkenness, with its legion of ills, by drying up the principal sources from which it flows. To one of these sources, and that the most active and powerful, I propose to ask your attention this evening. The occasion, I need not say, is a most worthy one; one that merits the warmest sympathy and support of every patriot and philanthropist, of every follower of Jesus Christ.

For what is intemperance, and what the extent and magnitude of its evils? Of these we all know something. We all know how it diseases the body; how it disturbs the equilibrium of the intellect; how it poisons the springs of generous affection in the heart, and lays a ruthless hand upon the whole moral and spiritual nature. What drunkenness does to its poor victim, and to those who are bound to him by the closest ties, you all know. All know, did I say? Let us thank God that few of you can know, or are likely to know, the inexpressible horrors which fill the soul of the inebriate, or the gloom and anguish of heart which are the portion of his family. You know enough, however, to feel that where this sin enters, there a blight falls on happiness, virtue and even hope. Look at the palpable shame and misery and guilt which collect within and about one drunkard's home; and then multiply their dreadful sum by the whole number of such homes which, at this moment, can be found in this Christian city, and you will have an accumulation of sin and sorrow, even at your doors, which no mortal arithmetic can guage, but which is sufficient to appal the stoutest heart and move to sympathy the coldest charity.

But whence does this vast and hideous evil come? To you, as a jury of inquest, standing over the victims it strikes down, I appeal for a verdict according to truth and evidence. Can it be said that they who are now cold in death, with a drunkard's shame branded on their memory, "died by visitation of God?" God sends no such curse even upon the guiltiest of his creatures. He may send pestilence and earthquake; he may send blasting and mildew; but he commissions no moral plague, like drunkenness, to carry desolation to the souls as well as bodies of men. This evil, alas! is self-invoked and self-inflicted.

And how? Do men rush deliberately, and with full purpose of heart, into such an abyss? Is there any one so lost to self-respect, to all prudence and duty, so devoid of every finer instinct and sentiment of our nature, that he can willingly sink down to the ignominy and the wo that are the drunkard's portion? I tell you nay. Every human being recoils, with involuntary horror and disgust, from the contemplation of such a fate. He shrinks from it as he would from the foul embraces of a serpent, and feels that he would sooner sacrifice everything than take his place beside the bloated and degraded beings who seem dead to all that is noble in our nature or hopeful in our lot. These are victims that have gone blindfold to their fate. Gentle is the declivity, smooth and noiseless the descent, which conducts them, step by step, along the treacherous way, till suddenly their feet slide, and they find themselves plunging over the awful precipice.

And what is that deceitful road? Or which is the perfidious guide who stands ever ready to turn aside the feet of the unwary traveler? Here, ladies and gentlemen, is the great question. To arrest an evil effectually, we mnst know its nature and cause. It is idle to lop off branches, while the trunk stands firm and full of life. It is idle to destroy noxious leaves or flowers, while the plant still pours forth its malignant humors at the root. If we would go to the bottom of this evil, if we would lay the axe to the very root of the baleful tree, we must see how and whence it is that unsuspecting multitudes are thus ensnared, never scenting danger till they begin to taste of death.

It will be admitted, I presume, by all who hear me, that, if there were no temperate drinking, there would be none that is intemperate. Men do not begin by what is usually called immoderate indulgences, but by that which they regard as moderate. Gradually and insensibly their draughts are increased, until the functions of life are permanently disturbed, the system becomes inflamed, and there is that morbid appetite which will hardly brook restraint, and the indulgence of which is sottish intemperance. Let it be remembered, then, that what is usually styled *temperate* drinking, stands as the condition precedent of that which is *intemperate.* Discontinue one and the other becomes impossible.

But what is the cause of moderate or temperate drinking? Is it the force of natural appetite? Rarely. Nine-tenths, if not ninety-nine hundredths, of those who use alcoholic stimulants, do it, in the first instance, and often for a long time, *not from appetite, but from deference to custom or fashion.* Usage has associated intoxicating drinks with good fellowship —with offices of hospitality and friendship. However false and dangerous such an association may be, it is not surprising that, when once established, it continually gathered strength; with some through appetite, with others through interest. It is in this way that what we term *Drinking Usages* have become incorporated with every pursuit in life, with the tastes and habits of every grade and class of society. In the drawing-room and dining-room of the affluent, in the public room of the hotel, in every place of refreshment, in the social gatherings of the poor, in the harvest field and the workshop, alcoholic liquor was at one time deemed essential. Too often it is deemed so still. Many a host and employer, many a young companion, shrinks even now from the idea of exchanging the kind offices of life without the aid of intoxicating liquors, as he would shrink from some sore offence against taste and propriety. Not to put the cup to your neighbor's lip, in one word, is to sin against that most absolute of earthly sovereigns, fashion.

Here, then, lies the gist of the whole difficulty. Fashion propagates itself downward. Established and upheld by the more refined and opulent, it is soon caught up by those in less conspicuous walks. It thus spreads itself over the whole face of society, and, becoming allied with other principles, is planted deep in the habits and associations of a people. It is preëminently so with *drinking usages*. Immemorial custom; the example of those whose education or position gives them a commanding sway over the opinions and practice of others; appetite, with them who have drunk till what was once but compliance with usage, is now an imperious craving; the interest of many, who thrive by the traffic in intoxicating drinks, or by the follies into which they betray men — here are causes which so fortify and strengthen these usages, that they seem to defy all change. But let us not despair. We address those who are willing to think, and who are accustomed to bring every question to the stern test of utility and duty. To these, then, we appeal.

Drinking usages are the chief cause of intemperance; and these usages derive their force and authority, in the first instance, wholly from those who give law to fashion. Let this be considered. Do you ask for the treacherous guide, who, with winning smiles and honeyed accents, leads men forward from one degree of indulgence to another, till they are besotted and lost? Seek him not in the purlieus of the low grog-shop; seek him not in any scenes of coarse and vulgar revelry. He is to be found where they meet who are the observed of all observers. There, in the abodes of the rich and admired; there, amidst all the enchantments of luxury and elegance; where friend pledges friend; where wine is invoked to lend new animation to gaiety and impart new brilliancy to wit; in the sparkling glass, which is raised even by the hand of beautiful and lovely woman, there is the most dangerous decoy. Can that be unsafe which is thus associated with all that is fair and graceful in woman, with all that is attractive and brilliant in man? Must not that be proper and even obligatory, which has the deliberate and time-honored sanction of those who stand before the world as the "glass of fashion," and "rose of the fair state?"

Thus reason the great proportion of men. They are looking continually to those who, in their estimation, are more favored of fortune or more accomplished in mind and manners. We do not regulate our watches more carefully or more universally by the town clock, than do nine-tenths of mankind take their tone from the residue, who occupy places towards which all are struggling.

Let the responsibiltty of these drinking usages be put, then, where it justly belongs. When you visit, on some errand of mercy, the abodes of the poor and afflicted; when you look in on some home which has been made dark by drunkenness,—where hearts are desolate and hearths are cold; where want is breaking in as an armed man; where the wife is heart-broken or debased, and children are fast demoralizing; where little can be heard but ribaldry, blasphemy and obscenity,—friends! would you connect effect with cause, and trace this hideous monster back to its true parent, let your thoughts fly away to some abode of wealth and refinement, where conviviality reigns; where, amidst joyous greetings and friendly protestations, and merry shouts, the flowing bowl goes round; and there you will see that which is sure to make drinking everywhere attractive, and which, in doing so, never fails, and cannot fail, to make drunkenness common.

Would we settle our account, then, with the *drinking usages of the refined and respectable?* We must hold them answerable for maintaining corresponding usages in other classes of society; and we must hold them answerable, further, for the frightful amount of intemperance which results from those usages. We must hold them accountable for all the sin, and all the unhappiness, and all the pinching poverty, and all the nefarious crimes to which intemperance gives rise. So long as these usages maintain their place among the respectable, so long will drinking and drunkenness abound through all grades and conditions of life. Neither the power of law aimed at the traffic in liquors, nor the force of argument addressed to the understandings and consciences of the many, will ever prevail to cast out the fiend drunkenness, so long as they who are esteemed the favored few uphold with unyielding hand, the practice of drinking.

Hence, the question, whether this monster evil shall be abated, resolves itself always into another question; and that is: will the educated, the wealthy, the respectable, persist in sustaining the usages which produce it? Let them resolve that these usages shall no longer have their countenance, and their insidious power is broken. Let them resolve that, wherever they go, the empty wine glass shall proclaim their silent protest; and fashion, which now commands us to drink, shall soon command us, with all-potential voice, to abstain.

Now, what is there in these usages to entitle them to the patronage of the wise and good? Are they necessary? Are they safe or useful?

Unless they can show some offset to the vast amount of evil which they occasion, they ought surely to be ruled out of court. But is any one prepared to maintain that these Drinking Usages are *necessary*—that it is necessary, or even *useful*, that men should use intoxicating liquors as a beverage? Do they add vigor to muscle, or strength to intellect, or warmth to the heart, or rectitude to the conscience? The experience of thousands, and even millions, has answered this question. In almost every age and quarter of the world, but especially within the last twenty-five years, and in our own land, many have made trial of entire abstinence from all that can intoxicate. How few of them will confess that they have suffered from it, either in health of body, or elasticity of spirits, or energy and activity of mind! How many will testify that in each of these respects they were sensible gainers from the time they renounced the use of all alcoholic stimulants!

But, if neither useful or necessary, can it be contended that these drinking customs are harmless? Are they not *expensive?* Many a moderate drinker, did he reckon up accurately the cost of this indulgence, would discover that it forms one of his heaviest burdens. No taxes, says Franklin, are so oppressive* as those which men levy on themselves. Appetite and fashion, vanity and ostentation, constitute our most rapacious tax-gatherers. It is computed by Mr. Porter, an English statistician of distinguished ability, but of no special interest in the subject which we are now discussing, that the *laboring people* of Great Britain, exclusive of the middle or higher classes, expend no less than £53,000,000 ($250,000,000) every year on alcoholic liquors and tobacco! There is little doubt that the amount directly or indirectly consumed in

---

* "My companion at the press," says Franklin, speaking of his life as a journeyman printer in London, "drank every day a pint before breakfast, a pint at breakfast, with his bread and cheese, a pint between breakfast and dinner, a pint at dinner, a pint in the afternoon about six o'clock, and another when he had done his day's work. I thought it a detestable custom; but it was necessary, he supposed, to drink *strong* beer, that he might be *strong* to labor. I endeavored to convince him that the bodily strength afforded by beer could only be in proportion to the grain or flour dissolved in the water of which it was made; that there was more flour in a pennyworth of bread; and, therefore, if he could eat that with a pint of water, it would give him more strength than a quart of beer. He drank on, however, and had four or five shillings to pay out of his wages every Saturday night for that vile liquor, — an expense which I was free from; *and thus these poor devils keep themselves always under.*"—*See Dr. Franklin's Life, written by himself.*

Pennsylvania* annually for the same indulgence equals $10,000,000,—a sum which, could it be saved for four successive years, would pay the debt which now hangs like an incubus on the energies of the Commonwealth. In wasting $250,000,000 every year, the laboring population of Britain put it beyond the power of any government to avert from multitudes of them the miseries of want. Were but a tithe of that sum wrenched from the hands of toil-worn labor, and buried in the Thames or the ocean, we should all regard it as an act of stupendous folly and guilt. Yet it were infinitely better that such a sum should be cast into the depths of the sea than that it should be expended in a way which must debauch the morals, and destroy the health, and lay waste the personal and domestic happiness of thousands. If the question be narrowed down to one of mere *material wealth*, no policy can be more suicidal than that which upholds usages, the inevitable effect of which is to paralyze the *productive* powers of a people, and to derange the proper and natural *distribution* of property. Remember, then, he who sustains these usages sustains the most prolific source of improvidence and want. He makes, at the same time, an inroad upon his own personal income, which is but a loan from God, entrusted to him for his own and others' good.

But these drinking usages are not only expensive; *they are unreasonable.* What is their practical effect? It is that others shall decide for us a question, which ought most clearly to be referred only to our own taste and sense of duty. We are to drink, whether it be agreeable to us or

---

* In Western Pennsylvania, one of the most valuable products is bituminous coal. Great quantities are sent down the Ohio, and are paid for in whiskey. I was informed by a distinguished citizen of that part of the state, that every year shows a balance against the producers of coal, and in favor of the distillers!

not; whether we think it right or not; whether we think it safe or not. Moreover—and this is sufficiently humiliating—we are to drink precisely *when*, and precisely *where*, others prescribe. It has been said that, in some parts of our country, one must either drink with a man who invites him or fight. It is not long since, in every part of it, one must either drink, when invited, or incur the frowns and jeers of those who claimed to be arbiters of propriety. And, even now, he or she who will not drink at all, or will drink only when their own reason and inclination bid, must not be surprised if they provoke invective or ridicule. And is a bondage like this to be upheld? Does it become free born Americans, who boast so much of liberty, to bow down their necks to a servitude so unrelenting, and yet so absurd?

A German nobleman once paid a visit to Great Britain, when the practice of toasting and drinking healths was at its height. Wherever he went, during a six months' tour, he found himself obliged to drink, though never so loth. He must pledge his host and his hostess. He must drink with every one who would be civil to him, and with every one, too, who wished a convenient pretext for taking another glass. He must drink a bumper in honor of the king and queen, in honor of church and state, in honor of the army and navy. How often did he find himself retiring with throbbing temples and burning cheek from these scenes of intrusive hospitality! At length his visit drew to a close; and to requite, in some measure, the attentions which had been lavished upon him, he made a grand entertainment. Assembling those who had done him honor, he gathered them round a most sumptuous banquet, and feasted them to their utmost content. The tables were then cleared. Servants entered with two enormous hams; one was placed at each end; slices were cut and passed round to each guest, when the host rose, and with all gravity said: "Gentlemen, I give you the king! please eat to his honor." His guests protested. They had dined; they were Jews; they were already surcharged through his too generous cheer. But he was inflexible. "Gentlemen," said he, "for six months you have compelled me to *drink* at your bidding. Is it too much that you should now *eat* at mine? I have been submissive: why should you not follow my example? You will please do honor to your king! You shall then be served with another slice in honor of the queen, another to the prosperity of the royal family, and so on to the end of the chapter."

But, waiving the *absurdity* and *costliness* of these usages, let me ask if they are *safe*. No one who drinks can be perfectly certain that he may not die a drunkard. Numbers, which defy all computation, have gone this road, who were once as self-confident as any of us can be. No one, again, who drinks, can be certain that he may not, in some unguarded hour, fall into a debauch, in which he shall commit some error or perpetrate some crime that will follow him, with shame and sorrow, all his days. How many a young man, by one such indiscretion, has cast a cloud over all his prospects for life! You have read Shakspeare's "Othello," the most finished and perfect, perhaps, of all his tragedies. What is it but a solemn Temperance lecture? Whence come all the horrors that cluster round the closing scenes of that awful and magnificent drama? Is it not from the wine with which Iago plied Cassio? What is Iago himself but a human embodiment of the Great Master of Evil? And, as that Master goes abroad over the earth seeking whom he may destroy, where does he find a more potent instrument than the treacherous wine cup? This dark tragedy, with its crimes and sorrows, is but an epitome, a faint transcript, of ten thousand tragedies which are all the time enacting on the theatre of our daily life. How many are there at this moment, who, from the depths of agonized and remorseful hearts, can echo the words of Othello's sobered but almost frenzied lieutenant, "O thou invisible spirit of wine! if thou hast no name to be known by, let us call thee devil!" "That men should put an enemy in their mouths to steal away their brains! That we should, with joy, pleasance, revel and applause, transform ourselves into beasts!" "Oh! I have lost my reputation! I have lost the immortal part of myself, and what remains is bestial,—my reputation, Iago, my reputation!" "To be now a sensible man, by and by a fool, and presently a beast! O strange! Every inordinate cup is unblessed, and the ingredient is a devil." In this land, and in our day, there are few cups which, for the young and excitable, are not "inordinate." Wines that are charged high with brandy, or brewed in the distillery of some remorseless fabricator, are never safe. Among wine proverbs, there are two which are now more than ever significant of truth: "The most voluptuous of assassins is the bottle;" "Bacchus has drowned more than Neptune."

It is not the opinion of "temperance fanatics" merely, that adjudges drinking to be *hazardous*. It is so in their estimation, who are close, practical observers and actors in life. Mr. Jefferson is said to have expressed his conviction—the result of long and various experience—that no man should be entrusted with office who drank. I have now before me evidence, still more definite, in the two-fold system of rates proposed to be applied in one of our largest cities by the same life insurance company. The one set of rates is adapted to those who use intoxicating liquors; the other, to those who do not use them at all. Suppose that you wish your life to be assured to the extent of $1000, and that you are twenty years of age. If you practice total abstinence, the rate will be $11.60 per annum; if you use intoxicating drinks, it will be $14.70. At twenty-five years of age, the rates will be as $13.30 to $17; at thirty years of age, as

$15.40 to $19.60. I have also before me the returns of two beneficial societies, in one of which the principle of total abstinence from all intoxicating liquors was observed, while in the other it was not. The result has been that, with the same number of members in each, the deaths in one, during a given period, were but *seventy-seven;* whereas, in the other, they were *one hundred and ten!* making the chances of life as ten to seven in their favor who practice *total abstinence.* This result need not so much astonish us, when we are told, on the authority of persons who are said to have made careful and conscientious inquiry, that, of all males who use intoxicating liquors, one in thirteen becomes intemperate.

Here, then, are results reached by men of business, when engaged in a mere calculation of probabilities. Drinking, according to their estimates, is hazardous—hazardous to life and property, hazardous to reputation and virtue. Is it not wise, then, to shun that hazard? Is it not our duty? Is not this a case in which the Savior's injunction applies: "*If thy right eye offend thee, pluck it out and cast it from thee; if thy right hand offend thee, cut it off and cast it from thee; for it is better for thee that one of thy members should perish, than that thy whole body should be cast into hell fire?*" We all consider it madness not to protect our children and ourselves against small-pox by vaccination; and this, though the chances of dying by the disease may be but one in a thousand, or one in ten thousand. Drunkenness is a disease more loathsome and deadly even than small-pox. Its approaches are still more stealthy; and the specific against it—total abstinence—has never failed, and cannot fail.

But let us admit for one moment, and for the sake of argument (to admit it on other ground would be culpable)—let us admit that *you can drink with safety to yourself. Can you drink with safety to your neighbor?* Are you charged with no responsibility in respect to him? You drink, as you think, within the limits of safety. He, in imitation of your example, drinks also, but passes that unseen, unknown line, within which, for him, safety lies. Is not your indulgence, then, a stumbling-block—ay, perchance, a fatal stumbling-block in his way? Is it not, in principle, the very case contemplated by St. Paul, when he said: "*It is good neither to eat flesh,* NOR TO DRINK WINE, *nor anything whereby thy brother stumbleth or is offended, or is made weak?*" Yonder are the young and inexperienced, without habits of self-control, and with fiery appetites. Would you have them do as you do? Yonder is one who is just on the verge of the precipice that will plunge him into shame and wo unutterable; are you willing that he should find in your daily potations a specious apology for his own? Or yonder is one who is already a bondman to this fearful vice, but who feels his debasement, and would gladly be once more free; will you do that in his presence which will discourage him from striking boldly for emancipation? Nay, it may be that he is even now struggling bravely to be free. He has dashed away the cup of sorcery, and is practicing that which, to him, is the only alternative to ruin. Is it well, Christian—follower of Him who sought not his own, and went about doing good—is it well that from *you* should proceed an influence to press him back to his cups?—that *you*, by your example, should proclaim, that not to drink is to be over scrupulous and mean spirited?—that at *your* table, in *your* drawing-room, he should encounter the fascination which he finds it so hard to withstand, so fatal to yield to?

Nineteen years ago, I knew an instructor who stood in relations most intimate to three hundred students of a college. The disorders which occasionally invade such institutions, and the disgrace and ruin which are incurred by so many promising young men, result almost exclusively from the use of intoxicating liquors. This fact had so imprinted itself on this instructor's mind, that he made a strenuous effort to induce the whole of this noble band to declare for that which was then considered the true principle—total abstinence from *distilled* spirits. Fermented stimulants were not included; but it was pointedly intimated that intoxication on wine or beer would be a virtual violation of the engagement. The whole number, with perhaps two or three exceptions, acquiesced; and, for a few months, the effect was most marked in the increased order of the institution and the improved bearing of its inmates. Soon, however, there were aberrations. Young men would resort occasionally to hotels, and drink champagne; or they would indulge in beer at eating-houses. The evil which, at one time, seemed dammed out, was about to force itself back; and the question arose, what could be done? Then that professor came to the conclusion that, for these young men at least, there was no safety but in abstinence from *all* intoxicating liquors. He had often protested against including wine in the same category with ardent spirits. But the wine these young men drank was as fatal to them and to college discipline as rum; and the simple alternative was between continued excesses, on the one hand, or total abstinence from all intoxicating beverage, on the other. Under such circumstances, this professor did not long hesitate. He determined to urge and exhort those for whose welfare he was so fearfully responsible, to the only course which was safe for them. But there was one huge difficulty in his way. It was the bottle of Madeira which stood every day upon his own table. He felt that, from behind that bottle, his plea in behalf of abstinence from all vinous potations would sound somewhat strangely. He was not ready to encounter the appeal from theory to practice, which all are so prompt to make—none more prompt than the young—when they deal with the teachers of unwholesome doctrine. He determined, therefore, to prepare himself for his duty, by removing every hindrance which his own example could place in the way of the impression which he was bent upon producing. Did he act well and wisely? Ye fathers and mothers, who know with what perils the young are encompassed when they go forth into the world, would you have advised him to cling to his wine? Or you, who may be about to commit a fiery and unstable son to a teacher's care and guidance, would you prefer that this teacher's example and influence should be *for* wine drinking or *against* it?

But if, in your judgment, that professor stands acquitted — nay, if you actually applaud his course, what, permit me to ask, is *your* duty?—yours, fathers and mothers! yours, sisters and brothers! yours, employers and teachers! There is not one of you but has influence over others, and that influence is much greater than you are apt to imagine. Is it not a sacred trust, which should never be abused? O parents! do you consider, as you ought, how closely your children observe all your ways, and how eagerly and recklessly they imitate them? Employers! do you estimate sufficiently your responsibility in regard to hirelings and domestic servants, who are prompt to adopt your habits and manners, but who seldom possess the self-control which your education and position constrain you to exercise? Your precepts, enjoining sobriety and moderation, pass for little. Your practice, giving color and countenance to self-indulgence, sinks deep into their hearts. One hour spent by you in thoughtless conviviality may plant the seeds of sin and ruin in those by whom you are attended! And the crowd of wives, mothers, sisters, daughters, that I see before me,— do *they* always consider with what wizard power they rule over man's sterner nature? It is our pride and privilege to defer to your sex. At all periods of life, and in all relations, you speak with a voice which penetrates to our gentler and nobler sentiments. Most of all is this the case when you burst into early womanhood, encompassed by bright hopes and fond hearts—when the Creator adorns you with graces and charms that draw towards you the dullest souls. Ah! how little do you appreciate, then, the sway which, for weal or wo, you wield over those of our sex who are your companions and friends! Is that sway always wise and holy? Is it always on the side of temperance and self-command? Alas! alas! could the grave give up its secrets, what tales of horror would it not reveal of woman's perverted influence—of woman thoughtlessly leading man, through the intoxicating cup, to the brink of utter and hopeless ruin! One case of the kind was mentioned to me lately. It is but one of many.

A young man, of no ordinary promise, unhappily contracted habits of intemperance. His excesses spread anguish and shame through a large and most respectable circle. The earnest and kind remonstrance of friends, however, at length led him to desist; and feeling that for him to drink was to die, he came to the solemn resolution that he would abstain entirely for the rest of his days. Not long after he was invited to dine, with other young persons, at the house of a friend. *Friend!* did I say? pardon me: he could hardly be a friend who would deliberately place on the table before one lately so lost, now so marvellously redeemed, the treacherous instrument of his downfall. But so it was. The wine was in their feasts. He withstood the fascination, however, until a young lady, whom he desired to please, challenged him to drink. He refused. With banter and ridicule she soon cheated him out of all his noble purposes, and her challenge was accepted. He no sooner drank than he felt that the demon was still alive, and that from temporary sleep he was now waking with tenfold strength. "Now," said he to a friend who sat next to him, "now I have tasted again, and I drink till I die." The awful pledge was kept. Not ten days had passed before the ill-fated youth fell under the horrors of delirium tremens, and was borne to a grave of shame and dark despair. Who would envy the emotions with which that young lady, if not wholly dead to duty and to pity, retraced her part in a scene of gaiety which smiled only to betray?

Let me not be misunderstood. I do not maintain that drinking wine is, in the language of the schools, *sin per se.* There may be circumstances under which to use intoxicating liquors is no crime. There have been times and places in which the only intoxicating beverage was light wine, and where habits of inebriation were all but unknown. But is that *our* case? Distillation has filled our land with alcoholic stimulants of the most fiery and deleterious character. Our wines, in a large proportion of instances, are but spurious compounds, without grape juice, and with a large infusion of distilled spirits, and even of more unhealthy ingredients. As long ago as the days of Addison, we read in the *Tatler* (No. 131) that in London there was "a fraternity of chemical operators, who worked under ground in holes, caverns and dark retirements, to conceal their mysteries from the observation of mankind. These subterranean philosophers are daily employed in the transmutation of liquors; and, *by the power of magical drugs and incantations, raising, under the streets of London, the choicest products of the hills and valleys of France. They can squeeze claret out of the sloe, and draw champagne out of an apple.*" The practice of substituting these base counterfeits for wine extracted from the grape has become so prevalent in this country, that well-informed and conscientious persons aver that, for every gallon of wine imported from abroad, ten or more are manufactured at home. "Five and twenty years ago," says the late J. Fennimore Cooper, "when I first visited Europe, I was astonished to see wine drunk in *tumblers.* I did not at first understand that half of what I had been drinking at home was brandy under the name of wine."

These adulterations and fabrications in the wine trade are not confined to our country or to England. They abound where the wine flourishes in greatest abundance. "Though the pure juice of the grape," says our eminent countryman, Horatio Greenough (the sculptor), can be furnished here (in Florence) for *one cent* a bottle, yet the retailers choose to gain a fraction of profit by the admission of water or drugs." He adds, "How far the destructive influence of wine, as here used, is to be ascribed to the grape, and how far it is augmented and aggravated by poisonous adulterations, it would be difficult to say." McMullen, a recent writer on wines, states that in France there are "extensive establishments (existing at Cette and Marseilles) for the manufacture of every description of wine, both white and red, to resemble the produce not only of France, but of all other wine countries. It is no uncommon practice with speculators engaged in this trade to purchase and ship wines, fabricated in the places named, to other ports on the continent; and, being branded and marked as the genuine wines usually are, they are then transshipped to the markets for which they are designed, *of which the United States is the chief.* Such is the extent to which this traffic is carried, that one individual has been referred to in the French ports who has been in the habit of shipping, four times in the year, twenty thousand bottles of champagne, *not the product of the grape, but fabricated in these wine-factories.* It is well known that the imposition of these counterfeit wines has arrived at such a pitch as to become quite notorious, and the subject of much complaint, in this country at least."*

---

* McMullen on Wines, p. 172.

In the presence of facts like these, I ask, what is our duty? Were nine out of ten of the coins or bank bills which circulate, counterfeit, we should feel obliged to decline them altogether. We should sooner dispense entirely with such a medium of circulation, than incur the hazard which would be involved in using it. And, even if we could discriminate unerringly ourselves between the spurious and the genuine, we should still abstain, *for the sake of others*, lest our example, in taking such a medium at such a time, encourage fabricators in their work of fraud, and lead the unwary and ignorant to become their victims. But, in such a case, abstinence would be practiced at great personal inconvenience. It is not so with abstinence from intoxicating drinks. That can subject us to no inconvenience worthy to be compared with the personal immunity with which it invests us, and with the consoling consciousness that we are giving no encouragement to fraud, and placing no stumbling block in the way of the weak and unwary.

The question, then, is not what may have been proper in other days or in other lands, in the time of Pliny or of Paul, but *what is proper now, and in our own land.* The apostle points us to a case in which *to eat meat* might cause one's brother to offend; and his own magnanimous resolution, under such circumstances, he thus avows, "*If meat make my brother to offend, I will eat no more while the world stands.*" Thus what may at one time be but a lawful and innocent liberty, becomes at another a positive sin. The true question, then—the only practical question for the *Christian* patriot and philanthropist—is this: "Intemperance abounds! Ought not my personal influence, whether by example or by precept, to be directed to its suppression? *Can* it be suppressed while our present drinking usuages continue? In a country where distilled liquors are so cheap and so abundant, and where the practice of adulterating every species of fermented liquor abounds—in such a country can any practical and important distinction be made between different kinds of intoxicating liquors? If abstinence is to be practiced at all, as a *prudential* or a *charitable* act, can it have much practical value unless it be *abstinence from all that can intoxicate?*" These questions are submitted, without fear, to the most deliberate and searching scrutiny.

Ladies and gentlemen, I conclude. Neither your patience nor my own physical powers will permit me to prosecute this subject. I devoutly hope that, in the remarks which I have now submitted, I have offended against no law of courtesy or kindness. I wish to deal in no railing accusations, no wholesale denunciations. When Paul appeared before the licentious Felix, he *reasoned* with him, we are told, of *temperance*. It is the only appeal that I desire to make. I might invoke your passions or your prejudices; but they are unworthy instruments, which he will be slow to use who respects himself; and they are instruments which generally recoil with violence on the cause that employs them. There is enough in this cause to approve itself to the highest reason and to the most upright conscience. Let us not be weary, then, in calling them to our aid. If we are earnest, and yet patient; if we speak the truth in love, and yet speak it with all perseverance and all faithfulness, it must at length prevail. But few years have passed since some of us, who are now ardent in this good work, were as ignorant or sceptical as those whom we are most anxious to convince. We then thought ourselves conscientious in our doubts, or even in our opposition. Let our charity be broad enough to concede to those who are not yet with us the same generous construction of motives which we then claimed for ourselves. And let us resolve that, if this noble cause be not advanced, it shall be through no fault of ours; that our zeal and our discretion shall go hand in hand; and that fervent prayer to God shall join with stern and indomitable effort to secure for it a triumph alike peaceful and permanent.

It was a glorious consciousness which enabled St. Paul, when about to take leave of those amongst whom he had gone preaching the kingdom of God, to say, "*I take you to record this day that I am pure from the blood of all men.*" May this consciousness be ours, my friends, in respect, at least, to the blood of drunkards! May not one drop of the blood of their ruined souls be found at last spotting our garments! Are we ministers of Christ? Are we servants and followers of Him who taught that it is more blessed to give than to receive? Let us see to it, that no blood guiltiness attaches to us here. We can take a course which will embolden us to challenge the closest inspection of our influence as it respects intemperance; which will enable us to enter without fear, on this ground at least, the presence of our Judge. May no false scruples, then, no fear of man which bringeth a snare, no sordid spirit of self-indulgence, no unrelenting and unreasoning prejudice deter us from doing that over which we cannot fail to rejoice when we come to stand before the Son of Man!

FROM PREFACE ON THE USE AND ABUSE OF ALCOHOLIC LIQUORS IN HEALTH AND DISEASE,

BY WM. B. CARPENTER, M. D., F. R. S., F. G. S.

A FAIR trial has been given, both in this country and in the United States, to societies which advocated the principle of *Temperance*, and which enlisted in their support a large number of intelligent and influential men; but it has been found that little or no good has been effected by them among the classes on whom it was most desirable that their influence should be exerted, except where those who were induced to join them really adopted the *total abstinence* principle. Though the author agrees fully with those who maintain that, *if* all the world would be *really temperate*, there would be no need of total abstinence societies, the author cannot adopt the inference, that those who desire to promote the temperance cause may legitimately rest satisfied with this measure of advocacy. For sad experience has shown that a large proportion of mankind *cannot*, partly for want of the self-restraint which proceeds from moral and religious culture, be temperate in the use of alcoholic liquors; and that the reformation of those who have acquired habits of intemperance *cannot* be accomplished by any means short of entire abstinence from fermented liquors. Further, experience has shown that in the present dearth of effectual education among the masses, and with the existing temptations to intemperance arising out of the force of example, the almost compulsory drinking usuages of numerous trades, and the encouragement which in various ways is given to the abuse of alcoholic liquors, nothing short of total abstinence can prevent the continuance, in the rising generation, of the terrible evils which we have at present to deplore. And, lastly, experience has also proved that this reformation cannot be carried to its required extent without the coöperation of the educated classes, and that their influence can only be effectually exerted by *example.* There is no case in which the superiority of example over mere precept is more decided and obvious than it is in this. "I practice total abstinence myself," is found to be worth a thousand exhortations; and the lamentable failure of the advocates who cannot employ this argument should lead all those whose position calls upon them to exert their influence, to a serious consideration of the claims which their duty to society should set up in opposition to their individual feelings of taste or comfort.

Among the most common objections brought against the advocate of the total abstinence principle is the following: "That the abuse of a thing good in itself does not afford a valid argument against the right use of it." This objection has been so well met by the late Archdeacon Jeffreys, of Bombay (in a letter to the *Bombay Courier*), that, as it is one peculiarly likely to occur to the mind of his medical readers, the author thinks it desirable to quote a part of his reply. "The truth is," he says, "that the adage is only true under certain general limitations; and that out of these, so far from being true, it is utterly false, and a mischievous fallacy. And the limitations are these: If it be found by experience that, in the general practice of the times in which we live, the abuse is only the solitary exception, whereas the right use is the general rule, so that the whole amount of good resulting from its right use exceeds the whole amount of evil resulting from its partial abuse, then the article in question, whatever it be, is fully entitled to the benefit of the adage; and it would not be the absolute and imperative duty of the Christian to give it up on account of its partial abuse. This is precisely the position in which stand all the gifts of Providence and all the enjoyments of life; for there is not one of them which the wickedness of man does not more or less abuse. But, on the other hand, if it be found by experience that there is something so deceitful and ensnaring in the article itself, or something so peculiarly untoward connected with the use of it in the present age, that the whole amount of crime and misery and wretchedness connected with the abuse of it greatly exceeds the whole amount of benefit arising from the right use of it, then the argument becomes a mischievous fallacy; the article in question is not entitled to the benefit of it, and it becomes the duty of every good man to get rid of it." After alluding to the evidence that this is preëminently the case with regard to alcoholic liquors, the

Archdeacon continues: "We have, then, established our principle in opposition to the philosophic adage; taking the duty of the citizen and the patriot even on the lowest ground. But Christian self-denial and Christian love and charity go far beyond this. St. Paul accounted one single soul so precious that he would on no account allow himself in any indulgence that tended to endanger a brother's soul: 'If meat make my brother to offend, I will eat no meat while the world standeth, lest I make my brother to offend.' 'It is good neither to eat flesh, nor to drink wine, nor anything whereby thy brother stumbleth, or is offended, or is made weak.' And we must bear in mind that flesh and wine are here mentioned by Paul as 'good creatures of God;' they are not intended to designate things evil in themselves. This saying of St. Paul is the charter of teetotalism; and will remain the charter of our noble cause so long as the world endures—so long as there remains a single heart to love and revere this declaration of the holy, self-denying Paul."

If, then, the author should succeed in convincing his readers that the "moderate" habitual use of alcoholic liquors is not beneficial to the healthy human system; still more, if they should be led to agree with him, that it is likely to be injurious—he trusts that they will feel called upon, by the foregoing considerations, to advocate the principle of total abstinence, in whatever manner they may individually deem most likely to be effectual. *He believes it to be in the power of the clerical and medical professions combined so to influence the opinion and practice of the educated classes as to promote the spread of this principle among the "masses" to a degree which no other agency can effect.* And he ventures to hope that, whether or not he carries his readers with him to the full extent of his own conclusions, he will, at any rate, have succeeded in convincing them that so much is to be said on his side of the question, that it can no longer be a matter of indifference what view is to be taken of it; and that, as "universal experience" has been put decidedly in the wrong with regard to many of the supposed virtues of alcohol, it is, at any rate, possible that its other attributes rest on no better foundation. In his general view of the case, he has the satisfaction of finding himself supported by the recorded opinion of a large body of his professional brethren; upwards of *two thousand* of whom, in all grades and degrees, from the court physicians and leading metropolitan surgeons, who are conversant with the wants of the upper ranks of society, to the humble country practitioner, who is familiar with the requirements of the artisan in his workshop and the laborer in the field, have signed the following certificate:

"We, the undersigned, are of opinion,

"1. That a very large proportion of human misery, including poverty, disease and crime, is induced by the use of alcoholic or fermented liquors as beverages.

"2. That the most perfect health is compatible with total abstinence from all such intoxicating beverages, whether in the form of ardent spirits, or as wine, beer, ale, porter, cider, &c.

"3. That persons accustomed to such drinks may, with perfect safety, discontinue them entirely, either at once, or gradually after a short time.

"4. That total and universal abstinence from alcoholic beverages of all sorts would greatly contribute to the health, the prosperity, the morality and the happiness of the human race."

No medical man, therefore, can any longer plead the *singularity* of the total abstinence creed as an excuse for his non-recognition of it; and, although a certain amount of moral courage may be needed for the advocacy and the practice of it, yet this is an attribute in which the author cannot for a moment believe his brethren to be deficient. Judging from his own experience, indeed, he may say that he has found much less difficulty in the course he has taken than he anticipated when he determined on it; and that he has met with a cordial recognition of its propriety, not merely on the part of those who participated in his opinions but did not feel called upon to act up to them in their individual cases, but also among others who dissented strongly from his scientific conclusions, and who consequently had no more sympathy with his principles than with his practice.

www.ingramcontent.com/pod-product-compliance
Lightning Source LLC
LaVergne TN
LVHW010131110826
845151LV00002B/325

* 9 7 8 1 4 2 5 5 4 0 0 2 9 *